ENGLISH LANGUAGE SERIES

A Linguistic Guide to English Poetry

Geoffrey Leech is Lecturer in the English Department and Secretary of the Communication Research Centre, University College London. From 1964-5, as a Harkness Fellow, he studied linguistics and transformational theory at the Massachusetts Institute of Technology. He is the author of *English in Advertising*, a previous volume in the English Language Series, and has written various essays and articles on style and varieties of English. He also has a particular interest in semantics, and has developed a new theoretical approach to the subject.

A Linguistic Guide to English Poetry

GEOFFREY N. LEECH

Reader in English : University of Lancaster

LONGMAN

LONGMAN GROUP LIMITED
London and Harlow

*Associated companies, branches and representatives
throughout the world*

© Longman Group Ltd (formerly Longmans, Green & Co Ltd) 1969

First published 1969
Second impression 1969

SBN 582 52211 0
*Made and printed in Great Britain by
William Clowes and Sons, Limited
London and Beccles*

Foreword

'There is not perhaps any *Figure of Speech* so pleasing, as THE METAPHOR', wrote the eighteenth-century linguistic thinker, James Harris. "'Tis at times the Language of *every Individual,* but *above all* is peculiar to *the Man of Genius.*'† Although backed by the testimony of Aristotle, this statement is of less interest to us than the exercise in stylistic comparison, suggestive of Quéneau, which precedes and occasions it. A *vulgar* utterance ('Don't let a lucky Hit slip; if you do, be-like you mayn't any more get at it') is set against an *affected* one ('Opportune Moments are few and fleeting; seize them with avidity, or your Progression will be impeded'), and both are contrasted with Brutus's expression of the same idea through his metaphor of taking a tide at the flood. Besides having 'intrinsic elegance', says Harris *(ibid.,* 197), such language as the third *flatters* the reader by leaving him 'to discover something *for himself*'.

More than metaphor is involved in the study of poetic language, and even so outstanding a philologist as Harris was deaf to the poetry of Chaucer ('so uncouth', p. 468), but it is nevertheless interesting to see linguistics and criticism, nearly two hundred years ago, taking a few modest steps to 'knit hands'. How near is this Miltonic figure to a full realization in our own times? The American scholar, Richard Ohmann, tells us scathingly that for all the progress in linguistic theory critics have retained their old benighted subjective habits: 'the most serviceable studies of style continue to proceed from the critic's naked intuition, fortified against the winds of ignorance only by literary sophistication and the tattered garments of traditional grammar. Especially damaging is the critic's inability, for lack of a theory, to take into account the deeper structural features of language, precisely those which should enter most revealingly into a stylistic description.'‡

---

† *Philological Inquiries* (London, 1781), 186.
‡ In *Word,* 20 (1964), 426.

We may or may not think it just that Ohmann should thus berate the critics, as we may or may not agree with how he assesses the potentiality of specific current linguistic theories; we must surely admit that the critics have a case in counter-claiming that much of the recent linguistic work on literature has been too elementary or trivial or laboriously irrelevant to merit their serious consideration, and at best too much preoccupied with the style of the most startlingly idiosyncratic writers. But it is beyond question that in recent years linguists have been turning their attention increasingly to literary texts, and in ways that are of increasing interest to critics, making possible, as Ohmann says, a 'refinement in the practice of stylistic analysis'. In these developments Geoffrey Leech has played a notable part, and for some years now his work has been in demand from editors of symposia in linguistic stylistics. In the present volume, however, he achieves something that is beyond what a symposium can by definition even attempt: a single mind, sensitive and well-read, applying a single view of linguistic structure discursively and in some depth to the analysis of a wide range of English poetry. His book will therefore be of immense value not only to the students of English literature for whom it has primarily been written but also to more senior readers: the critics who wish to see something of what linguistics is coming to offer their discipline; and Mr Leech's fellow linguists who cannot fail to profit from his example.

And so, like his previous successful volume, this book is greatly to be welcomed in the series in which it appears. As our language and literature have come to be studied more and more on a world-wide basis, there has arisen an acute need for more information on the language and the ways in which it is used. The English Language Series seeks to meet this need and to play a part in further stimulating the study and teaching of English by providing up-to-date and scholarly treatments of topics most relevant to present-day English – including its history and traditions, its sound patterns, its grammar, its lexicology, its rich variety in speech and writing, and its standards in Britain, the USA, and the other principal areas where the language is used.

University College London　　　　　RANDOLPH QUIRK
August, 1968

Preface

This book is designed as an introductory course in stylistics for students of English, and is based on my own experience of teaching the subject to first-year undergraduates. Although it is 'introductory' in the sense of 'starting from scratch', it does not pretend to give a general survey of current approaches to the study of literary style; instead, it aims at developing one particular approach, from introductory generalities down to the practical details of textual interpretation. What I hope will emerge from these pages, in outline, is a general scheme for the discussion of the language of literary texts, and a framework of reference on linguistic matters for anyone interested in the interpretation of poetry.

I emphasize that the linguistic and critical aspects of literary studies are here regarded as complementary, the first being a tool of the second. One of my motives for writing this book is an impatience with those who, whether as linguists or as critics, have by intolerance or lack of imagination fostered the view that the two disciplines of literary criticism and linguistics work against, rather than for, one another. It is my hope that this book may help to clear away some of the fog of misunderstanding, as well as providing for a real teaching need in university English courses.

The first two chapters are perhaps noticeably easier than the others; they cover ground which will be familiar to many students of English, but are a necessary preparation for the more carefully analytic approach of later chapters.

Passages of poetry for further discussion are suggested at the end of each chapter. My intention is that these should be treated quite freely, according to the needs and temperament of individual teachers or students. It should perhaps be pointed out that a thoroughly fruitful discussion of each example requires some knowledge of the poem's background – biographical, intellectual, social, etc. They cannot, therefore, be compared with textbook exercises for which the textbook itself is a complete preparation. Ideally, the discussion of each piece should be preceded by background exposition in much greater detail than my occasional explanatory notes can provide.

My debt to Randolph Quirk is far larger than that which a writer conventionally owes to his editor; he has given unfailing encouragement and guidance on all matters, from the most general issues of theory to the most practical points of presentation and typography. I am also very grateful to Frank Kermode, head of my department, for his interest and advice; to John Chalker and Frank Fricker for valuable comments from a literary viewpoint; to Sidney Greenbaum for a thorough reading of the book in typescript, and for summarizing for my benefit an article in Hebrew by U. Ornan; also to Roger Fowler for a detailed critique of Chapter 7; and to my father-in-law George Berman for kindly acting as proof-reader. What I owe to Winifred Nowottny through her book *The Language Poets Use* will be plain from almost every chapter of this one; but in addition I have a more personal debt to her, having been under her tutelage as a student at the University of London, and having had the unforgettable pleasure of attending the lectures upon which she later based her book. To other colleagues in the English Department of University College London I am grateful for giving me the benefit of their specialist knowledge on various points of literary appreciation.

Finally, I acknowledge, without too much shame, the help of *The Penguin Dictionary of Quotations* by J. M. and M. J. Cohen as a hunting-ground for suitable illustrations.

University College London   GNL
August, 1968

Acknowledgments

We are grateful to the following for permission to reproduce copyright material: George Allen & Unwin Ltd and the Viking Press Inc for an extract from *The Gift of Tongues* by Margaret Schlauch, Copyright 1942, Margaret Schlauch; author and author's agents for an extract from *Epigram: On His Books* by Hilaire Belloc; The Bodley Head and Random House Inc for an extract from 'The Sirens' from *Ulysses* by James Joyce; Curtis Brown Ltd and Curtis Brown, New York for *Letters from Iceland* by W. H. Auden and Louis MacNeice, Copyright © 1937 W. H. Auden and Louis MacNeice, renewed 1965 W. H. Auden; Jonathan Cape Ltd and Harcourt, Brace & World Inc for an extract from 'Lessons of the War: 1. Naming of Parts' from *A Map Of Verona* by Henry Reed; J. M. Dent & Sons Ltd and New Directions for extracts from 'From Love's First Fever to her Plague', 'Fern Hill', 'Ceremony after a Fireraid', 'Vision and Prayer', 'A Grief Ago', 'This Bread I Break' from *Collected Poems* by Dylan Thomas, Copyright 1939, 1946 by New Directions, 1945 by Trustees of the Copyrights of Dylan Thomas, and from *Under Milk Wood* by Dylan Thomas, Copyright 1954 New Directions; Faber & Faber and Harcourt Brace & World Inc for 'seeker of truth' poem 3 of *73 Poems* and 'pity this busy monster, manunkind' from *Selected Poems 1923–1958* by e. e. cummings (American title *Poems 1923–1954*), Copyright 1944 by e. e. cummings, and for extracts from 'East Coker', 'The Waste Land', 'The Hollow Men', 'Marina', 'The Love Song of J. Alfred Prufrock' from *Collected Poems 1909–1962* by T. S. Eliot; Faber & Faber and Oxford University Press Inc for 'Prayer before Birth' from *Collected Poems of Louis MacNeice*; Faber & Faber and Random House Inc for 'Bantams In Pine-Woods' and 'Metaphors of a Magnifico' from *The Collected Poems of Wallace Stevens*, Copyright 1923, renewed 1951 by Wallace Stevens, for 'The Wanderer' and 'A Summer Night' by W. H. Auden from *Collected Shorter Poems 1927–1957*; Grove Press Inc for 'Oread' by Hilda Doolittle from *Collected Poems*, Copyright © 1957 by Norman Holmes Pearson; The Trustees of the Hardy Estate, Macmillan & Co. Ltd and The Macmillan Companies of Canada and New York for 'In the Study' and 'Ah, Are you Digging on my Grave' from *Collected Poems of Thomas Hardy*, Copyright 1925 The Macmillan Co; Macmillan & Co. Ltd for 'Poem Without a Main Verb' from *Weep Before God* by John Wain; author, author's agents and the Estate of the late Mrs Frieda Lawrence and The Viking Press Inc for an extract from 'Snake' from *The Complete Poems of D. H. Lawrence, Vol. 1* (edited U.S.A by Vivian De Sola Pinto and F. Warren Roberts), Copyright 1923, 1951 by Frieda Lawrence; MacGibbon & Kee and New Directions for 'The Right of Way' from *Collected Earlier Poems* by William Carlos Williams, Copyright 1938 William Carlos Williams; The Marvell Press for 'Toads' from *The Less Deceived* by Philip Larkin; The Executors of Alice Meynell for 'The Rainy Summer' by Alice Meynell; Harold Owen, Chatto & Windus Ltd and New Directions for an extract from 'Strange Meeting' from The Collected Poems of Wilfred Owen, Copyright © 1963 Chatto & Windus; The proprietors of *Punch* Publications for a limerick, © *Punch*; author, author's agents and Holt, Rinehart & Winston Inc for 'Grass' from *Cornhuskers* by Carl Sandburg, Copyright 1918 by Holt, Rinehart & Winston Inc, 1946 by Carl Sandburg;

author, author's agents and The Macmillan Co of New York for 'Easter 1916' Copyright 1924, The Macmillan Co., 1952 by Bertha Georgie Yeats, for 'Leda and the Swan', Copyright 1928 by The Macmillan Co., 1956 by Georgie Yeats, for 'An Irish Airman Foresees His Death', Copyright 1919 by The Macmillan Co., 1946 by Bertha Georgie Yeats, from *The Collected Poems of W. B. Yeats*.

Contents

To the Memory of my Mother,
Dorothy Leech

Introduction

As a name for what this book is about, STYLISTICS is perhaps unfortunately pretentious; but there is no convenient alternative for it. I mean by 'stylistics' simply the study of literary style, or, to make matters even more explicit, the study of the use of language in literature. When we discuss 'style', we often have in mind the language of a particular writer, a particular period, a particular genre, even a particular poem. My plan, on the other hand, is to disregard these limiting factors and to investigate the general characteristics of language, and especially the English language, as a medium of literary expression.

0.1 THE 'LANG.-LIT.' PROBLEM

Such a course of study, one may claim, is central to those subjects in a modern curriculum ('English', 'German', 'Latin', etc.) which have as their titles the names of languages. What is entailed in these subjects, in the case of English almost as much as in the case of foreign or dead languages, is the study of language as a complement and aid to the study of literature. We generally suppose that the literature cannot be examined in any depth apart from the language, any more than the language can be studied apart from the literature. In the case of foreign languages or the English language of remote periods, this assumption is not difficult to justify, for it is obvious that a literary work cannot be properly understood without a thorough knowledge of the language which is its medium of expression. But there is a deeper reliance of literary studies on linguistic studies than this. Most critical discussions of literature revolve, at some stage, round appeal to linguistic evidence – that is, the evidence of words and sentences which actually occur on the printed page, in literary texts. The type of critical activity known as 'practical criticism' or 'explication de texte' relies more heavily on linguistic evidence than others. In addition, much of the basic vocabulary of literary criticism ('metaphor', 'figurative', 'antithesis', 'irony', 'rhythm', etc.) cannot be explained without recourse to linguistic notions. As a meeting-ground of linguistic and literary studies, stylistics is the field within which these basic questions lie.

All too often it is felt that the studies of language and literature, in English departments and elsewhere, pursue divergent paths, each under its own momentum, and fail to cohere within a single discipline. The problem of integration, which, for short, has been called the 'lang.-lit.' problem, has been aggravated in modern times by the decline of the teaching of RHE-TORIC,[1] and of the whole tradition of education enshrined in the classical 'Art of Rhetoric' and 'Art of Poesy'. What these manuals sought to do was to teach self-expression and literary composition through precept and the observation of the practice of great orators and writers. They combined a chief function of *prescription* (i.e. telling the student how to perform a task) with a lesser function of *description* (i.e. describing how it has been done successfully in the past). Nowadays, the emphasis has come to fall more and more on the *descriptive* aspect of literary studies – on the detailed explication of texts – rather than on the teaching of composition. Still surviving representatives of the rhetorical tradition today are the standard manuals of literary technique and of composition. These can be useful as reference books, but without the support of some more solid theoretical foundation and a deeper understanding of language, they cannot provide the kind of insight which the present age requires.

There is an interesting parallel today between the decay of traditional rhetoric and the decay of traditional grammar – both inherited from classical times. Traditional English grammar, as taught in schools, has been mainly prescriptive, like traditional rhetoric: that is, it has tended to lay down fixed rules as to what is 'correct' and 'incorrect' English. Now, partly through the growing influence of the discipline of general linguistics, this dogmatism has been broken down, and people have become more interested in what grammatical usage actually exists, rather than what usage 'ought to' exist; in other words, descriptive grammar has been replacing prescriptive grammar. None the less, a certain gap is felt in the educational system, for many schoolteachers who have lost confidence in the traditional grammar have not so far found a teachable replacement for it. In the same way, I believe, a void exists at university level in the study and teaching of stylistics. It is true that general linguistics, as a vigorous and developing field of study, has roused the interest of literary scholars, and that students of linguistics have been turning their attention more and more to the study of language in literature. But there has been much failure of communication, and the goals of literary and linguistic scholars, in approaching literary works, have often seemed too wide apart for fruitful co-operation.

Moreover, when a traditional body of theory falls into disrepute, the subject itself seems to suffer a similar eclipse. Just as many people today see no point in teaching grammar, so there is a tendency amongst some literary scholars to underestimate the importance to literary studies of such subjects as versification and rhetorical figures, and to treat them as matters of 'mere technique'. It is worth while observing that poets themselves have generally taken 'technique' very seriously: 'Let the neophyte know assonance and alliteration, rhyme immediate and delayed, simple and polyphonic, as a musician would expect to know harmony and counterpoint and all the minutiae of his craft.'[2] This advice from Ezra Pound to the would-be creative writer might be addressed with equal fitness to any student of literature.

0.2 A DESCRIPTIVE RHETORIC

It may be clear by now that what I am advocating, as one of the best services linguistics can at present pay to literary studies, is a 'descriptive rhetoric'. By this I mean a body of theory and technique devoted to the analysis of the characteristic features of literary language, and to the explanation of terms in the critic's vocabulary, where this can be done, using the linguist's insights at a level where they become useful to the student of literature. The present book, limited as it is in breadth of scope and depth of detail, will be, I hope, a step in this direction.

It may be helpful, in this light, to discuss two much criticized aspects of the traditional handbook of rhetoric. The first of these is its preservation of, and seeming reverence for, a vocabulary of unnecessarily difficult technical terms. Beside such well-known words as 'metaphor' and 'irony', as names for rhetorical figures, are many more forbidding Greek labels like 'epanalepsis', 'homoioteleuton', and 'antistrophe'. It would be foolish to lay any store by the mastery of this cumbersome terminology in an age when the classical languages and cultures are little studied. However, because such terms have a certain currency in literary scholarship, and serve a real communicative purpose, they cannot be altogether discarded. It would be even more foolish, in the present age, to try to replace the classical terms by a completely new terminology, as George Puttenham, the Elizabethan literary theorist, did in his *Arte of English Poesie*.[3] As a considerable part of the present book is concerned with what are traditionally known as 'rhetorical figures' or 'figures of speech',[4] it is as well to bear in mind from the start that the technical names for these figures are not sacrosanct, nor have their definitions been laid down once and for all time. In fact, the definitions of rhetorical terms have always been notorious for vagueness and inconsistency. My main preoccupation will be not how to define these terms, but how to get at the realities behind them – that is, the basic characteristics of poetic language.

Connected with this is a second weakness of traditional rhetoric – its cultivation of what I am tempted to call the 'train-spotting' or 'butterfly-collecting' attitude to style. This is the frame of mind in which the identification, classification, and labelling of specimens of given stylistic devices becomes an end in itself, divorced from the higher goal of enriching one's appreciation and critical understanding of literature. The response conveyed by 'Aha, there's an instance of *hysteron proteron*' is one of satisfaction without enlightenment. This train-spotting mentality was particularly prevalent in Elizabethan times,[5] but its persistence to the present day is shown in the survival in modern textbooks of figures like *hendiadys*, which we can value only as curiosities. Hendiadys (Greek for 'one-by-two') consists in the use of a co-ordinating construction where a structure of modification would be strictly appropriate: 'charmed by bright eyes *and* a woman' instead of 'charmed by the bright eyes *of* a woman'. It is so rare that I have found no certain instance of it in English literature.

There is danger of train-spotting whenever anyone tries, as I do in this book, to deal with the general properties of poetic language, without particular attention to a given text, a given writer, or a given period. With such a programme, one cannot help (except by avoiding illustrations altogether) quoting short passages, lifted from their contexts, simply as instances of this or that stylistic feature. The corrective to this use of labelled specimens lies in the opposite approach, whereby a student considers a characteristic of language only within the context of the poem to which it belongs, as a contribution to its total communicative effect. This is the method of 'practical criticism'.

However, both these approaches, the isolating and the synthesizing of stylistic effects, are necessary roads to the understanding of language in literature. We cannot appreciate how a poem fits together, unless we have first found the means to take it to pieces. Detailed exegesis of poems uses up more space than this book can accommodate, so I cannot avoid a certain bias towards specimen-collecting. But in the section called 'Examples for Discussion' at the end of each chapter, the student is invited to redress the balance for himself, by putting the content of that chapter and previous chapters to work on the explication of lengthier passages of poetry, some-times of whole poems. I therefore stress at this point the importance of these exercises, which are indispensable to the plan of the book.

0.3 POETIC LANGUAGE AND 'ORDINARY' LANGUAGE

The investigation of poetic language cannot proceed very far unless we have some notion of the relation between the kind of language which occurs in poetry, and other kinds of language. Here, if anywhere, we would expect linguistics, as the study of language in general, to help; for the subject matter of linguistics is all language – language as used not only in literary composition, but in everyday gossip, in scientific reports, in commercial or political persuasion, and in a multitude of other more or less mundane functions. The literary critic, on the other hand, concentrates on that relatively minute, but inordinately precious body of texts which are thought worthy of preservation as 'literature', to be studied for their own sake, rather than for their extrinsic value as (say) guide books or politi-cal tracts. Both the critic and the linguist are to some extent involved in the same task of describing and explaining linguistic communications: but in comparison with that of the critic, the linguist's perspective is broad and unspecialized. His approach to literature may be in many ways a crude one, but it results in generalizations and particular observations which could not easily be made from the critic's point of view.

As the position of poetic language with respect to 'ordinary' language is the subject for discussion in the first and second chapters, I shall merely anticipate here themes important to this book as a whole by observing that the relation between the two is not a simple one, and has at least three as-pects:

1. Poetic language may violate or deviate from the generally observed rules of the language in many different ways, some obvious, some subtle. Both the means of and motives for deviation are worth careful study.

2. The creative writer, and more particularly the poet, enjoys a unique freedom, amongst users of the language, to range over all its communica-tive resources, without respect to the social or historical contexts to which they belong. This means, amongst other things, that the poet can draw on the language of past ages, or can borrow features belonging to other, non-literary uses of language, as Ezra Pound and T. S. Eliot, for example, have

made use of the English of banal, prosy conversation in some of their poems.

3. Most of what is considered characteristic of literary language (for example, the use of tropes like irony and metaphor) nevertheless has its roots in everyday uses of language, and can best be studied with some reference to these uses.

Just as there is no firm dividing line between 'poetic' and 'ordinary' language, so it would be artificial to enforce a clear division between the language of poetry, considered as verse literature, and that of other literary kinds. I shall not hesitate to make use of prose illustrations where they are apposite, but in general the topics to be discussed can be more strikingly exemplified by verse extracts.

0.4. A POSSIBLE MISGIVING

I shall try now to forestall a misgiving which may arise in the mind of a reader who thinks of modern intellectual life in terms of the dichotomy of the 'two cultures', arts and science, with literary scholarship in the one camp and linguistics in the other. The analytic approach to literature might appear to such a mind objective and clinical, bent on destroying the sublime mysteries of poetry, and on reducing the study of literature to a set of lifeless mechanical procedures.

To allay that fear, I would firstly suggest that the division between arts and science, like that between 'lit.' and 'lang.', is to be fought rather than accepted.

Secondly, objectivity for its own sake is by no means a goal of science. In fact, though objectivity may be a theoretical requirement of science, a scientist (particularly in linguistics, if that is to be counted a science) in practice can rely so much on his own intuition for discovery and on his own judgment for corroboration, that his method of investigation may prove hardly distinguishable from that, say, of a literary commentator. Linguistics and literary criticism, to the extent that they are both concerned with explaining what and how a poem communicates, perform much the same task, but at a rather different level of abstraction.

Thirdly, insight or understanding is a much more important goal, in any human endeavour, than being objective. Statements of objective fact (for example, that there are eighty-two occurrences of the word *the* in the fourth canto of the first book of *The Faerie Queene*) can be as inane in the domain of style as anywhere else. I am fairly untroubled by the thought that I may be criticized for being unobjective, unscientific, or even unlinguistic. But if this book fails to enlighten, and thereby to sharpen appreciation of poetry, it will fail utterly.

Notes

1 The earlier history of poetics and rhetoric(a subject which has often had a much wider scope than literary technique) can be traced, in so far as they concern English literature, in J. W. H. ATKINS's volumes *Literary Criticism in Antiquity*, Vols. I and II, Cambridge, 1934; *English Literary Criticism: the Medieval Phase*, Cambridge, 1943; and *English Literary Criticism: the Renaissance*, London, 1947. Relatively modern representatives of the rhetorical tradition are A. BAIN, *English Composition and Rhetoric*, London, etc., 1887; and SIR H. GRIERSON, *Rhetoric and English Composition*, London, 1944. The 'rhetoric and composition' type of textbook has flourished independently in the USA up to the present day. See, for example, C. BROOKS and R. P. WARREN, *Fundamentals of Good Writing: a Handbook of Modern Rhetoric*, London, 1952.
2 E. POUND, 'Retrospect', in *Modern Poets on Modern Poetry*, ed. J. SCULLY, Fontana Library, 1966, 33.
3 See G. PUTTENHAM, *Arte of English Poesie*, ed. G. D. WILLCOCK and A. WALKER, Cambridge, 1936. Puttenham coined such homespun terms as *cuckoo-spell* (for *epizeuxis*), *over-reacher* (for *hyperbole*), and *insertour* (for *parenthesis*).
4 'Figures of speech' is here used in a loose, modern sense. In the past this expression has been used more narrowly in a sense corresponding to *schemes* (see §5.1), and so has excluded devices such as metaphor or hyperbole.
5 Consider, for example, a gloss by the Elizabethan commentator 'E.K.' on a passage from the January Eclogue of Spenser's *The Shepheardes Calender:* 'a pretty Epanorthosis in these two verses, and withal a Paronomasia or playing with the word. . . .'

One

Poetry and the Language of Past and Present

Poetic language 'should be the current language heightened, to any degree heightened and unlike itself, but not . . . an obsolete one.'   [*Gerard Manley Hopkins*][1]
'The language of the age is never the language of poetry.'   [*Thomas Gray*][2]

These two pronouncements by poets will serve to introduce our present theme.[3] They differ in emphasis, and indeed seem to contradict one another. This conflict leads us to wonder what is the degree of general truth in each assertion: a question to which an answer will be sought in this and the next chapter. They also testify to the keen interest poets themselves have taken in the relation between the language of poetry and the language of everyday communication.

1.1 VARIETIES OF ENGLISH USAGE

So often, in discussions of poetic language, people compare it with non-poetic ('ordinary', 'everyday', 'orthodox') language, without going into the question of what this latter category contains. A glance at the diversity of English usage outside literature will help to put things in the right perspective.

1.1.1 *Dialects*

Everyone is familiar with one kind of diversity in language: that of co-existing dialects. A language such as English contains not only different regional dialects, used by the inhabitants of different areas, but also social dialects, or varieties of English characteristic of a particular social class or section of the community – forces slang, for example, or the language of schoolchildren.

The question of what dialect to use has generally been a simple one for

English poets: ever since the fifteenth century, and more clearly than ever today, there has been a privileged dialect, a STANDARD ENGLISH, to which any writer wishing to command the attention of a wide educated audience has naturally turned. This standard English cuts across the boundaries of regional dialects, and is, in fact, international: American, Indian, Australian, and British writers make use of what, except for minor features of local currency, may be considered the same standard dialect. In the history of English literature since the Middle Ages, only one poet of unquestioned greatness, Robert Burns, has chosen to write his best work outside the standard dialect. Other poets, notably Rudyard Kipling and Thomas Hardy, have made extensive use of dialect in 'character' poems.

1.1.2. Registers: Usage according to situation

More central than dialect to the present topic is the diversity of English usage not according to the background of the speaker or writer, but according to the situation in which he is prompted to use language. It is usual to distinguish, amongst the circumstances which affect our use of English, the MEDIUM of communication (especially whether by speech or writing), the SOCIAL RELATION between the participants, and the ROLE of the communication.[4]

The social relation between the participants (that is, for the most part, between the author and his audience) determines what we may call in a broad sense the TONE of the discourse – whether it is colloquial or formal, familiar or polite, personal or impersonal, and so on. The ROLE of a piece of language is the place it has in the manifold patterns of human activities and institutions. Types of language which can be more obviously pigeon-holed as performing different roles are legal English, scientific English, liturgical English, advertising English, the English of journalism, all corresponding to public institutions which we acknowledge and identify with little difficulty. All these varieties of English may be comprehended in the notion of REGISTER, which, as language 'according to *use*', complements that of dialect, or language 'according to *user*'.[5]

Whereas each of us may be said to speak a recognizable dialect of English, he also has at his command, then, a range of registers, or usages, amongst which he can move, as speaker or writer, without difficulty, and indeed, often unconsciously. We rarely notice, for instance, how our manner of speech is transformed when we turn from conversation with a close friend or member of our family to talk to a stranger. In addition, we have a passive familiarity with a further range of registers (e.g. of advertising, of income tax forms, of sermons) within which we are rarely, if ever, called upon to perform the function of authorship. We can recognize almost instinctively the salient qualities of these types of English, so that, incidentally, we are able to compose or respond to parodies of them. When we find ourselves in a given communication situation, we automatically switch ourselves into the 'set of mind' for producing or receiving messages in the appropriate register. Any deviation from expected patterns of linguistic behaviour will bring about a reaction of disorientation and surprise.

It is evident that literature is to be fitted into this special framework as constituting a special *role* of language (although, as we shall see in Chapter 11, this in a sense amounts to an invitation to the poet to invent what role he pleases). Like the other roles mentioned above, the literary role corresponds to a distinct social or cultural function, the aesthetic function, for which a distinct form of linguistic behaviour is expected. As we are not concerned with appraisal, either within literature or outside it, there is no need to feel that there is disrespect in associating poetry with journalism, advertising, income tax forms, etc., in this fashion. Nor need anyone feel that the status of literary activity as a social institution is jeopardized by the difficulty of defining its function in society, or of drawing a clean line between literature and other kinds of linguistic composition on the fringes of literary art. For the present purpose, what makes a piece of writing literature is simply its treatment *as* literature by writer and reader – the fact that they both bring to it the assumptions, expectations, and standards which apply to literature rather than (say) to a deed of covenant, or a monograph on the ecology of eels.

Registers, like dialects, are different 'Englishes': they are distinguished by special features of semantics, vocabulary, grammar, sometimes even of pronunciation. For instance we recognize the sentence 'the bus we got on was the one he'd got off' as colloquial in tone because of a number of lexical and grammatical features:

1. the idiomatic phrases *get on* and *get off*;
2. the contraction of *he had* to *he'd*;
3. the lack of relative pronouns in the relative clauses 'we got on' and 'he'd got off';
4. The placement of the prepositions at the end of these clauses. (This is a necessary concomitant of 3.)

A corresponding formal version, with none of these features, might be: 'The bus which we boarded was that from which he had alighted.' This will probably strike most people as pompous, because the subject matter of the sentence is not of a sort to be treated formally. The Englishes of different roles are most clearly differentiated by special vocabulary: legal English by fossilized forms like *hereinafter*, in addition to an extensive technical vocabulary; scientific language by its innumerable technical terms, generally composed of Greek elements, and sometimes of grotesque length, like *phosphonochloridothioic (acid)*. Grammatical differences, also, are not wanting: there is a striking survival in religious English, for example, of the second person singular pronoun *thou/thee/thy/thine*, with its attendant verb forms *shouldst*, etc., although these have long been obsolete in most other varieties of English.

Not that these rules of religious English, colloquial English, etc., have been ascertained to the extent of those of general English usage, which have long been codified in grammars and dictionaries. The conventions of such subdivisions of the language lie in more or less unanalysed feelings about what is appropriate in a certain situation. Medical students probably learn without special tuition that 'His tummy is all upset' or 'He's got a bit of a head' is not the sort of thing to put in a medical report. Disregarding conventions of this kind does not lead to misunderstanding so much as to embarrassment or amusement. If on receiving a formal wedding invitation 'Mr and Mrs Gordon Jones . . .' I reply familiarly in writing 'Thanks a lot – so sorry I can't make it', this is a faux pas similar to that of turning up at the wedding without a jacket, or wearing tennis shoes at a ball.

These 'Englishes' are difficult to describe precisely, because they shade into one another, and have internal variations which could, if wished, lead to interminable sub-classification. For instance, we could not, on any reasonable principle, draw a strict line between the English of journalism, and the English of belles lettres or of general educational writing; or, to take another example, between formal and colloquial English – for there are innumerable degrees of formality and informality in language. The analogy of regional dialects is instructive on this point: rigid geographical frontiers between one dialect and another are exceptional.

These remarks are especially applicable to literature. Consider the futility of trying to draw an exact boundary between novels counting as 'literature', and the mass of popular fiction; or within literature, between lyric, epic, and other poetic genres.

Another thing we have to take into account is how rigid and restricting are the special habits of usage in different situations, more particularly in different roles. It would be misleading to suggest that in science, the law, or journalism, acceptable performance depends on slavishly following the dictates of convention: in all these spheres, a certain latitude is allowed, in which individual freedom and individual talent can assert itself. However, roles of language differ widely in how generous the latitude is: it is useful to draw a distinction here between LIBERAL roles, in which the pressure to linguistic conformity is weak, and STRICT roles, in which it is strong. The language of legal documents and the language of religious observance are the clearest examples of strictness in this special sense. In these roles, not only is a certain usage strictly insisted on, but often also a certain exact form of wording. Representatives of the opposite tendency are the roles of feature journalism, fiction writing, and general educational writing, in which good linguistic performance is measured not so much by one's ability to use the conventions properly, as by one's ability to escape from the conventions altogether. In these liberal roles, originality counts in the writer's favour; the conventions on the other hand, are considered marks of unoriginality, and are condemned by the use of terms like 'cliché', 'hackneyed', 'jargon', 'journalese'. From a historical viewpoint, strictness often means conservatism, and hence the cherishing of archaic forms of language, whereas liberalism goes with a ready acceptance of innovation.

1.2 LINGUISTIC CONVENTION IN POETRY

How does this contrast between liberal and conservative trends apply to the language of literature? The obvious reaction to this question would be to place literature, and above all poetry, at the liberal extremity of the scale: there is no other variety of language in which originality is so prized and dogged orthodoxy so despised; poetry is the mode of composition which is creative *par excellence*. The task of a linguist trying to discover by objective means the underlying conventions of poetic composition in English would be a thankless one, since each new poem he examined would be apt to contradict any generalizations he had been able to make. Rules in poetry are made only to be broken. So, he might conclude, there is no such thing as a literary register, a code of accepted usage, in literature.

Yet if this is a correct assessment of the liberal climate of literary language today, such a degree of freedom has not always existed. In most periods of the history of English literature, quite a strong sense of linguistic appropriateness has informed the making and judging of poetry. The rival tendencies of conservatism and liberalism have tugged in opposite directions. The liberal spirit holds sway at the present time, but in other periods, notably the Anglo-Saxon period and the eighteenth century, a distinctly conservative tendency prevailed.

1.2.1 *The Trend of Conformity*

To help us to appreciate the importance of the conformist (that is, conservative) tendency in poetic language, we may note a certain resemblance
between literature and the institutions which typify conservatism in language: law and religion. Like them, literature is a sphere in which the linguistic transactions of past ages are stored up reverently for their value to
posterity. Scriptures, statutes, and literary classics are three kinds of text
which are preserved for future ages word by word and sentence by sentence. They are more than historical documents, surviving as dead exhibits
in museums and libraries: they remain alive from generation to generation,
and speak in as authoritative a voice to one age as to another.

It is not surprising that ARCHAISM, the survival of the language of the
past into the language of the present, is a feature of these time-defying roles
of language. We have already noticed it in the *hereinafter* of legal English
and the *thou* forms of religious English. The archaic ingredient of poetic expression was noted long ago by Aristotle, and has persisted through much
of the history of English poetry. There is a difference between the occurrence of archaism in literature and its occurrence elsewhere, in that literary
archaism is often inspired by the wish to follow the model of a particular
writer or school of writers of the past. Nevertheless in the period 1600–
1900 there vaguely existed what could be called a 'standard archaic usage'
for English poetry, not based on the style of any one writer.[6] It is true that
the individual influences of Spenser and Milton played a leading part in the
establishment of this traditional pattern of usage, but later poets modified
it, and the archaic element was renewed at various times by poets who
found new inspiration in the literature of past ages: for example, Chatter-
ton, Coleridge, D. G. Rossetti, Morris. This tradition kept alive in poetry
such words as *behold, betimes, burthen, damsel, eftsoons, eld, ere, fain, hither,
lief, oft, quoth, smite, sprite, unto, wight, wot, yonder,* long after they fell into
general disuse.[7] But this retention of older forms was by no means confined to vocabulary. Examples of obsolete grammatical features retained
up to the later nineteenth century are the second person pronouns *ye* and
thou; the verbal endings (*e*)*st* and (*e*)*th*; and the old negative and interroga-
tive forms without an auxiliary, as in 'I know not' and 'Saw you anything?'. In addition, there survived grammatical variants such as '*tis*, '*twas*,
'*gainst, ne'er, e'en, o'er, spake, holp,* -*èd* (the past tense or past participle ending pronounced as a separate syllable, as in *clothèd*). Many of these variants
were obviously useful stock-in-trade for the versifier; they offered him
alternatives with one more or less syllable than the normal form, and so

made regular scansion easier. Even in orthography, archaic inclinations were fostered: under the antiquarian influences of the late eighteenth century, *chant* could appear as *chaunt*, and *mariner* as *marinere* (in Coleridge's poem).[8]

My use of the past tense above implies that archaism, as a regular component of poetic expression, is no longer with us. Indeed, I take it that the 'Spenserian' tradition of poetic expression eventually petered out towards the beginning of this century. Hardy, Yeats, and Bridges are perhaps the last major poets to have had any recourse to it. If the old-fashioned usages outlined above can be said to be part of the present-day English language, this is probably due more to the Authorized Version of the Bible, the Book of Common Prayer, and the Shakespearean canon, than to the outmoded conventions of poetic usage.

1.2.2 *The Function of Archaism*

The examples of archaism I have given are poetic clichés which became threadbare a long time ago. Are they to be taken seriously today, as relevant to our appreciation of the poetry of past ages, or simply to be made fun of, in mock-Spenserian utterances such as 'Hence, loathèd wight'? We must take them seriously if we are to explain something of what, in the past, has been considered the poetic HEIGHTENING of language. Archaic language is naturally invested with a dignity and solemnity which comes from its association with the noble literary achievements of the past. It also gives a sense of cultural continuity. In religious life, this has recently been illustrated by the loss many people have felt wherever the New English Bible has replaced the Authorized or even the Revised Version. We may deplore this sense of the grandeur of old-fashioned language as a spurious emotion; we may belittle it by parody or by turning it into 'olde worlde' quaintness; but we still have to recognize that it exists, and that it has existed in a stronger form in the past.

The connection between archaism and the sublime is shown in the tendency of certain nineteenth-century prose writers to modulate into 'biblical' or 'poetical' language at points of emotional climax. But, of course, the step from the sublime to the ridiculous is short. When archaic diction had become a mere mannerism, an incongruity between loftiness of tone and poverty of emotion (often found, for example, in Victorian ballads and translations of German lieder) helped to bring it into disrepute.

1.2.3 *Poetic Language and 'Poetical' Language*

The conformist aspect of poetic language, of which archaism is an important part, is what we normally read into the adjective 'poetical', if we want
to use that adjective in a slightly derogatory way. 'Poeticalness', on such
an understanding, bears the same relation to poetry as 'journalese' bears to
journalism: it sums up, in one word, all that is stale, hackneyed, or lacking
in originality in that form of writing.

However, if we connect conformity with staleness in this way, we take
a characteristically modern attitude. This is to be contrasted with the typical attitude of the eighteenth century – the period of the ascendancy of so-
called POETIC DICTION, when standards of the 'poetical' and 'unpoetical'
in language were seriously observed. Gray reflected the assumptions of the
age when he wrote (in a letter to Richard West, quoted at the beginning
of this chapter): 'Our poetry . . . has a language peculiar to itself; to which
almost every one that has written, has added something by enriching it
with foreign idioms and derivatives: Nay, sometimes words of their own
composition or invention'. Poetic language, he seems to suggest, is a
treasury in which has been collected all that is best in the language of the
past; it is a precinct set off from the 'ordinary' language of the day; the
poet, who is a custodian of this heritage, may nevertheless be allowed in
some small way to contribute to it. It is perhaps the daring tone in which
Gray makes this last concession to the liberal point of view that most clearly
reveals the strength of his conservatism.

As in all conservative roles, the set of conventions which make up
'poetical' usage have both a positive and negative aspect. The positive aspect consists of features which belong to the register of poetry, but are
rarely, if ever, found elsewhere in the language. Examples are special
poetical words, such as *billow, main* (='the sea'), *nymph, slumber, steed,
swain, verdant, woe,* as well as many of the archaisms already mentioned.
These, we may say, are parts of the language 'specialized' to the role of
poetry, and if they are ever used outside poetry (e.g. for comic purposes),
they carry strong overtones of 'poeticalness'. The poetic diction of the
Augustan age was also noted for favourite expressions such as *watery store,
fleecy care, feather'd race.*[9] These are periphrases for 'sea', 'sheep', and
'birds' respectively. Typically, such periphrases consist of a descriptive adjective followed by a collective or abstract noun. Also characteristic of this
periphrastic diction are nouns used in peculiar senses: *care* used in the sense
of 'what is cared for', for example, in *fleecy care* and *woolly care.*[10]

Again, one should not be misled by the term 'diction' into thinking that this specialized poetic usage is only a matter of vocabulary or phraseology. *Gulph* and *ghyll* (the latter 'apparently introduced by Wordsworth')[11] are examples of special poetical spellings, by the side of *gulf* and *gill*. Certain syntactic constructions which probably owe their currency to Milton's idiosyncratic influence are also virtually confined to poetry. An example is that of *nor* following an affirmative clause, in the sense 'and . . . not', as in Browning's 'Flat thus I lie nor flinch' [*Ivàn Ivànovich*].

Along with the positive specialization we have to consider the negative, exclusive side of poetry's 'language peculiar to itself'. It is difficult to determine what is excluded from the repertoire of the poet, that is, all that lies in the 'unpoetical' sections of the language; but such tacit proscription is attested whenever we have the intuition, in the words of Donald Davie, that 'words are thrusting at the poem and being fended off from it'.[12] This is certainly the feeling one gets on reading this stanza from Gray's *Ode on a Distant Prospect of Eton College*:

> Say, Father Thames, for thou hast seen
>   Full many a sprightly race
> Disporting on thy margent green,
>   The paths of pleasure trace;
> Who foremost now delight to cleave
> With pliant arm, thy glassy wave?
>   The captive linnet which enthral?
> What idle progeny succeed
> To chase the rolling circle's speed
>   Or urge the flying ball?

Here the everyday spectacle of children at play is described in far from everyday language; almost all the common words a person would normally use for this purpose, such as *children*, *play*, *swim*, *bank*, *water*, *hoop*, *roll*, *throw*, *catch*, *bird*, are avoided by the poet.

1.2.4 *Grand, Middle, and Plain Styles*[13]

The subject of linguistic appropriateness has not been neglected by the literary theorists of the past. The doctrine of DECORUM, or fittingness of style, has been passed down to us from the rhetoricians of Greece and Rome, who applied it first to oratory and then to written language. This is not so much concerned with the relation between literary and 'ordinary' language, as with the relation between various styles of literary expression. Generally three styles were distinguished: the GRAND, MIDDLE, and PLAIN styles. They can be associated with the registerial factor of tone, and can be considered three stages on a scale of poetic elevation. The analogy of clothing can again give some idea of what was meant by the three styles: we may think of the plain style as the working dress of language, and the grand style as ceremonial dress for a state occasion. For the middle style, between the two, the watchword was elegance – perhaps respectable clothes for a night out. The archaisms and other features contributing to poetic heightening belonged more to the grand style than to the others. Plain style was most like colloquial speech, but even here some degree of literary artistry (felicitous choice and arrangement of words, etc.) was usually insisted on.

Like most of the classifications of rhetoric, this one was variously interpreted and elaborated by writers of different periods. I have merely picked out what seem to be the most constant and significant elements of the theory. The idea that there are just three literary styles seems to have no justification apart from the sanction of tradition. Why should there be three, rather than four, or five, or an unlimited number? In the past two centuries, the code of decorum has been so vaguely conceived as to be of no particular use either to writer or critic. Nevertheless, it is useful to be reminded that whilst poetic language has to be distinguished from other kinds of English usage, there are further divisions to be made within poetic language itself. Previous ages have been much more conscious of these than we are today.

1.2.5 *The Routine Licences of Verse Composition*

We come now to a point at which it is necessary to deal more carefully with the division between poetry and prose literature. The bland characterisation of poetry as 'verse literature' in §0.3 above located this distinction in the apparently superficial matter of whether a given composition has a discernible metre, rhyme scheme, or stanza form, or even whether it is arranged in verse lines on the printed page. One might assume from this that there is no fundamental difference between poetic language and prose language, except that the features typifying literary composition tend to be more pervasive and pronounced in poetry than in prose.

But the difference is a little more subtle than this. Looking back over the span of English literature since Chaucer, we note that certain freedoms of language have been traditionally sanctioned in verse, but not in prose. These enter the study of poetic language at a rather low level: in fact, they belong to the mere mechanics of verse composition. Their obvious function is to compensate the poet for his loss of freedom in submitting himself to the discipline of verse composition; to furnish him with a wider set of choices than are normally available in English and thus to give him a better chance of squeezing his language into a predetermined mould of versification. If he rejects these 'routine licences', as we may call them, the task of versification is that much more difficult.

One such licence has already been exemplified: the retention in the poetic register of alternative forms (such as *'tis* for *it is*, *ne'er* for *never*, *oft* for *often*, *wingèd* for *winged*) containing a different number of syllables. Of the types of shortening shown in these examples, the omission of an initial part of a word or phrase is called APHESIS, the omission of a medial part SYNCOPE, and the omission of a final part APOCOPE. I do not mean to suggest that the shorter variant is necessarily derived historically from the longer one: *oft*, for example, is an older form than *often*.

Another freedom poets have enjoyed by custom is that of arranging syntactic elements in an irregular order (HYPERBATON): for example, placing an adjective after the noun it qualifies (*cities fair*) instead of before (*fair cities*). Jumbled clause structures have been taken so much for granted in verse, that we scarcely notice them. The opening two stanzas of Cowper's *The Diverting History of John Gilpin* contain three examples:

> John Gilpin was a citizen
> Of credit and renown,
> *A train-band captain eke was he*
> Of famous London town.

> John Gilpin's spouse said to her dear,
> 'Though *wedded we have been*
> These twice ten tedious years; yet *we*
> *No holiday have seen.*'

The sections in italics each contain the main clause elements subject (S), verbal (V), and object/complement (C), which in prose, as in ordinary speech, would almost certainly occur in the order S V C. Cowper gives us three separate variations of that order: C V S, C S V, and S C V. Only when we see Mrs Gilpin's remark written as prose, do we fully realize that no citizen's wife would have uttered, in reality, sentences of such odd structure: 'Though wedded we have been these twice ten tedious years, yet we no holiday have seen.' It would perhaps be going too far to suggest that in verse the elements may be scrambled into any order whatsoever: one would scarcely meet, even in a poem, such a violent disorganization as that of (say) 'have been though wedded we' or 'been have we wedded though'. Yet poets have exercised great freedom in this matter.

Some poets have claimed a greater degree of this kind of freedom than others. Spenser, of all major English poets, probably claimed most: in *The Faerie Queene* he was not averse, for instance, to leaving out a normally obligatory definite article or other grammatical determiner if it threatened the metre:

> Let all that live hereby be counselled
> To shunne Rocke of Reproch, and it as death to dred!
>   [II.xii.9]

In justification, if it is accepted as such, we can point to Spenser's achievement of sustaining an exacting verse form through the longest good poem in the English language. In contrast, the poets of the present century have veered far away from Renaissance artifice, preferring to reject these conventional peculiarities of poetic expression together with the rigidity of metre and complexity of verse form which made them necessary.

These matters belong, as I have said, to the mechanics of composition – to the level of craftmanship rather than art. Yet the point that has been made – that by the very act of writing in verse an author can claim special exemptions from the laws of normal usage – is by no means trifling. The feeling of 'heightening' in poetic language is, in part, nothing more than the consciousness that it is strange and arresting by the side of common usage. Since the bread-and-butter licences of versification in themselves bring about an alienation of poetic language from everyday language, we can see how verse may be accepted as the vehicle for a much more daring departure from linguistic norms than prose, and hence for the singularity of expression and concentration of meaning which contribute to 'heightening' in a more profound sense. Consequently, even the visual signal that a text is verse and not prose, its irregular lineation on the page, is sufficient to call up in a reader a whole range of expectations which would otherwise be absent.

Examples for discussion

[NOTE: *The topics suggested here cannot be investigated thoroughly without the use of reference books. Nevertheless, the exercise will be of some profit, I hope, to readers who rely simply on their own knowledge of the language past and present.*]

1. Identify archaisms (grammatical, etc., as well as lexical) in the following two stanzas by Byron. To help in this, attempt a paraphrase of the first stanza in everyday modern English. Disregarding the factor of versification, what is gained or lost by such a paraphrase?

> Whilome in Albion's isle there dwelt a youth,
> Who ne in virtue's ways did take delight;
> But spent his days in riot most uncouth,
> And vex'd with mirth the drowsy ear of Night.
> Ah me! in sooth he was a shameless wight,
> Sore given to revel and ungodly glee;
> Few earthly things found favour in his sight
> Save concubines and carnal companie,
> And flaunting wassailers of high and low degree.

> Childe Harold was he hight: – but whence his name
> And lineage long, it suits me not to say;
> Suffice it, that perchance they were of fame,
> And had been glorious in another day:
> But one sad losel soils a name for aye,
> However mighty in the olden time;
> Nor all that heralds rake from coffin'd clay,
> Nor florid prose, nor honeyed lies of rhyme,
> Can blazon evil deeds, or consecrate a crime.
>   [*Childe Harold's Pilgrimage*, I]

2. Distinguish conventional features of poetic language in the following passage (in which the goddess Venus is arguing the superiority of love to war). As in (1) above, a paraphrase in 'unpoetical' language will help to determine the extent of the conventionality, and its value (if any). Arthos and Groom (see the Notes below) are useful books to consult on eighteenth-century poetic diction.

> No savage joy th'harmonious hours profane!
>   Whom love refines, can barbarous tumult please?
> Shall rage of blood pollute the sylvan reign?
>   Shall Leisure wanton in the spoils of Peace?

> Free let the feathery race indulge the song,
>   Inhale the liberal beam, and melt in love:
> Free let the fleet hind bound her hills along,
>   And in pure streams the watery nations rove.
>   [James Beattie, *Judgement of Paris*, 1765]

3. Show, on the basis of linguistic evidence, why this poem strikes one as colloquial and familiar in tone, rather than formal or elevated. Does it contain any lines which could not be heard in everyday speech?

Why should I let the toad *work*
 Squat on my life?
Can't I use my wit as a pitchfork
 And drive the brute off?

Six days of the week it soils
 With its sickening poison –
Just for paying a few bills!
 That's out of proportion.

Lots of folk live on their wits:
 Lecturers, lispers,
Losels, loblolly-men, louts –
 They don't end as paupers;

Lots of folk live up lanes
 With fires in a bucket,
Eat windfalls and tinned sardines –
 They seem to like it.

Their nippers have got bare feet,
 Their unspeakable wives
Are skinny as whippets – and yet
 No one actually *starves*.

Ah, were I courageous enough
 To shout *Stuff your pension!*
But I know, all too well, that's the stuff
 That dreams are made on:

For something sufficiently toad-like
 Squats in me, too;
Its hunkers are heavy as hard luck,
 And cold as snow,

And will never allow me to blarney
 My way to getting
The fame and the girl and the money
 All at one sitting.

I don't say, one bodies the other
 One's spiritual truth;
But I do say it's hard to lose either,
 When you have both.
    [Philip Larkin, *Toads*]

Notes

1   Letter to Robert Bridges, 14 August 1879.
2   Letter to Richard West, April 1742.
3   Both passages are quoted in Chapter 15 of R. QUIRK, *The Use of English* (2nd edn.), London, 1968. That chapter is the source of many of the ideas and examples in Chapters 1 and 2 of this book, and I here declare my great indebtedness to its author.
4   This threefold system of register analysis has appeared in various forms in various publications. The term 'tone' is here preferred to alternatives 'style' and 'tenor', which are required for other purposes in this book. See M. A. K. HALLIDAY, A. MCINTOSH, and P. STREVENS, *The Linguistic Sciences and Language Teaching*, London, 1964, 90–4; N. E. ENKVIST, J. SPENCER, and M. J. GREGORY, *Linguistics and Style*, London, 1965, 86. The most thorough and extensive treatment of English register to date is D. CRYSTAL and D. DAVY, *Investigating English Style*, London, 1969.
5   M. A. K. HALLIDAY, A. MCINTOSH, and P. STREVENS, *op. cit.*, 87.
6   In this discussion of poetic tradition, I have drawn freely on the wealth of information in B. GROOM, *The Diction of Poetry from Spenser to Bridges*, Toronto, 1955.
7   GROOM, *op. cit.*, gives lists of archaisms under relevant authors: 14, 75, 159–61, 212–3, 228, 254–5, 257–8.
8   *Ibid.*, 257–8.
9   *Ibid.*, 110, 114, 115.
10 *Ibid.*, 104. A valuable source book for eighteenth-century poetic diction is J. ARTHOS, *The Language of Natural Description in Eighteenth Century Poetry*, Ann Arbor, 1949.
11 GROOM, *op. cit.*, 161.
12 D. DAVIE, *Purity of Diction in English Verse*, London, 1952, 5.
13 For the history of this subject, consult the index of J. W. H. ATKINS, *Literary Criticism in Antiquity*, 2 Vols., Cambridge, 1934, and of other volumes by the same author on the history of English literary criticism.

Two

The Creative Use of Language

We now pass from the conservative to the liberal, from the derivative to the creative aspect of poetic language. The latter is the more important and interesting subject, and with few interruptions will occupy the rest of this book. The poet is nothing if not creative, and since language is his medium, one might well ask how he could be creative without using language in some sense creatively.

2.1 THE ESCAPE FROM BANALITY

Poetic tradition and poetic originality are contrary forces: we may characterize the creative impulse of the artist, on one dimension, as a flight from the banality of 'a worn-out poetical fashion' [Eliot, *East Coker*]. To revitalize the language of poetry, the poet draws directly on the resources of the contemporary language. As Eliot said, 'Every revolution in poetry is apt to be . . . a return to common speech'.[1] This description he applied not only to his own revolution, but to that of Wordsworth, and to that of Dryden and his older contemporaries, Waller and Denham.

The effect of the return to ordinary language in the present century has been far-reaching. The feeling that there are intrinsically poetical and unpoetical sectors of the language has been repudiated. Much of the old paraphernalia of poetic expression (e.g. archaism) has been overthrown, and poets have eagerly delved into the most unlikely resources, such as the terminology of aeronautics and finance. Pound, Eliot, and the poets of the thirties showed their determination to be rid of orthodox restrictions of choice by making use of flagrantly prosy and vulgar aspects of everyday usage. In the new poetry of the fifties, this flamboyance has given way to a more sober and easy acceptance of colloquialism, even slang, as a fit medium of poetic expression. A good example is Philip Larkin's *Toads*, given complete as an example for discussion at the end of the last chapter. Its idiomatic familiarity of tone is in many ways typical of recent British poetry.

On the other hand, poetic language cannot come too close to the 'ordinary language' of the day – if it does, it runs the danger of another kind of banality, an undistinguished style which is perhaps easier to illustrate from one of Wordsworth's well-known experiments, such as *Simon Lee, the Old Huntsman*, rather than from contemporary poetry. So we may think of the successful poet as avoiding banality on two dimensions: the banality of the poetic convention of the past; and the banality of the everyday usage of the present. These two forces pull in opposite directions, and there is rarely a firm balance between them. It appears that the steady weight of conservatism has to be counteracted, from time to time, with a jerk in the direction of 'the language of ordinary men'. The progress of poetic language is something like a canal climbing a hill by a series of locks: the surface of the water, remaining horizontal, cannot help diverging from the land contour it attempts to follow, and a lock (in this simile, a poetic revolution) has to raise it every now and then by brute force towards the level of the land surface.

2.2 TWO MEANINGS OF 'CREATIVE'

As I dealt in the last chapter with the pull of tradition, I turn in this one to the equivocal relation between the poet's language and the everyday language of his day. The two meanings of 'creative' I shall deal with, therefore, are concerned with only the second of the two kinds of banality which were the subject of the last section. A writer may be said to use language creatively [a] if he makes original use of the established possibilities of the language; and [b] if he actually goes beyond those possibilities, that is, if he creates new communicative possibilities which are not already in the language. Linguistic creativity in either of these senses may be paraphrased by 'inventiveness' or 'originality'. It is characteristic of all registers which have liberal tendencies, and supremely, of poetic language.

The following two eccentric utterances will help to show what is meant by this distinction:

1. The polar bears of the Arctic ice-cap have recently taken to wearing false eyelashes as a protection against snow-blindness.
2. Eins within a space and a wearywide space it wast ere wohned a Mookse.

In linguistics, it has recently become widely accepted that a language such as English has theoretically infinite resources, i.e. consists of an infinite number of sentences, most of which have actually never been uttered.[2] This claim, though it seems extravagant at first, becomes credible when we consider that the largest English dictionaries, although they contain hundreds of thousands of entries, do not record the whole of contemporary vocabulary; and that any sentence whatever can be made into another, longer, sentence, by the addition of one of any number of possible modifiers, or co-ordinative elements. If this is accepted, then we, as speakers of English, have the capability of using language 'creatively' in the purely linguistic sense of making up sentences which we have never heard uttered before. I have made use of this capability in making up sentence (1) above, which is in all likelihood original, if only because of the unlikelihood of the event it describes. But more generally, practically every book we read (although there are no means of confirming this) must contain numerous sentences which have never occurred outside that book (if we discount reprints, quotations, etc.).

Sentence (2) above, for which James Joyce[3] is responsible, is as undoubtedly unique as sentence (1): no one, except by the oddest coincidence, could have thought up that particular sequence of symbols before Joyce did. But it is original in a more radical sense than sentence (1), which was regularly formed according to the rules of English. Joyce's sentence breaks the rules of the language so markedly, that one would be in doubt whether to treat it as written 'in English' at all.

It may be objected that linguistic creativity, in either of these senses, need be nothing more than eccentricity. A literary effect, on this score, seems to be levelled to the status of a spelling mistake, a malapropism, or some other kind of linguistic aberration. This is true; to get from a linguist's to an artist's idea of creativity, we have to assess the significance, or communicative value of a linguistic deviation: something which will not be discussed until §4.2.1. None the less, being linguistically creative is the means to being creative in the literary sense; in fact, there is a rough correspondence, as we shall see, between the two linguistic meanings of 'creative' and two types of literary expression: the 'prosaic' and the 'poetic'.

2.3 THE QUALITIES OF PROSE IN POETRY

Often it is felt that poetry and prose are basically different kinds of writing: that the difference between them is not just a question of versification, not just a matter of the greater degree of linguistic boldness and compression of significance to be found in poetry, but of something fundamentally different in the character of the linguistic effort involved. If it is valid to think, in this way, of 'good poetry' and 'good prose' as separate ideals, then these can be associated with the two types of linguistic creativity. Now we are using 'prosaic' and 'poetic' in the sense 'having the qualities *typical* of prose/poetry', so that there is no contradiction in talking of 'prosaic poetry' or 'poetic prose': indeed, people often feel the need to talk of such categories. Just as prose has sometimes aspired to be poetic, so prosaic strength has sometimes been an ideal in poetic composition. 'Prosaic strength' (Donald Davie's phrase)[4] is a fitting term to apply to writing which explores the expressive resources of the language to the full, without noticeably exceeding them. Poetry which excels in this property can be said to have 'the qualities of good prose'.[5]

    Although anyone who speaks English has the ability, in theory, to produce and understand an infinite number of English sentences, in practice we make very limited use of this inventive capacity, finding it easier to rely on a limited repertoire used over and over again. The elements of the repertoire can be words, or whole sentences; but most typically they are pieces of intermediate length, consisting of perhaps three or four words. Consider, for example, the answer I might make to a request for the name of a plumber in my home town: 'You might try having a look through the Classified Directory.' In making this suggestion, I would not be aware of consciously picking one expression rather than another; the reply is almost effortless and automatic. It breaks down into three fixed locutions: *You might try ———ing; hav——— a look through;* and *the Classified Directory.* I have used each of these chunks many times before; in using them here I have called only on my memory, not on my skill to invent new combinations of elements. To make up the whole utterance, I have merely threaded them together in their right order.

    Such prefabricated sentences are an inevitable part of casual, spontaneous communication, which would be intolerably laboured if every word were individually weighed and chosen. But in serious writing, of course, they are generally considered the mark of bad prose style – a sign of intellectual feebleness or slovenliness. George Orwell had this kind of thing in mind, with particular reference to political propaganda, when he denounced 'Gumming together long strips of words which have already been set in order by someone else, and making the results presentable by sheer humbug'.[6] Orwell felt that cliché-ridden writing, following the ready-made grooves of past communications, stultifies the intellect of author and audience, and debases the language so misused. The fixed phrases, runs this argument, become mere counters substituting for the mental effort that should attend the serious use of language, and the words making up the counters lose their independent semantic force. Hackneyed phrases like *each and every one of us*, or *bring to a satisfactory conclusion*, become formulae in which the individual meanings of *each*, *satisfactory*, etc., are virtually unconsidered.

The mechanical, humdrum, repetitive element in everyday communication is anathema to a literary artist, whose task is to restore and enhance the value of the debased linguistic currency; in Eliot's phrase translated from Mallarmé, to 'purify the dialect of the tribe' [*Little Gidding*]. A respected literary style is one in which each choice of vocabulary or grammar is arrived at by exercise of the writer's judgment and sensibility. Indeed, every serious, premeditated use of language, unless it is totally inept, goes some way towards the ideal of a style in which linguistic choices precisely fit their purpose, and bear their full weight of meaning. The phrase 'le mot juste', which comes to mind in this connection, is misleading if it suggests that acceptable prose style is merely a matter of choosing the right words – it is rather a question of drawing freely from all the expressive resources of the language, lexical, grammatical, even orthographic and phonological, for the purpose in hand.

To illustrate this quality in its typical habitat, I shall turn to a short passage from a modern novel, *Under the Net* by Iris Murdoch[7]:

> While I was thinking these thoughts a little stream was running softly somewhere in my mind, a little stream of reminiscence. What was it? Something was asking to be remembered. I held the book gently in my hands, and followed without haste the course of my reverie, waiting for the memory to declare itself.

This describes an unremarkable experience, which could be briefly described in pedestrian language as 'trying to track down something in the back of your mind'. What makes Iris Murdoch's account *un*pedestrian is partly a negative matter – the very absence of memorized chunks like *track down* and *in the back of your mind*. More positively, it gives a precise, vivid account of the experience by apt choice of vocabulary (*reminiscence, reverie*), and by a syntax which imitates the thought process being recalled: 'What was it? Something was asking to be remembered.' The style approaches poetic boldness in the personification of a memory which 'asks to be remembered' and eventually 'declares itself', but otherwise contains no unorthodox features. The description of the memory as a 'stream . . . running softly' freshly recreates a much-used metaphor found in phrases like *stream of consciousness* and *flow of ideas*. The adverb *softly* and the phrase *without haste* in this passage seem to me good examples of very ordinary expressions which are endued with strength of meaning within an appropriate literary context.

The Augustan period of English literature has been aptly called the 'age of prose', for it was during this period that 'prosaic strength' was particularly admired and cultivated not only in prose, but in poetry. Indeed, Pope's well-known definition of wit, 'What oft was thought but ne'er so well express'd' [*An Essay on Criticism*, 298], seems to sum up the kind of virtue we expect to find in the prose of Iris Murdoch, as of most other serious prose writers. The aim of 'prosaic' writing is to realize in an apt and illuminating form the common experience of man. We see this aim strikingly realized in the following character sketch from *Absalom and Achitophel*, a passage in which Dryden seems to weigh up each word with a delicate balance, so as to describe with probing accuracy the character of a public figure (the Earl of Shaftesbury) he assumes to be known to his readers:

> Of these the false Achitophel was first,
> A name to all succeeding ages curst.
> For close designs and crooked counsels fit,
> Sagacious, bold, and turbulent of wit,
> Restless, unfixt in principles and place,
> In pow'r unpleased, impatient of disgrace;
> A fiery soul, which working out its way,
> Fretted the pigmy body to decay:
> And o'er-informed the tenement of clay.
> A daring pilot in extremity;
> Pleas'd with the danger, when the waves went high
> He sought the storms; but, for a calm unfit,
> Would steer too nigh the sands to boast his wit.

As with most good prose, the positive qualities of this piece of verse are difficult to define. We can again point negatively to the absence of commonplace diction. For example, the three adjectives in the fourth line, *sagacious, bold,* and *turbulent,* each add a deliberate, precise stroke to the verbal portrait: they are far from being chosen mechanically, like the adjectives of many a spontaneous thumbnail sketch produced in conversation: *terribly kind and helpful; tall, dark, and handsome,* etc. On the other hand there is no violent departure from accepted usage. Figurative language, where it occurs, is of a traditional kind: the metaphor of the 'ship of state', for example, is found in classical literature. Much of the strength of the passage comes from Dryden's deployment of verse form in relation to syntax, in order to give the right kind of contrastive emphasis to each significant lexical item. There is a great deal more to be said about Dryden's skill in this description – but I hope I have made my point about the 'prosaic' toughness typical of Restoration and Augustan poetry.[8]

Although it is to Dryden and Pope that one turns for masterpieces of prosaic poetry, the solid, unpretentious qualities of good prose are perhaps more of an essential part of poetry than we realise. 'No poet', says Eliot in *The Music of Poetry*, 'can write a poem of amplitude unless he is a master of the prosaic.'[9]

2.4 DEGREES OF LINGUISTIC AUDACITY

As we have seen, it is useful, from some points of view, to think of language as a code of rules which can either be observed or broken. But this all-or-nothing view of linguistic deviation has its limitations; in the last section, for example, the reader may have been struck by the difficulty of deciding whether a given metaphor is the invention of a writer or an established part of language. My aim in this last section is to show how this analogy of language to a fixed code has to be modified. But first of all, I shall reformulate the distinction that has already been made, between choice within the language and choice outside the language, borrowing in a loose way the communication engineer's concept of 'information'.

'Information' in this sense can be equated with the communicative weight of each linguistic choice, independent of *what* meaning is conveyed. The amount of 'information' in a piece of language is related to the predictability of one linguistic choice from another. In ordinary pedestrian communications (for instance, in routine business letters), this predictability is high, and the amount of 'information' transmitted is comparatively small. In serious prose, on the other hand, the selections made have on the average a low predictability, and the amount of 'information' conveyed is fairly large. We can confirm this, impressionistically, by noting that a single glance at a business letter is often enough to tell a reader the substance of its message, whereas a page of literary prose has to be read with careful scrutiny: it conveys too much 'information' to take in on a superficial reading.

An actual violation of a rule of the language, however, belongs to a dimension of choice for which information theory makes no provision. By the standards of the accepted linguistic code, any selection which is not one of the selections allowed by the rules has a null probability: in other words, its occurrence within the language is impossible. But for a poet, the question of whether to obey the rules of the language or not is itself a matter of choice. This is shown visually in the 'special paradigm' of fig. [b] below as opposed to the 'normal paradigm' of fig. [a], which illustrates the set of possibilities regularly available in the language. The example is a famous case of linguistic deviation in poetry, Dylan Thomas's phrase 'a grief ago':[10]

fig. [*a*] NORMAL PARADIGM

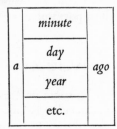

fig. [*b*] SPECIAL PARADIGM

a	minute day year etc.	NORMAL	ago
	grief	DEVIANT	

The poet in this phrase has gone beyond the normal range of choice represented in fig. [a], and has established, for the occasion, the paradigm represented by fig. [b]. The word *grief*, being placed in a position normally reserved for nouns of time-measurement, has to be construed as if it *were* a noun of time-measurement.

I have here taken a case favourable to the all-or-nothing view of linguistic rules. The rule Dylan Thomas ignores, in its most general form, may be expressed as follows: 'Only phrases based on nouns of time-measurement may enter into the construction --- *ago*', and it seems quite a straightforward matter to determine when this rule has been observed, since the nouns of time measurement *minute*, *day*, etc., constitute quite a small, listable group. Yet even in this case, we have to consider the question 'How deviant?' rather than simply 'Deviant or normal?'. Take for example the following phrases:

1. many moons ago
2. ten games ago
3. several performances ago
4. a few cigarettes ago
5. three overcoats ago
6. two wives ago
7. a grief ago
8. a humanity ago

These violations of the rule just stated are listed in order of (in my judgment) diminishing acceptability. At the 'most normal' end, expressions like 'many moons ago' have become so entrenched in the poetic idiom of the language that one needs a separate dictionary entry for *moon* to cater for it: 'the length of time between one new moon and the next' (i.e. 'lunar month'). The next two examples, 'ten games ago' and 'several performances ago', are perfectly plausible in appropriate situations – say at a tennis match and at an operatic production. 'A few cigarettes ago', 'three overcoats ago', and 'two wives ago' are slightly more bizarre, but it is not in the least inconceivable that someone should want to measure his existence in terms of the life of a cigarette, of an overcoat, or of a marriage. Only example (8) is so weird as to make it almost possible to say 'this phrase could not occur'. The more acceptable of these expressions can be paralleled by other quasi-acceptable time phrases such as 'since the bomb', 'before electricity', and 'after Freud'.

A more obvious illustration of degrees of abnormality is provided by metaphor. The newly minted poetic metaphor violates the usage recorded in the dictionary by creating an unorthodox (figurative) sense of a word or expression. But there is a world of difference between this and a 'dead' metaphor which has lost most of its analogical force, has passed into general currency, and has ended up being included in the dictionary as a recognized use; for instance, 'the *eye* (of a needle)' '*killing* time', 'he *swallowed* his pride'. And of course, there are all degrees of moribundity between these two extremes. The opening line of Gray's *Elegy* illustrates some of the intermediate stages:

The curfew tolls the knell of parting day

There are at least three metaphors here, although people will differ in attributing to them any degree of 'live' figurative power. First, *curfew* is not used in its primary historical sense of 'bell announcing the time for extinction of fires (according to medieval regulation)', but for a bell which *resembles* that bell in being rung at evening time. Actually, this second sense is given in the *Concise Oxford Dictionary* as a recognized meaning of *curfew* ('ringing of bell at fixed evening hour, still surviving in some towns'), although I was unaware of this until recently, and had assumed that the metaphor was original. Secondly, 'parting day' is mildly figurative to the extent that we feel *parting* to apply primarily to the departure of a person or physical object, and only secondarily, by metaphorical extension, to time. Thirdly, the expressions 'the curfew' and 'parting day' are separated by 'tolls the knell of', which is metaphorical with respect to both of them. The curfew, being itself a bell-ringing event, cannot literally toll a bell. So we must take 'tolls the knell' in the more abstract sense of 'announces the extinction of', which entails a figurative comparison between proclaiming the end of the day, and announcing a person's funeral rites. None of these metaphors approaches anywhere near the daring of (for example) Shakespeare's

<blockquote>
put a tongue
In every wound of Caesar, that should move
The stones of Rome to rise and mutiny.
[*Julius Caesar*, III.ii]
</blockquote>

Indeed, one may read Gray's line almost without noticing anything metaphorical about it at all. Yet none of the metaphors it contains are quite 'spent'.

A different kind of gradable unorthodoxy arises in syntax, and may be exemplified from the very last line of Hopkins's *The Wreck of the Deutschland*:

Our hearts' charity's hearth's fire, our thoughts' chivalry's throng's Lord.

The most striking linguistic feature of this line is the number of times the genitive construction is repeated: three successive genitives occur in each parallel half-line. The genitive construction in English is one of those which can be indefinitely repeated, each genitive being dependent on its successor; so that to trace an extremely distant family connection, I might embark upon a reiterative structure such as 'my uncle's brother's niece's grandfather's stepson's wife's ...'. This could theoretically go on *ad infinitum*, but in practice one very rarely has cause (or, in the interests of comprehension, dares) to make up a sequence of more than two genitives. Thus each of Hopkins's twin structures might be placed at position 3 on a scale of oddity as follows:

1. *A*'s *B*   (least odd)
2. *A*'s *B*'s *C*
3. *A*'s *B*'s *C*'s *D*

4. *A*'s *B*'s *C*'s *D*'s *E*   (more and more odd)
    etc.

Another, non-literary example of this kind of deviation is the last verse of the nursery rigmarole *This is the House that Jack Built*. In this case, the recursive structure is less baffling to the intellect, because it is composed not of genitives, but of relative clauses, which follow rather than precede the noun they modify. We would scarcely say that any rule of the language has been broken in such cases – rather, a theoretical possibility within the rules of the language has been realized to an extent which is in practice extremely unusual.

We are now able to see the difficulty of determining the exact limits to what is permitted to happen within the English language, and to realize that my earlier distinction between creativity within the language and outside the language (and hence the distinction between 'prosaic' and 'poetic' styles of writing) was something of an idealization. It is more realistic to think of degrees of linguistic audacity ranging between the extreme creative exuberance of a Dylan Thomas or a James Joyce, and the sober restraint of a Dryden or a Pope. Perhaps these two tendencies can be associated with the elusive concepts of 'Classicism' and 'Romanticism'. Ezra Pound suggests that classical writers, in one sense, are those that look 'for the *least possible* variant that would turn the most worn-out and commonest phrases of journalism into something distinguished'.[11] In that case, it is no coincidence that Gray, the representative of eighteenth-century classicism, should prove a ready source of examples of the milder, semi-assimilated type of metaphor.

Examples for discussion

1. Consider in what respects the following passages of twentieth-century poetry can be interpreted as personal testimonies of the poet's struggle to 'escape from banality'. (They are discussed in R. Quirk, *The Use of English*, 262–3.)

So here I am, in the middle way, having had twenty years –
Twenty years largely wasted, the years of *l'entre deux guerres*–
Trying to learn to use words, and every attempt
Is a wholly new start, and a different kind of failure
Because one has only learnt to get the better of words

For the thing one no longer has to say, or the way in which
One is no longer disposed to say it. And so each venture
Is a new beginning, a raid on the inarticulate
With shabby equipment always deteriorating
In the general mess of imprecision of feeling,
Undisciplined squads of emotion.
> [T. S. Eliot, *East Coker*]

And from the first declension of the flesh
I learnt man's tongue, to twist the shapes of thoughts
Into the stony idiom of the brain
To shade and knit anew the patch of words
Left by the dead who, in their moonless acre,
Need no word's warmth.
> [Dylan Thomas, *From Love's First Fever to her Plague*]

2. Pick out commonplace, idiomatic phrases of spoken English in Philip Larkin's
Toads, quoted in Examples for Discussion on page 21. In the light of the discussion
in §2.3, consider why the poem is not vulnerable to the charge of banality,
although it contains many of these 'prefabricated chunks' of language.

3. Draw diagrams similar to that of fig. [b] in §2.4 ('a grief ago') for the italicized
phrases in the following passages by Dylan Thomas:

[a] A dog barks in his sleep, *farmyards away.*
> [*Under Milk Wood*, p. 22]

[b] *All the moon long* I heard, blessed among stables, the nightjars . . .
> [*Fern Hill*]

[c] Cry,
Child *beyond cockcrow*
> [*Ceremony After a Fireraid*]

[d]   Who
      Are you
    Who is born
   In the next room
   So loud to my own
> [*Vision and Prayer*]

[e] Or, masted venus, through the paddler's bowl
Sailed up the sun
> [*A Grief Ago*]

Alternative diagrams may be necessary. What clues do the diagrams furnish for the
interpretation of the phrases? (You will find the full contexts for these passages in
the printed edition of *Under Milk Wood* (London, 1954) and *Collected Poems 1934-*

1952. Further help in interpretation is provided by W. Y. Tindall, *A Reader's Guide to Dylan Thomas*, London, 1962.)

Notes

1   T. S. ELIOT, 'The Music of Poetry', *Selected Prose*, Penguin Books, 1953, 58.
2   See N. CHOMSKY, *Syntactic Structures*, The Hague, 1957, 2; *Topics in the Theory of Generative Grammar*, The Hague, 1966, 11–12.
3   From *Finnegan's Wake*: 'Tales Told of Shem and Shaun', *The Essential James Joyce*, ed. H. LEVIN, London, 1948, 524.
4   D. DAVIE, *Purity of Diction in English Verse*, London, 1952, 62–9. My use of the phrase is comparable to Davie's although formulated in different terms.
5   See *ibid.*, 27–8.
6   G. ORWELL, 'The Language of Politics', *Collected Essays*, London, 1961, 361.
7   IRIS MURDOCH, *Under the Net*, London, 1954, 92.
8   See D. DAVIE, *op. cit.*, 29–90.
9   T. S. ELIOT, *Selected Prose*, 59.
10   For a different approach to 'a grief ago', see S. R. LEVIN, 'Poetry and Grammaticalness', *Proceedings of the IXth International Congress of Linguists*, ed. H. G. LUNT, The Hague, 1964, 308–14.
11   E. POUND, *A.B.C. of Reading*, London, 1951, 54.

Three

Varieties of Poetic Licence

In the phrase POETIC LICENCE we concede the poet's right to ignore rules and conventions generally observed by users of the language. I have already found myself discussing two very different kinds of poetic licence: in Chapter 1, the routine licences which are part of the traditional equipment of the versifier; and in Chapter 2, the creative licence, whereby a poet may transcend the limits of the language to explore and communicate new areas of experience.

The liberties poets have taken with the language have been of immense variety and have sometimes (especially in modern times) reached pathological degrees of abnormality. There is a world of difference between acknowledging a degree of poetic licence, and saying that 'anything goes' in the language of poetry. As with a legal code, if transgressions are too frequent and too violent, the system breaks down.

There are limits not only in the degree of freedom, but also in the types of freedom exercised. Certainly, poetic licence is displayed more at some levels of linguistic patterning than at others. An example of a type of rule-breaking which seems to have little value in poetry is the kind of ungrammaticality illustrated in: 'I doesn't be liking he.' Three rules at least are broken in this 'pidgin' utterance: the verbal element fails to agree with its subject in person, *be* is wrongly negated by means of the auxiliary *do* as if it were a lexical verb like *take*, etc., and the pronoun *he* is in the subjective case. It is not immediately apparent why this type of deviation strikes us as a mistake – as something a foreign learner of the language might be capable of saying, but not a poet; but I shall return to that question in §3.2.2.

My object in this chapter is to illustrate and discuss different kinds of poetic licence.[1] In doing so, I shall not entirely ignore aspects of the language which seem to offer the poet little opportunity for creative improvisation; but my main interest will lie in those areas which lend themselves to this purpose.

3.1 ANATOMY OF LANGUAGE

A survey of different kinds of poetic licence must begin with the question of what kinds of rule or conventional restriction can be infringed. This in turn leads us back to more fundamental questions: What is the nature of language? How is it constituted? What different kinds of rules in language have to be recognized? My preliminary task is therefore to attempt a very short, simplified account of how a language such as English may be broken down into various levels of organization, and how these levels combine together. I should add that there are as many ways in which such an account could be given as there are different theories of how language works. The following sketch is a composite one, which aims to be non-controversial.[2]

One thing on which there seems to be little disagreement nowadays is that the traditional method of breaking language down into two components, form and meaning, is inadequate. Instead, a roughly tripartite model is usually preferred[3]:

fig. [*c*]

REALIZATION	FORM	SEMANTICS
Phonology	Grammar and Lexicon	(Denotative or Cognitive) Meaning
Graphology		

The reader may perhaps best understand this diagram by imagining himself in the position of someone trying to learn the language for the first time, and asking himself, 'What different kinds of knowledge do I have to acquire, before I can say I know English, and am able to use it properly?'

3.1.1 *The Three Main Levels: Realization, Form, Semantics*

Since knowledge of a language is traditionally condensed into two kinds of book, the dictionary and the grammar book, we may start by observing that to know a language competently, a speaker is required to have memorized a vocabulary in that language, and to have learnt a set of rules showing how the items of the vocabulary are to be used in constructing sentences. These two parts, the LEXICON and the GRAMMAR, together comprise the FORMAL aspect of the language.

But dictionaries and grammar books do not entirely restrict themselves to specifying the lexicon and grammar in this sense. They also give other kinds of information a learner needs to know: how to pronounce and write the forms of the language, that is, how to give them physical realization; and also what they mean. Thus three main types of rule have to be known: rules of FORM, of REALIZATION (phonological or graphological), and of SEMANTICS.

The same three-level model applies both to the productive and receptive processes of language: to listening and reading as much as to speaking and writing. The only difference between these processes is that the types of rule are applied in the opposite order, as indicated in fig. [d], which for simplicity represents the spoken language alone:

fig. [d]

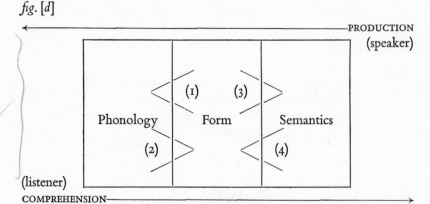

There is no point in going into details as to why language has come to be analysed on three major levels rather than two. But it may be useful to give examples of locutions which are identical on one level and different on another, neighbouring level. These will illustrate the functions of each level, and will also go some way towards suggesting why it is necessary to have three levels at all. The four possibilities to consider are drawn on the diagram above, and are listed with corresponding numbers below:

1. *Homophony.* Same pronunciation, different form (e.g. *light* adj. and *light* noun).
2. *Differentiation.* Same form, different pronunciation (e.g. the noun *envelope* pronounced either as 'envelope' or as if 'onvelope'; in poetry, *over* and *o'er*, etc.).
3. *Synonymy.* Same meaning, different form (e.g. *none the less, nevertheless, all the same*).

4. *Multiple Meaning (Polysemy).* Same form, different meaning (e.g. *light* = (1) 'undark', and (2) 'unheavy').

These four many-one relations apply not only to words, but to sentences and longer utterances. The remark 'His designs upset her', for example, has four possible meanings: [*a*] 'His drawings disturbed her'; [*b*] 'His intentions disturbed her'; [*c*] 'His drawings disturb her'; [*d*] 'His intentions disturb her'. One ambiguity arises from the homophony of the two forms *upset* (present tense) and *upset* (past tense), whereas the other arises from the polysemy of *designs*. Hence lurking in 'His designs upset her' there are two homophonous sentences, and each of these has two distinct meanings.

3.1.2. *Phonology and Graphology*

As English sentences can be transmitted by writing as well as by speech, a competent performer needs to know both how to pronounce and how to write the language. The term 'graphology' is somewhat wider than the more usual term 'orthography', as it refers to the whole writing system: punctuation and paragraphing as well as spelling. To a great extent, English graphology imitates phonology – that is, the written version of the language is a visual coding of its spoken version. But as everyone knows, English spelling does this in a very irregular manner, and sometimes makes distinctions which are not heard in speech (e.g. between *ceiling* and *sealing*). Moreover, punctuation does not mirror features of spoken English in any obvious manner; it has not so far been shown, for instance, that there is anything in speech corresponding to the paragraph. Because graphology has to some extent its own rules and structure independent of pronunciation, it is perhaps best treated as a separate level of realization side by side with phonology, as shown in fig. [c]. The two levels are thus in an 'either–or' relationship, in contrast to the 'both–and' relationship between grammar and lexicon. But this does not mean that a written text has no implications of spoken performance. Indeed, we know well enough that in poetry, phonological effects, including those of versification, can be appreciated in silent reading, as well as in reading aloud.

3.1.3 *Meaning and Significance*

Now I move to the right-hand box of fig. [c], to semantics, or the study of meaning. I must make it clear that the word MEANING is to be used in this book in the narrow sense of 'cognitive', 'logical', or 'denotative' meaning:

that is, the kind of meaning that is the concern of the dictionary-maker. This contrasts with a very broad use of the term often encountered in literary studies, where the 'meaning' of a poem, a line, a word, etc., may include everything that is communicated by it. This I shall prefer to call the SIGNIFICANCE or (more explicitly) TOTAL SIGNIFICANCE of a piece of language. I make this distinction, to avoid confusions which have sometimes accompanied the use of such words as 'meaning' in reference to literature.

The (cognitive) meaning of an utterance or text is a part of its total significance, but how important that part is depends very much on the communicative situation. Scientific and technical varieties of English approach as close as they can to a type of communication in which nothing is significant except cognitive meaning. In personal conversation, however, allowance has to be made for other, non-cognitive elements, especially of emotive and attitudinal import. In poetry, so many special avenues of communication between writer and reader are used, that cognitive meaning may seem to be only a small part of the entire communication. Yet it would be quite absurd to insist that cognitive meaning counts for nothing in poetry. Whilst we can reasonably assert that the word *cloud* in Wordsworth's 'I wander'd lonely as a cloud' conveys something additional to what it would convey in a weather forecast, there is no need to go to the extreme of claiming that the meteorologist's and poet's uses of the terms have nothing in common. If all words were deprived of cognitive content in poetry, they would be reduced, in communicative power, to the level of exclamations like *alas, ouch*, and *tally-ho*.

It has been a widely accepted doctrine for some time in literary criticism that a poem or piece of poetry cannot be paraphrased. The debates which have revolved around this doctrine show how confusion can result from an undiscriminating use of terms like 'meaning' in literary discussion. But if we bear in mind the above distinction between meaning and significance, the whole issue is clarified. Of course, on the plane of cognitive meaning a poem can be paraphrased: representing the 'sense' of a passage (i.e. its cognitive content) in different words is in fact a recognized classroom exercise. But if by 'paraphrase' we understand 'giving the whole *significance* of a passage in different words', then the doctrine which attacks the 'paraphrastic heresy' is no doubt correct.

3.1.4 *Ancillary Branches of Linguistics*

The box diagram in fig. [c] depicted the domain of DESCRIPTIVE LINGUISTICS[4]; that is, of that central aspect of linguistics which is concerned with the description of linguistic patterns in the abstract, without reference to how, where, when, etc., they are used. The three additional branches of DIALECTOLOGY, REGISTER STUDY, and HISTORICAL LINGUISTICS deal with three different dimensions on which these patterns are liable to vary. DIALECTOLOGY is the study of dialect, that is, how language varies according to its user; REGISTER STUDY is concerned with variations according to the function of language in society (the concept of register is widened here to include how language expresses the feelings and attitudes of the user); HISTORICAL LINGUISTICS charts the development of language through time. These three 'ancillary' studies are essentially *comparative*, because they compare the different ways in which language is used according to circumstances. The rules of any of the three major levels are apt to be restricted by conditions of dialect, style, or time.

Descriptive linguistics, we might say from another point of view, deals only with knowledge of the language, not with the knowledge of how to use it. Certainly the linguistic expertise of our hypothetical learner of English will be somewhat limited unless his knowledge extends to these three additional factors. Without some experience of them, he will not only commit grave social errors, but will miss many of the more subtle aspects of linguistic communication. These debilities will above all handicap his understanding of literary texts, in which associations of register, social class, historical period, etc., are used for deliberate effect, and are especially significant.

When we note that *caitiff* has archaic connotations, *roster* military connotations, *tootsy* nursery connotations, we merely observe how words of limited use acquire the flavour of the circumstances to which their use characteristically belongs. *Tootsy*, improbably transplanted into a poem, would carry its nursery background with it. When we talk of 'connotative meaning', we refer, in part, to this power of a word, sentence, etc., to conjure up the typical context of its occurrence. But this is not the whole explanation of 'connotation', for this term is used not only of the associations which go with the use of the linguistic item itself, but also of the associations of what it refers to. If, for instance, *night, blood, ghost, thunder*, are said to have 'sinister connotations', it is surely because this suggestive quality belongs to the things themselves – night, blood, ghosts, and thunder – (and hence, by association, to the words) rather than just to the words. The sinister aura would be felt (no doubt more powerfully) in pictorial or auditory representations of these things, just as much as it is in the words denoting them. In my opinion, linguistics can say nothing about this latter kind of associativity, which is nevertheless of undeniable importance in poetry.

3.2 TYPES OF DEVIATION

We are now equipped for a cursory survey of different types of linguistic deviation in poetry, starting with the central level of linguistic form, and moving from there to the other levels shown in fig. [c].

3.2.1 *Lexical Deviation*

Neologism, or the invention of new 'words' (i.e. items of vocabulary) is one of the more obvious ways in which a poet may exceed the normal resources of the language. Not that it is the prerogative solely of the poet: journalists, copywriters, and scientists, to mention three other types of linguistic practitioners, are for various reasons renowned for lexical invention. Even ordinary citizens in ordinary conversations quite often stumble into neologism as the readiest way to express their feelings or opinions. We call new words NONCE-FORMATIONS if they are made up 'for the nonce', i.e., for a single occasion only, rather than as serious attempts to augment the English wordstock for some new need. The poet's lexical innovations can mostly be placed in the category of nonce-formations, although obviously poetic neologisms are inclined to be less ephemeral than conversational ones, for a successful poem will be read time and time again, by the poet's contemporaries and by succeeding generations. Quite a number of widely used English words apparently originated in poetry: examples are *blatant* [Spenser], *assassination* [Shakespeare], *pandemonium* [Milton], and *casuistry* [Pope].

It is misleading to suggest that neologism is a 'violation of lexical rule'; a more correct explanation is that an existing rule (of word-formation) is applied with greater generality than is customary: that the usual restrictions on its operation are waived in a given instance. Let us take as an example the English rule of word-formation which permits the prefixation of *fore-* to a verb, to convey the meaning 'beforehand', as in *foresee, foreknow, foretell,* and *forewarn.* If this rule were completely free in its application, we would use verbs such as *foresell* ('sell in advance') or *foreappear* ('appear in advance') without even noticing their oddity. But the rule is in fact limited to a small group of items, so that when T. S. Eliot [in *The Waste Land*, III] augments the group by using the verb *foresuffer* in the line 'And I Tiresias have foresuffered all', this strikes us as a novelty, and as a surprising extension of the expressive possibilities of the language. If there were no limitations of vocabulary of this kind, there would be no such thing as a finite list of words constituting the lexicon of the language.

The most common processes of word-formation are affixation (the addition of a prefix or suffix to an item already in the language), and compounding (the joining together of two or more items to make a single compound one). In the following phrase from Hopkins's *The Wreck of the Deutschland* both compounding and affixation are used to similar effect:

the widow-making unchilding unfathering deeps.

The privative use of *un-* here in the sense 'take off/away from' can be paralleled in *unhorse, unfrock, unleash*, etc. (compare Lady Macbeth's *unsex*). *Widow-making* is a compound on the pattern of *music-loving, tub-thumping, prize-winning*, etc. Another means of extending the vocabulary, of especial importance in English, is FUNCTIONAL CONVERSION, which might be better described as 'zero affixation'. Functional conversion consists in adapting an item to a new grammatical function without changing its form. Hopkins makes as striking use of this as of other methods of word-formation, as the following examples show:

And storms *bugle* his fame	[*The Wreck of the Deutschland*]
Let him *easter* in us	[*The Wreck of the Deutschland*]
The just man *justices*	[*As Kingfishers Catch Fire*]
The *achieve* of, the mastery of the thing	[*The Windhover*]

It is interesting that in this last example, *achieve* is chosen in preference to the very common abstract noun *achievement*, and that this choice makes all the difference between poetic vigour and prosaic flatness. Daring use of functional conversion is also a feature of Shakespeare's style. In *Antony and Cleopatra*, for example, Antony tries to goad his henchman Eros into killing him, by envisaging Eros as a spectator of his humiliation in Caesar's triumph: 'Would'st thou be *window'd* (i.e. placed in a window) in great Rome, and see / Thy master thus ...' Later in this play, Cleopatra anachronistically foresees her impersonation by child-actors on the Shakespearean stage with 'I shall see some squeaking Cleopatra *boy* my greatness'.[5]

As with metaphor, the degree of strangeness one feels with a lexical innovation varies greatly from item to item, and from context to context. Some types of word-formation have been so common in poetry that they cause little surprise in the reader, and may almost be classified as routine licences (see §1.2.5). Spenser often prefixed *a-* and *en-* to words which required an extra syllable to fill their allotted place in the metrical scheme. He was likewise fond of adjectives in *-y, -less, -full*, and nouns in *-ment*. Some of these affixes remained especially productive in the poetry of the following two or three centuries. Spenser, too, helped to introduce into English poetic diction the propensity for compounds like *shaggy-bearded* (*goats*), *firie-mouthed* (*steeds*), etc.[6]

To find what else, apart from custom, is involved in the strangeness of a new formation, we must first turn to the general question of the purpose and effect of neologism in poetry. It is wrong, at least in most cases, to suppose that the intended meaning could not have been conveyed without lexical invention. To return to Hopkins's 'the widow-making unchilding unfathering deeps': the cognitive meaning of this could have been rendered 'the deeps which deprive (wives) of husbands, (children) of fathers, and (parents) of children'. The longwindedness of this paraphrase, however, reveals the degree of compression and economy which can be achieved by affixation and compounding. But I think that there is another, more important if rather elusive factor, which may be called the 'concept-making' power of neologism. If a new word is coined it implies the wish to recognize a concept or property which the language can so far only express by phrasal or clausal description. Eliot's *foresuffered* is not just a new word, but the encapsulation of a newly formulated idea: that it is possible to anticipate mystically the suffering of the future, just as it is possible to *foresee*, *foretell*, or have *foreknowledge* of future events. Similarly, Hopkins's three epithets seem to invest the sea with three awe-inspiring qualities. The paraphrase by means of a relative clause simply describes tragic happenings connected with the sea, whereas *widow-making*, *unchilding*, and *unfathering* seem to attribute to the sea properties which are as inseparable from it as are the properties of wetness, blueness, and saltness. The oddity of neologisms is related to the general usefulness of the concepts they represent: *widow-making* strikes us as stranger than *cloth-making* or *rabbit-catching*, because we would rarely wish to classify aspects of the universe by their tendency to make people into widows, whereas we might quite easily want to characterize objects (e.g., a machine or a snare) by their ability to make cloth or catch rabbits.

3.2.2 *Grammatical Deviation*

To distinguish between the many different types of grammatical deviation, it is as well to start with the line traditionally drawn between MORPHOLOGY (the grammar of the word) and SYNTAX (the grammar of how words pattern within sentences). Despite the many morphological extravagances such as *museyroom*, *intellible*, and *eggtentical* in Joyce's *Finnegan's Wake*, linguistic oddities in the former category are rare enough in English poetry to be passed over here.

In syntax, there is first a difference between the type of deviation illustrated in §2.4 ('Our heart's charity's hearth's fire') – an exploitation of the potential complexity of repetitive structure to an unusual degree – and a simple 'yes'/'no' case of ungrammaticality, as with 'I doesn't like him'. Secondly, there is, according to recent thinking on syntax, a distinction of great importance between the DEEP STRUCTURE and the SURFACE STRUCTURE of a sentence.[7] I shall not go into the exact theoretical nature of this distinction, but simply observe that the deep structure directly reflects the meaning of the sentence, whereas the surface structure relates to the way in which a sentence is actually uttered. For example, in the passive sentence 'Gladstone was revered by his supporters', the identification of the 'logical subject' ('his supporters') belongs to the deep or underlying structure, whereas the identification of the 'grammatical subject' ('Gladstone') belongs to the surface structure. Deep structure may be characterized as the 'semantic end' of syntax, and surface structure as the 'phonological end', as it specifies the actual forms which are uttered, and the sequence in which they occur.

Violations of surface structure are 'superficial' not only in the technical sense, but also in the sense that they have no fundamental effect on the way in which a sentence is understood. Into this category fall violations which could be described as 'bad' or 'incorrect' grammar, and also the examples of syntactic rearrangement (hyperbaton) discussed in §1.2.5. 'I doesn't like him' strikes us as a poor attempt at 'I don't like him'; 'He me saw' as a strange variant of 'He saw me'.

Examples of violation of deep structure are *a grief ago* (see §2.4) and the other phrases of Dylan Thomas appended to Chapter 2 (Examples for Discussion, page 21). In these cases, a position reserved for words of a certain class is filled by a word from a different class. Most deviations of deep structure can be treated as cases of 'mistaken selection'; and the interpretation of the deviation consists not in mapping the deviant form on to a single normal form which it most closely resembles, but rather in relating it to a whole class of normal forms which could replace it in that position.

A rather different case of 'misclassification' is that which arises in this line from *The Wreck of the Deutschland*:

Thou hast bound bones and veins in me, *fastened me flesh*

What is peculiar about the second half of this line is the occurrence of the verb *fasten* in a construction (Subject + Verbal + Object + Object Complement) into which it does not normally fit. *Fasten* belongs to the class of straightforward transitive verbs regularly followed by a single object. How then do we interpret it when followed by two nominal elements? One way is to treat it as if reclassified as a factitive verb – that is, as a member of the class of verbs such as *make*, *crown*, *elect*, which regularly take both an object and an object complement. It is then construed, approximately, as 'to make (me) into (flesh) by fastening'. This line demonstrates, however, how interfering with regular linguistic classifications can lead to ambiguities of structure. A second, perhaps more plausible, way to make sense of this deviation would be to take *me* as an indirect object and *flesh* as a direct object. Then the analogy will not be to the construction of 'crown him king', but to that of 'cook him dinner'. A rough paraphrase in this case would be 'fasten flesh for me', i.e. 'for my benefit'.

I shall close this very incomplete survey of grammatical deviation in poetry with a glance at various 'asyntactic' styles which have made their appearance in modern literature. These mainly seem to have the function of impressionistically evoking psychological states. In *The Wanderer*, apparently modelled on the Anglo-Saxon poem of the same name,[8] W. H. Auden evolves a subjectless, articleless style which suggests to me the exile's loss of a sense of identity and of a co-ordinated view of life:

> There head falls forward, fatigued at evening,
> And dreams of home,
> Waving from window, spread of welcome,
> Kissing of wife under single sheet;
> But waking sees
> Bird-flocks nameless to him, through doorway voices
> Of new men making another love.

The disjointed syntax of this passage has something in common with that of the style Joyce uses to represent the interior monologue of Leopold Bloom in *Ulysses* (see the Examples for Discussion at the end of this chapter, page 53).

3.2.3 *Phonological Deviation*

Patterns of phonology are even more 'on the surface' than those of surface syntactic structure, so it is not surprising that phonological deviation in English poetry is of limited importance. Not that this is true of all languages: in some American Indian cultures, notably that of the Nootka, literary recitation is clearly marked off from ordinary speech by a set of deviant phonological characteristics.[9]

In English, the only irregularities of pronunciation we need note are conventional licences of verse composition: elision, aphesis, apocope, etc. (see §1.2.5) and special pronunciation for the convenience of rhyming, as when the noun *wind* is pronounced like the verb *wind*. It appears also that certain nineteenth-century poets placed word stresses in unusual places: *balúster* [Tennyson], *bastárd* [Browning], and *Júly* [D. G. Rossetti].[10] Whether this was merely for exigencies of metre, out of archaic affectation, or out of obedience to some obscure principle of euphony, is hard to determine.

3.2.4 *Graphological Deviation*

To the extent that spelling represents pronunciation, any strangeness of pronunciation will be reflected by a strangeness of written form. But there is also a kind of graphological deviation which need have no counterpart in speech. The key example of this might seem too obvious to mention: it is the characteristic line-by-line arrangement of poetry on the printed page, with irregular right-hand margins. The typographical line of poetry, like the typographical stanza, is a unit which is not paralleled in non-poetic varieties of English: it is independent of, and capable of interacting with, the standard units of punctuation. This interaction is a special communicative resource of poetry.

It is clear that when lines on the page do not correspond to any phonological reality, as in *vers libre*, verse lineation becomes a structuring device with no justification beyond itself. Two American poets who explore possibilities of purely visual patterning in poetry are William Carlos Williams and E. E. Cummings. Cummings is well known for his use of other types of orthographic deviation: discarding of capital letters and punctuation where convention calls for them, jumbling of words, eccentric use of parentheses, etc. For him, capitalization, spacing, and punctuation become expressive devices, not symbols to be used according to typographic custom; he uses the compositor's case as an artist's palette. Some of his more extreme experiments in visual poetry resemble coded messages which, for their decipherment, call upon the kind of skill we use in solving crossword-puzzles and anagrams. The following example, by contrast, is mild and simple:

seeker of truth

follow no path
all paths lead where

truth is here

[No. 3 of *73 Poems*]

The brevity of this poem (which, by the way, because of its semi-rhyme, does not abandon the phonological basis of verse) enables me to point to one particular use to which graphological deviation can be put. An ambiguity arises from a clash between the units of sense indicated by lineation and by syntax. According to the lineation, the poem ends with a statement 'truth is here'; but according to the syntax, 'truth is' must belong to the clause begun in the previous line, and so 'here' is left on its own as an exclamatory conclusion. The whole significance of the poem pivots on this ambiguity, which of course could not have arisen if the poet had used conventional capitalization and punctuation.

3.2.5 *Semantic Deviation*

W. B. Yeats thought that an irrational element was present in all great poetry. It is indeed, almost as commonplace to regard a poem as a kind of inspired nonsense, as 'a piece of sophisticated looniness' (Theodore Roethke's pleasing description of a composition by Wallace Stevens).[11] This is the characteristic of poetry we have under focus when we consider the topic of semantic deviation.

It is reasonable to translate 'semantic deviation' mentally into 'nonsense' or 'absurdity', so long as we realize that 'sense' is used, in this context, in a strictly literal-minded way: that is, in a way which would find favour with a mathematician or logician. Wordsworth's 'The child is father of the man' is far from nonsensical by the generous standards of poetic appreciation: indeed, its very face-value oddity lends it abnormal power of significance. But by the deliberately unimaginative standards of the philosopher, it is impossible for X to be Y's father while X is a child and Y is a man.

We may approach this from another direction by saying that the superficial absurdity of Wordsworth's apophthegm forces the reader to look beyond the dictionary definition for a reasonable interpretation: he has to understand *father* in another sense than that of 'progenitor'. This is clearer in the case of an equally celebrated paradox, Keats's 'Beauty is truth, truth beauty', which equates, as baldly and bluntly as in a mathematical formula, two philosophically important abstractions: 'beauty=truth'. This definition of 'truth' and 'beauty' in terms of one another is, needless to say, at odds with what any dictionary attempting to record customary usage would say. For example, when we say 'This story is beautiful' we decidedly do not imply 'This story is true'. Keats is proposing some mystical unity of concepts which are ordinarily treated as distinct.

In poetry, TRANSFERENCE OF MEANING, or METAPHOR in its widest sense, is the process whereby literal absurdity leads the mind to comprehension on a figurative plane. It is by far the most important single factor in that transcendence of the normal resources of communication by which I characterized poetic language in Chapter 2. So important an element of poetic language is it that poets and critics alike have tended to consider it the only thing that really matters in poetry. Whilst this is taking the claims of metaphor too far, it is obviously too central an aspect of poetic language to be dealt with in one minor section of this chapter, and I therefore postpone an extended treatment of it until Chapter 9.

3.2.6 *Dialectal Deviation*

I have dealt with deviation in all the departments of the box diagram in fig. [c], page 37, so it only remains to consider the validity of the concept of poetic licence in those other aspects of linguistic study I have called 'ancillary'.

DIALECTISM, or the borrowing of features of socially or regionally defined dialects, is a minor form of licence not generally available to the average writer of functional prose, who is expected to write in the generally accepted and understood dialect known as 'Standard English'. But it is, of course, quite commonly used by story-tellers and humorists. For the poet, dialectism may serve a number of purposes.

In *The Shepheardes Calender*, Spenser's use of homely provincial words like *heydeguyes* (a type of dance), *rontes* ('young bullocks'), *weanell* ('newly weaned kid or lamb'), and *wimble* ('nimble')[12] evokes a flavour of rustic naivety in keeping with the sentiments of pastoral. In Kipling's army ballads and Hardy's Wessex ballads, dialectism is almost inseparable from the writer's plan of depicting life as seen through the experience and ethos of one particular section of English-speaking society.

3.2.7 *Deviation of Register*

Modern poets, as we noted in Chapter 1, have asserted their freedom from constraints of 'poetical' language. It is therefore to the present age that we turn for the most striking examples of poetic licence in the domain of register. It is not that borrowing language from other, non-poetic registers, is a new invention, but that poets of the present century have exploited this device with an unprecedented audacity. Could any form of language outrage stylistic decorum more violently than the coarseness of Philip Larkin's phrase 'stuff your pension' in *Toads* (quoted on page 21), or the drab clichés of officialdom in Ezra Pound's line (from *Homage to Sextus Propertius*, XII) 'For a much larger Iliad is in the course of construction (and to Imperial order)'?

Register borrowing in poetry is almost always accompanied by the further incongruity of REGISTER MIXING, or the use in the same text of features characteristic of different registers. Eliot in *The Waste Land* (III) juxtaposes high-flown poetical diction and stock journalistic phraseology:

> The nymphs are departed.
>
> . . .
>
> Departed, have left no addresses.

A more subtle example is the following two lines from Auden's *Letter to Lord Byron* [II, 19]:

> And many a bandit, not so gently born
> Kills vermin every winter with the Quorn.

Winifred Nowottny, in *The Language Poets Use*,[13] makes the penetrating observation that 'Kills vermin' here is a singular expression because it mixes two usages: in the euphemistic parlance in which one refers to animals as vermin, one speaks of killing as 'keeping down', 'destroying', 'dealing with', etc. This incongruity, which contributes considerably to the satirical force of the couplet, can very easily be overlooked. In a similar connection, Mrs Nowottny quotes the opening of *Lessons of the War: 1. Naming of Parts* by Henry Reed[14]:

> To-day we have naming of parts. Yesterday,
> We had daily cleaning. And to-morrow morning,
> We shall have what to do after firing. But to-day,
> To-day we have naming of parts. Japonica
> Glistens like coral in all of the neighbouring gardens,
>   And to-day we have naming of parts.

Here the effect of mingling two registers – that of rifle instruction and that of lyrical description – is ironical in a bolder, more clear-cut, but nevertheless equally effective way. The first four lines, but for the last word *japonica*, might have been taken verbatim from a rifle-instructor's mono-logue. They have the naively repetitive syntax of an inept style of lectur-ing, and contain the mechanically produced regulation army phrases, which, one feels, should be printed in capitals to show their status as headings lifted from the instruction booklet: 'Naming of Parts', 'Daily Cleaning', 'What to Do After Firing'. It is in the last line, where the regulation language is yoked by co-ordination to the descriptive language, that the irony reaches its full concentration.

Sometimes an incongruity lies not so much in the relation of a piece of language to its linguistic context as in its relation to its subject matter. In Eliot's line 'He, the young man carbuncular, arrives' [*The Waste Land*, III] the poetic heightening of the syntax (shown particularly in the inver-sion of adjective and noun) ironically belittles the character and event de-scribed. The adjective *carbuncular*, too, despite its polysyllabic resonance, is ludicrously incompatible with the lofty sentiments the syntax leads us to expect. This clash between matter and manner is the basis of the mock heroic style cultivated in the eighteenth century, although in the latter part of that period mock heroic became a convention in itself, a stereotyped pose of mock-seriousness not necessarily combined with satirical intent.

3.2.8 *Deviation of Historical Period*

We have noted the poet's ability to range over the multifariousness of the language without respect to boundaries of dialect and register. To com-plete the picture, we must also note (as, indeed, we have already done to some extent in the discussion of archaism, §1.2.1) that he has 'the freedom of the language', in the same sense that he is not restricted to the language of his own particular period, as is the case with more commonplace types of linguistic transaction. It might be said, in fact, that the medium of Eng-lish poetry is the English language viewed as a historical whole, not just as a synchronous system shared by the writer and his contemporaries. James Joyce thought that a writer must be familiar with the history of his lan-guage – that he must, in short, be a philologist. T. S. Eliot expressed a similar point of view, in more general terms, when he insisted that 'no poet . . . has his complete meaning alone. His significance, his appreciation is the appreciation of his relation to dead poets and artists'.[15] Such senti-ments help to explain why many poets have felt that they share the same language, the same communicative medium, as poets of earlier generations, whatever important changes the language may have undergone in the meantime.

What a poet sees as his linguistic heritage may even include dead languages such as Latin and Greek. A type of historical licence current in the period of neo-classical culture following the Renaissance was the use of a word of Latin origin in a sense reconstructed from the literal Latin meanings of its elements. Examples of such etymological reinterpretations in Milton are: *inspiring* (= 'breathing in'), *induce* (= 'lead in'), 'with *serpent error* wand'ring' ('crawling', 'creeping'), 'Bush with frizzl'd hair *implicit*' ('entwined').[16]

Archaism as the 'survival of the language of the past into the language of the present', is of course an institutionalized licence of poetry, and may perhaps be distinguished from linguistic anachronism, or the conscious and calculated resurrection of language belonging to a bygone age. A clear case of anachronism in language (consisting largely in quotation from Sir Thomas Elyot's *The Governour*) occurs in the following passage from T. S. Eliot's *East Coker*:

> The association of man and woman
> In daunsinge, signifying matrimonie –
> A dignified and commodious sacrament,
> Two and two, necessarye coniunction,
> Holding eche other by the hand or the arm
> Which betokeneth concorde.

The alternation between ancient and modern, emphasized by spelling, is similar in inspiration and effect to the register mixing which Eliot employs extensively, both in this poem and elsewhere. The point of the device, in the larger context of the poem, is clear: it 'says' that progression through time is cyclic, and that present and past are ultimately one.

Archaism and anachronism in other periods of literature are difficult to separate. For example, in the language of Coleridge's *The Ancient Mariner*, there is a certain amount of deliberate revival of obsolete usage, for historical colouring; but there is also some reliance upon standard archaisms current in the poetry of the day.

3.3 CONCLUSION

Our gamut of categories has not exhausted the numerous ways in which English poets may deviate from the norms of English. An instance of a type of licence for which no allowance has been made in the foregoing scheme is the interpolation of bits of living foreign languages, conspicuously practised by Pound and Eliot in some of their poems, and illustrated in Walt Whitman's 'Allons! we must not stop here!' [*Song of the Open Road*]. However, I shall not attempt to extend the catalogue beyond this point: instead, I shall use Whitman's exhortation to spur the reader on to the next chapter, where my aim will be to correct the negative emphasis of this chapter by paying attention to the constructive communicative value of linguistic deviation.

Examples for discussion

1. Say as precisely as possible how the following passage of 'interior monologue' from James Joyce's *Ulysses* deviates from the syntax of normal discursive prose (see §3.2.2):

> Bloom looked, unblessed to go. Got up to kill: on eighteen bob a week. Fellows shell out the dibs. Want to keep your weathereye open. Those girls, those lovely. By the sad sea waves. Chorusgirl's romance. Letters read out for breach of promise. From Chickabiddy's own Mumpsypum. Laughter in court. Henry. I never signed it. The lovely name you.   [From *The Sirens*]

2. Identify types of linguistic deviation in the following. Discuss how they contribute to the total significance of each passage:

[*a*] [Part of a passage satirizing Wordsworth's *The Waggoners*]

> If he must fain sweep o'er the ethereal plain,
>   And Pegasus runs restive in his 'Waggon',
> Could he not beg the loan of Charles's Wain?
>   Or pray Medea for a single dragon?
> Or if, too classic for his vulgar brain,
>   He fear'd his neck to venture such a nag on,
> And he must needs mount nearer to the moon,
>   Could not the blockhead ask for a balloon?
>   [Byron, *Don Juan*, III, 99]

[*b*]

> No worst, there is none. Pitched past pitch of grief,
> More pangs will, schooled at forepangs, wilder wring.
> Comforter, where, where is your comforting?
> Mary, mother of us, where is your relief?
> My cries heave, herds-long; huddle in a main, a chief
> Woe, world-sorrow; on an age-old anvil wince and sing –
> Then lull, then leave off. Fury had shrieked 'No ling-
> ering! Let me be fell: force I must be brief'.

O the mind, mind has mountains; cliffs of fall
Frightful, sheer, no-man-fathomed. Hold them cheap
May who ne'er hung there. Nor does long our small
Durance deal with that steep or deep. Here! creep,
Wretch, under a comfort serves in a whirlwind: all
Life death does end and each day dies with sleep.
                    [A sonnet by G. M. Hopkins]

[c]
pity this busy monster, manunkind,

not.   Progress is a comfortable disease:
your victim(death and life safely beyond)

plays with the bigness of his littleness
– electrons deify one razorblade
into a mountainrange;lenses extend

unwish through curving wherewhen till unwish
returns on its unself.
                    A world of made
is not a world of born – pity poor flesh

and trees,poor stars and stones,but never this
fine specimen of hypermagical

ultraomnipotence.   We doctors know

a hopeless case if – listen:there's a hell
of a good universe next door;let's go
                    [A complete poem by E. E. Cummings]

Notes

1   Cf. a survey of types of deviation in S. R. LEVIN, 'Internal and External Deviation in Poetry', *Word*, 21.2 (1965), 225–39. (In this chapter we are only concerned with what Levin calls 'external deviation'.)
2   The conception of language represented here follows, more than any other, that of the 'Neo-Firthian' movement in Great Britain; see especially M. A. K. HALLIDAY, A. MCINTOSH, and P. STREVENS, *The Linguistic Sciences and Language Teaching*, London, 1964, 9–12.
3   Compare the diagram in HALLIDAY, MCINTOSH, and STREVENS, *op. cit.*, 18.
4   HALLIDAY, MCINTOSH, and STREVENS (*op. cit.*, 15–19) use the term 'descriptive linguistics' in a similar sense.

5   B. GROOM, *The Diction of Poetry from Spenser to Bridges*, Toronto, 1955, 43–4.

6   GROOM, *op. cit.*, 7–8.

7   See N. CHOMSKY, *Aspects of the Theory of Syntax*, Cambridge, Mass., 1965, 16–18.

8   It has been pointed out, however, that the opening line of this poem is derived from a medieval homily entitled *Sawles Warde*. (M. W. BLOOMFIELD, 'Doom is Dark and Deeper than Any Sea-Dingle', *Modern Language Notes*, 63 (1948), 549–552).

9   See LEVIN, *op. cit.*, 229 and n.

10 GROOM, *op. cit.*, 217, 237, and 254.

11 C. BROOKS and R. P. WARREN, eds., *Conversations on the Craft of Poetry*, New York, 1961, 59 (quoted in H. GROSS, *Sound and Form in Modern Poetry*, Ann Arbor, 1964, 228).

12 In the June, February, September, and March Eclogues respectively. See C. L. WRENN, 'On re-reading Spenser's *Shepheardes Calender*', conveniently reprinted in his *Word and Symbol*, London, 1967, 108–9.

13 W. NOWOTTNY, *The Language Poets Use*, London, 1962, 41.

14 *Ibid.*, 37–8.

15 T. S. ELIOT, 'Tradition and the Individual Talent', *Selected Prose*, Penguin Books, 1953, 23.

16 GROOM, *op. cit.*, 81–2.

Four

Foregrounding and Interpretation[1]

'Poetry's unnatural', said Mr Weller; 'No one ever talked poetry 'cept a beadle on boxin' day.'[2] In concentrating on the abnormalities of poetic language in Chapter 3, we saw that there is truth, in a sense, in at least the first part of Mr Weller's remark. But what we have to consider in this chapter is something beyond Mr Weller's matter-of-fact wisdom: how the apparently unnatural, aberrant, even nonsensical, is justified by significance at some deeper level of interpretation. This question has been raised informally in earlier chapters, especially in connection with the Examples for Discussion, for to have tried to separate deviance altogether from significance would have been a very artificial exercise. But we need to give the subject more careful attention.

4.1 FOREGROUNDING

First, however, I wish to place linguistic deviation in a wider aesthetic context, by connecting it with the general principle of FOREGROUNDING.

4.1.1 *Foregrounding in Art and Elsewhere*

It is a very general principle of artistic communication that a work of art in some way deviates from norms which we, as members of society, have learnt to expect in the medium used.[3] A painting that is representational does not simply reproduce the visual stimuli an observer would receive if he were looking at the scene it depicts: what is artistically interesting is how it deviates from photographic accuracy, from simply being a 'copy of nature'. An abstract painting, on the other hand, is interesting according to how it deviates from mass-produced regularities of pattern, from absolute symmetry, etc. Just as painting acts against a background of norms, so in music there are expected patterns – of melody, rhythm, harmonic progression, abstract form, etc., and a composer's skill lies not in mechanically reproducing these, but in introducing unexpected departures from them. As a general rule, anyone who wishes to investigate the significance and value of a work of art must concentrate on the element of interest and surprise, rather than on the automatic pattern. Such deviations from linguistic or other socially accepted norms have been given the special name of 'foregrounding',[4] which invokes the analogy of a figure seen against a background. The artistic deviation 'sticks out' from its background, the automatic system, like a figure in the foreground of a visual field.

The application of this concept to poetry is obvious. The foregrounded figure is the linguistic deviation, and the background is the language – the system taken for granted in any talk of 'deviation'. Just as the eye picks out the figure as the important and meaningful element in its field of vision, so the reader of poetry picks out the linguistic deviation in such a phrase as 'a grief ago' as the most arresting and significant part of the message, and interprets it by measuring it against the background of the expected pattern (see §2.4). It should be added, however, that the rules of the English language as a unity are not the only standard of normality: as we saw in Chapter 1, the English of poetry has its own set of norms, so that 'routine licences' which are odd in the context of English as a whole are not foregrounded, but rather expected, when they occur in a poem. The unique creative innovations of poetry, not the routine deviations, are what we must chiefly have in mind in this discussion of foregrounding.

Deliberate linguistic foregrounding is not confined to poetry, but is found, for example, in joking speech and in children's games. Literature is distinguished, as the Czech scholar Mukařovský says, by the 'consistency and systematic character of foregrounding',[5] but even so, in some non-literary writing, such as comic 'nonsense prose', foregrounding may be just as pervasive and as violent (if not more so) as it is in most poetry:

> Henry was his father's son and it were time for him to go into his father's business of Brummer Striving. It wert a farst dying trade which was fast dying.

Even in this short passage from *John Lennon in his own Write*,[6] there are several instances of orthographic, grammatical, and semantic deviation. If a longer passage were considered, it would be seen that the linguistic foregrounding is far from being spasmodic or random – it follows a certain rationale of its own. It is difficult to analyse what is meant by foregrounding being 'systematic', but the notion is intuitively clear in the feeling we have that there is some method in a poet's (and even in John Lennon's) 'madness'.

4.1.2 *An Example*

A convincing illustration of the power of foregrounding to suggest latent significance is furnished by those modern poets (especially Pound and Eliot) who make use of the stylistic device of transposing pieces of ordinary, non-poetic language into a poetic context. A famous example of this kind of register-borrowing is the bar-parlour monologue in 'A Game of Chess' [*The Waste Land*, III]:

> When Lil's husband got demobbed, I said –
> I didn't mince my words, I said to her myself, . . .
> Now Albert's coming back, make yourself a bit smart.
> He'll want to know what you done with that money he gave you
> To get yourself some teeth. He did, I was there . . .

The very fact that this passage occurs in a poem, incongruously rubbing shoulders with other, more respectably literary types of English, causes us to pay it the compliment of unusual scrutiny. Here it is foregrounded, whereas if it had been overheard in a pub or on a bus, it would not have been. We find ourselves not paying heed to its meaning *qua* casual gossip, but rather asking what is the point of its inclusion at this place in the poem? What is its relevance to its context? What is its artistic significance, in the light of what we have understood of the rest of the poem? This method of composition recalls the painter's technique of 'collage'; in particular, the gumming of bits of newspaper, advertisements, etc., on to the surface of a painting. Because a piece of newspaper, whatever its content, appears in the unwonted setting of a painting, we look at it with more attention, and with a different kind of attention, from that of the careless eye we would cast upon it in a customary situation. The same applies to Eliot's literary collage.

4.2 INTERPRETATION

Poetic foregrounding presupposes some motivation on the part of the writer and some explanation on the part of the reader. A question-mark accompanies each foregrounded feature; consciously or unconsciously, we ask: 'What is the point?' Of course, there may be no point at all; but the appreciative reader, by act of faith, assumes that there is one, or at least tends to give the poet the benefit of the doubt. On the other hand, we must not forget the Mr Wellers of this world, who shrug their shoulders at each question-mark, and take poetry to be a kind of outlandish nonsense. The problem we now have to consider is the problem which stands astride the gap between linguistic analysis and literary appreciation: *When is a linguistic deviation (artistically) significant?*

4.2.1 *The Subjectivity of Interpretation*

To the foregoing question I wish to consider three answers.

ANSWER 1: *When it (i.e. the deviation) communicates something.* According to this definition of significance, practically all deviation is significant. Consider the following three cases:

[a] My aunt suffers from terrible authoritis.
[b] Like you plays?
[c] The Houwe [*sic*] of Commons.

The linguistic abnormalities in these examples are most likely to be taken as errors, as trivial hindrances to communication. But unintentionally, they may convey quite a bit of information. The first, if we take it to be an example of malapropism (*authoritis* for *arthritis*), at least tells us something about the education, character, etc., of its perpetrator. In the second example, the ungrammaticality probably suggests that its author is a foreigner with an imperfect command of English. The third example, occurring in a printed text, informs us that the printer has made a mistake, that the author is a careless proof-reader, etc. Such mistakes may, of course, be deliberately imitated for artistic or comic effect, as in the case of Mrs Malaprop herself:

> An aspersion upon my parts of speech! Was ever such a brute! Sure, if I reprehend anything in this world, it is the use of my oracular tongue and a nice derangement of epitaphs.
> [Sheridan, *The Rivals*, III.iii]

However, it is clear that even the most trivial and unmotivated deviation may communicate information of a kind.

ANSWER 2: *When it communicates what was intended by its author.* This definition of 'significant' narrows the first one to exclude solecisms, malapropisms, and other sorts of linguistic blunder. It insists that a deviation is significant only when deliberate. But the one main difficulty about this answer is that the intention of the author is in practice inaccessible. If he is dead, his intention must remain for ever unknown, unless he happens to have recorded it; and even a living poet is usually shy of explaining 'what he meant' when he wrote a given poem. There is, moreover, a widely held view that what a poem signifies lies within itself and cannot be added to by extraneous commentary.[7] In any case, must a poet's own explanation be treated as oracular? An interesting case of conflicting interpretations is reported in Tindall's *A Reader's Guide to Dylan Thomas*.[8] In Thomas's *A Grief Ago* there occurs a puzzling compound *country-handed*:

The country-handed grave boxed into love.

Edith Sitwell discerned in the compound a 'rural picture of a farmer growing flowers and corn', whereas Thomas himself said that this was quite contrary to his intention, and that he had envisaged the grave in the likeness of a boxer with fists as big as countries. Should we accept Thomas's 'correction' as the last word on the subject? Or should we not rather accept Edith Sitwell's interpretation as being valid and artistically significant in its own right?

ANSWER 3: *When it is judged or felt by the reader to be significant.* This answer, anticipated above, is on the face of it the most unsatisfactory of all: it merely says that the significance of a poem lies ultimately in the mind of the reader, just as beauty is said to lie in the eye of the beholder. Yet I think we are forced back on this definition by the failure of the other two to circumscribe what people in practice take to be significant in a poem. We may go further, and say that not only *whether* a deviation has a sensible interpretation, but *what* interpretation it is to be given, is a subjective matter. Not that I am advocating the critical anarchy of every man's opinion being as good as his neighbour's: there is such a thing as a consensus of interpretative judgment, in which certain experts (critics) have a bigger voice than laymen, and in which the voice of the poet, if heard, is probably the most authoritative of all.

This conclusion, however much of an anticlimax it may seem, is salutary if it teaches us the difference between the objectivity (at least in spirit) of linguistic analysis, and the subjectivity (in the last resort) of critical interpretation.[9] It should also teach us that linguistics and literary criticism, in so far as they both deal with poetic language, are complementary not competing activities. Where the two meet is above all in the study of foregrounding.

4.2.2 *The 'Warranty' for a Deviation*

Assuming that a deviation can be given a sensible and constructive interpretation, let us now examine more precisely how a particular interpretation is arrived at. In detail, this is a matter of critical theory rather than stylistics, and I can do no more here than sketch, in a general way, the processes involved.

A linguistic deviation is a disruption of the normal processes of communication: it leaves a gap, as it were, in one's comprehension of the text. The gap can be filled, and the deviation rendered significant, but only if by an effort of his imagination the reader perceives some deeper connection which compensates for the superficial oddity. In the case of metaphor, this compensation is in the form of analogy. Donne's line (from *The Apparition*)

Then thy sick taper will begin to wink

contains two violations of literal meaningfulness: the idea of a taper being 'sick', and the idea of a taper being capable of winking. The warranty for these deviations lies in a figurative interpretation of 'sick' and 'wink', whereby we appreciate analogies between someone who is ill and a candle which is burning out, and between the flickering of a candle and the batting of an eyelid. The search for a warranty can go further than this. We can ask how these comparisons contribute to the total effectiveness of the poem; but for the moment we shall only investigate what can be called the *immediate* warranty for a deviation.

Another kind of deviation is illustrated in the bizarre word-blends and neologisms of Joyce's *Finnegan's Wake*, e.g. *museyroom, wholeborrow, Gracehoper*. In these cases the immediate warranty can be divided into two parts. The first is the apprehension of a linguistic connection – actually a phonological resemblance – between the invented word and one or more well-established items of vocabulary: *museum, wheelbarrow, grasshopper*. The second is the attempt to match this linguistic connection with some connection outside language, perhaps some referential connection between the invented words and the 'proper' words we map on to them. Thus *museyroom* suggests, appropriately enough, that a museum is a room in which one muses, just as in [a] of §4.2.1, *authoritis* might suggest a writing-bug which afflicts my aunt as cripplingly as arthritis.

4.3 PARALLELISM

Linguistic deviation as we have studied it (i.e. the waiving of rules or conventions of language) is not the only mechanism of linguistic foregrounding. The effect of obtrusion, of some part of the message being thrust into
the foreground of attention, may be attained by other means. A pun, for
instance, is a type of foregrounding:

When I am dead, I hope it may be said:
'His sins were scarlet, but his books were read'.
[Hilaire Belloc, *On his Books*]

This epigram contains no violation of linguistic rules, but we are conscious,
at its conclusion, of two simultaneous interpretations 'read' and 'red'. Our
attention, that is to say, is focused upon a phonological equivalence which
would normally be unobserved.

Now I want to concentrate on a type of foregrounding which is in a
sense the opposite of deviation, for it consists in the introduction of extra
regularities, not irregularities, into the language. This is PARALLELISM in the
widest sense of that word.[10]

4.3.1 *Parallelism as Foregrounded Regularity*

To explain what I mean by 'extra regularities', I shall take as an example
the alliterative pattern of repeated *f*s in Coleridge's line 'The furrow followed free' [*The Ancient Mariner*].

To the extent that any use of language consists in obeying rules, regularity or 'ruledness' is a property of language in general, both inside and
outside poetry. One of the ways in which language shows itself to be re-
ducible to rule is in the possibility of segmenting a text into structurally
equivalent units: for example, syllables (in phonology) and clauses (in
grammar). Thus a text can be analysed as a pattern, on different layers, of
repeated similar structures:

fig. [*e*]

A. ðə fʌ-rou fɔ-loud friː   phonemic transcription
B. cv cv-cv cv-cvc ccv   syllable structure
C. × | ∕ × | ∕ × | ∕   rhythmic structure
D. × | f́ × | f́ × | f́   alliterative pattern

Line *A* of the diagram gives a phonemic transcription of Coleridge's line:
it records the actual units of sound in the order in which they are articu-

lated. These sounds, as everyone knows, are not represented one-for-one by the letters of a written text; for example, the two *l*s of *followed* stand for only a single sound. (The combination /ou/ counts as a single sound.)

Line *B* shows the same sequence of sounds (phonemes), but this time they are identified simply as consonants (c) or vowels (v). When the sounds are classified in this way, a pattern of like structures emerges. This patterning may be explained by segmenting the sequence into syllables, and specifying the limited range of structures a syllable in English may have as follows:

$$(c)\ (c)\ (c)\ v\ (c)\ (c)\ (c)\ (c)$$

In this formula, parentheses indicate elements which may or may not be present. Rendered verbally, it says that an English syllable consists of a vowel or diphthong preceded by 0, 1, 2, or 3 consonants and followed by 0, 1, 2, 3, or 4 consonants. (An alternative, and more convenient way of representing this is $C^{0-3}\ V\ C^{0-4}$.) A maximum initial consonant cluster is found in *strong* /str-/, and a maximum final cluster is found in *sixths* /-ksθs/. Hyphens in this line, as in the one above, indicate boundaries between one syllable and the next, if they are within the same unit of rhythm (see below).[11]

Line *C* symbolizes a second layer of phonological patterning in the line, showing how it breaks down into a sequence of stressed syllables (/) and unstressed syllables (×). Again underlying the pattern there is a general principle of organization comparable to that of syllable structure: each rhythm-unit, or 'measure', as we may call it, contains one and only one stressed syllable, and optionally a number of unstressed syllables, up to a maximum of about four. The boundaries between the measures are marked by vertical bars, analogous to bar-lines in music rather than to foot-boundaries in traditional scansion. The purpose of analysing rhythm in this way will be clearer in §7.1, when we come to discussing its place in versification; for the moment, we shall take it that every measure begins with a stressed syllable. (It happens in this example that bar-lines coincide with word boundaries.)

We see from the above analysis how the phonological patterning of the English language can be described by means of a hierarchy of units. The smallest units, PHONEMES, are the individual vowels and consonants (/f/, /g/, /u/, etc.) of which larger units, SYLLABLES are composed. Syllables themselves, classified as stressed or unstressed, are the elements of still larger units, the units of rhythm here called MEASURES. A fourth unit of even greater extent, a unit of intonation, may also be distinguished, but is of only limited interest in the study of poetry. A similar hierarchy of units, sentence, clause, phrase, word, etc., may also be set up to describe grammatical patterns.[12]

The alliterative structure written out in line D is a pattern superimposed, so to speak, on the patterning already inherent in the language. It consists in the recurrence of a particular phoneme, /f/, at the beginning of every stressed syllable in the line. Another extra regularity is the metrical pattern of alternating stressed and unstressed syllables: DI-DUM-DI-DUM-DI-DUM. There is no rule in the language stating that this must be the case, any more than it is a rule of English that all stressed syllables must start with /f/.

Metre and alliteration are only two of many examples of the type of linguistic foregrounding which consists in making a text more organized than it has to be by virtue of the rules of the language. A further example, this time a syntactic one, is seen in the second line of this couplet:

Ill fares the land, to hastening ills a prey,
Where *wealth accumulates* and *men decay*.
[Goldsmith, *The Deserted Village*]

The relevant units in this case are not measures or syllables, but clauses. The italicized parts of the line have identical syntactic structures: each consists of a single-word subject followed by a single-word predicate. Where the language allows for a choice from a variety of structures (Subject + Verbal, Subject + Verbal + Object, Subject + Verbal + Indirect Object + Object, etc.), the poet insists on an exact repetition. The term 'parallelism' is above all associated with this sort of syntactic repetition.

Parallelism in its broad sense is precisely the opposite, as I have said, of the kind of foregrounding found in 'a grief ago', as discussed in §2.4. In the latter case, where a certain range of selections is available in the language, the poet makes a selection beyond this range. With parallelism, where the language allows him a choice, he consistently limits himself to the same option.

4.3.2 *How Much Regularity?*

Foregrounding is rarely an all-or-nothing matter. Just as there are degrees of foregrounded irregularity (see §2.4), so there are degrees of foregrounded regularity. There is a trivial parallelism in a sentence like 'He found his key and opened the front door', which contains two consecutive Verbal + Object constructions. But this construction is in any case so frequent in English that we tend not to notice the pattern, and would scarcely consider it contrived for artistic effect. In contrast, the degree of patterning is quite marked in the saying 'No news is good news', for the repetition of the same syntactic pattern Modifier + Noun is here accompanied by the same lexical choice of *news*. An even stronger foregrounding of regularity occurs in Othello's 'I kissed thee ere I killed thee', where the two clauses have (1) identical structures (Subject + Verbal + Object), (2) the exact verbal correspondences of *I* and *thee*, (3) corresponding past tense suffixes (*-ed*), and (4) a phonological congruence between *kissed* and *killed*. We may notice also that the parallelism of 'wealth accumulates' and 'men decay' in Goldsmith's line resides not just in the identity of clause structures (Subject + Verbal) but in the fact that each element of the clause consists of only one word. If we altered each clause so that this second condition no longer applied (e.g. 'wealth has accumulated' and 'good men decay') the pattern would be considerably weaker because there would no longer be such a close grammatical correspondence. These examples give some idea of what factors enter into the assessment of how strong a parallelism is: whether it extends to both lexical and grammatical choices; whether it operates simultaneously on different layers of structure; whether it involves patterning on both phonological and formal levels.

4.3.3 *Patterns of Identity and Contrast*

The importance of parallelism as a feature of poetic language almost rivals that of deviation. Gerard Manley Hopkins went so far as to claim that the artifice of poetry 'reduces itself to the principle of parallelism'.[13] It is certainly the principle underlying all versification. We would therefore like to inquire carefully into its nature and function, as we inquired into those of linguistic deviation.

It is first of all important to note a difference between parallelism and mechanical repetition. As Roman Jakobson has said,[14] 'any form of parallelism is an apportionment of invariants and variables'. In other words, in any parallelistic pattern there must be an element of identity and an element of contrast. The element of identity requires little comment: it is clear that any superimposed pattern of the kinds illustrated in §4.3.1 above sets up a relation of equivalence between two or more neighbouring pieces of a text, as indicated here by the horizontal brackets:

The furrow followed free

```
×  /    ×  /    ×  /
/  f    /  f    /  f
```

Where wealth accumulates and men decay
......Subject + Verbal......Subject + Verbal

What is probably less obvious is that this identity does not extend to absolute duplication. The exact repetition of a sentence, as in the chanting of crowds ('We want Alf! We want Alf!' ... etc.) is not counted as parallelism, because parallelism requires some *variable* feature of the pattern – some contrasting elements which are 'parallel' with respect to their position in the pattern.

Having made this distinction, we may further observe that parallelism is typical of many other aspects of human culture apart from literature. The eighteenth-century German writer Johann Gottfried von Herder defended the characteristic parallelism (in meaning as well as form) of the Hebrew Psalms against the charge of monotony and redundancy with the words: 'Haben Sie noch nie einen Tanz gesehen?' ('Have you never seen a dance?').[15] Similarly in music:

The opening bars of Beethoven's Fifth Symphony forcefully illustrate the patterning of constants and variables which is basic to almost all aspects of musical form.[16] In this case it is the rhythmic figure ♩♫♫♩ with a fall on the last note which is the invariant part of the theme; the actual tonal values of the notes make up the variable element.

Proverbs, slogans, nursery rhymes, and many other 'sub-literary' uses of language also abound in parallelism. Songs and ballads are extremely parallelistic in design, and this is amply reflected in the stanza from *The Ancient Mariner* (an imitation of ballad style) from which our example of alliteration was taken:

The fair breeze blew, the white foam flew,
The furrow followed free;
We were the first that ever burst
Into that silent sea.

It would take a page to list the many interlocking foregrounded patterns – metre, end-rhyme, internal rhyme, alliteration, and syntactic parallelism – in this short passage.

4.3.4 *The Interpretation of Parallelism*

It is impossible to summarize the function of parallelism in a way which will cover all the diverse examples of its occurrence, inside and outside poetry. Linguistic parallelism is very often connected with rhetorical emphasis and memorability. In nursery rhymes and ballads, it affords an artless kind of pleasure in itself, and probably has and needs no further justification. We tend to dismiss this kind of pleasure as of no account in the appreciation of poetry, but I think it would be wrong to dismiss completely the feature of the language of literature which links it most closely to the language of music – the other major art-form which exists on the dimension of time.

Nevertheless, people generally feel that if a parallelism occurs in a poem, some deeper motive or justification for it should be sought. The feeling is all the stronger because most prose writers are inclined to go out of their way to avoid gratuitous effects of this kind: alliteration, rhyme, etc., are felt to be a positive distraction and hindrance to communication unless they are artistically justified. The parallelisms of versification belong to a class of extra regularities which, like routine licences, are not foregrounded in poetry. But we may assume that in general, *foregrounded regularities* like *foregrounded irregularities*, require an interpretation.

The assignment of significance to a parallelism rests upon a simple principle of equivalence. Every parallelism sets up a relationship of equivalence between two or more elements: the elements which are singled out by the pattern as being parallel. Interpreting the parallelism involves appreciating some external connection between these elements.[17] The connection is, broadly speaking, a connection either of similarity or of contrast. In Goldsmith's line 'Where wealth accumulates and men decay' it is obviously one of ironic contrast. Other examples of a contrastive connection are:

> He raised a mortal to the skies;
>   She drew an angel down.
>   [Dryden, *Alexander's Feast*]

> To err is human, to forgive, divine.
>   [Pope, *An Essay on Criticism*]

It is to cases like these, in which formal parallelism is combined with an implication of contrast, that the term ANTITHESIS is most readily applied. If, on the other hand, Goldsmith's line had been parodied 'Where wealth diminishes and men decay', the connection would have been understood as one of similarity: the two states of affairs go together, in fact the one seems to follow from the other. A third possibility is shown in a further parody: 'Where wealth accumulates and men obey.' This is puzzling because on the face of it there is no connection between the two verbs which the pattern sets in opposition to one another; yet we find ourselves trying to grope towards an interpretation, by imagining a situation in which the one might be taken as complementary or in contrast to the other. In interpreting parallelism, as in interpreting deviation, human nature abhors a vacuum of sense.

Another expectation raised by syntactic parallelism is that if there are more than two phases to the pattern, it moves towards a climax. This expectation is fulfilled in the following passage from *The Merchant of Venice* [III.i]

> If you prick us, do we not bleed? if you tickle us, do we not laugh? if you poison us, do we not die? and if you wrong us, shall we not revenge?

where the portentousness and emotive force of *revenge*, coming after *bleed*, *laugh*, and *die*, is underlined by a slight verbal variation in the pattern; the replacement of *do* by *shall*. The passage would have been not just less effective but downright unsatisfactory if (disregarding the position of *and*) the lines had been put in the opposite order.

A slightly more complicated case is that of this celebrated quotation from Robert Burns's *To a Mouse*:

> The best laid schemes o' mice an' men
> Gang aft a-gley.

The relation of equivalence here is between *mice* and *men*, which correspond not only syntactically, but phonologically, in that they are both monosyllables beginning with /m/. The phonological foregrounding, or 'chiming', of two words in this way is quite a common poetic effect. The reinforcing connection between *mice* and *men* is twofold. We firstly appreciate the referential contrast between man, the supreme head of animal creation, and the mouse, one of the tiniest, timidest, most inconsequential of creatures. But secondly, helped by the conjunction *and* which links the two words, we appreciate a similarity between man and mouse, who in the sentiment of this passage are levelled to the same status of vulnerability to fate. What the parallelistic bond between the two seems to say is that creatures superficially different are basically the same.

The interpretation of parallelism is like the interpretation of deviation in being divisible into an *immediate* interpretation and a *wider* interpretation, which takes into account its relation to other foregrounding, and ultimately to the whole work in which it appears. For an example of wider reinforcement, we return to Othello's words 'I kissed thee ere I killed thee', in which the parallelism strongly urges a connection between *kissed* and *killed*. This is similar to the 'mice and men' example in that it combines contrast with similarity. Kissing and killing have opposed connotations, the former being associated with love, and the latter with hatred and aggression. On the other hand, the sentence as a whole suggests that they are similar: that kissing and killing are compatible actions. On a wider scale, therefore, this parallelism summarizes with great concentration the paradox of Othello's jealousy, and the irony of his final tragedy.

Examples for discussion

1. What instances of linguistic foregrounding, both of regularity (parallelism) and of irregularity (deviation) can be identified in the following. How are the foregrounded features interpreted, and how do their individual interpretations fit into the total interpretation of each passage or poem? Discuss, with reference to these examples, the meaning of 'consistency of foregrounding' in poetry.

[a]   *Justice*
   I cannot skill of these Thy ways;
Lord, Thou didst make me, yet thou woundest me;
Lord, Thou dost wound me, yet Thou dost relieve me;
Lord, Thou relievest, yet I die by Thee;
Lord, Thou dost kill me, yet Thou dost reprieve me.

   But when I mark my life and praise,
   Thy justice me most fitly pays;
For I do praise Thee, yet I praise Thee not;
My prayers mean Thee, yet my prayers stray;
I would do well, yet sin the hand hath got;
My soul doth love Thee, yet it loves delay.
   I cannot skill of these my ways.
       [George Herbert]

[b]
And I, forsooth, in love! I, that have been love's whip;
A very beadle to a humorous sigh;
A critic, nay, a night-watch constable;

A domineering pedant o'er the boy;
Than whom no mortal so magnificent!
This whimpled, whining, purblind, wayward boy;
This senior-junior, giant dwarf, Dan Cupid
Regent of love-rhymes, lord of folded arms,
The anointed sovereign of sighs and groans,
Liege of all loiterers and malcontents,
Dread prince of plackets, king of codpieces,
Sole imperator and great general
Of trotting paritors: – O my little heart! –
And I to be a corporal of his field,
And wear his colours like a tumbler's hoop!
                    [*Love's Labour's Lost*, III.i]

(The above passage, spoken by Berowne, is discussed from a linguistic point of view by Mrs Nowottny, in *The Language Poets Use*, 5–6.)

2. Search the following passages for patterns of formal parallelism. Describe each parallelism, using a notation on lines already illustrated in §4.3.3 for representing parallel sequences of formal items or grammatical categories; for example, the pattern of 'A tim'rous foe and a suspicious friend' (Pope, *Epistle to Dr Arbuthnot*) can be symbolized '*a* + Adjective + Noun *and a* + Adjective + Noun'. Be wary of confusing parallelism with co-ordination, and of assuming that every parallelism of meaning must be accompanied by a parallelism of syntactic construction. Consider the interpretation of formal parallelism in these passages.

[*a*] BRUTUS: Romans, countrymen, and lovers! hear me for my cause, and be silent, that you may hear: believe me for mine honour, and have respect for mine honour, that you may believe: censure me in your wisdom, and awake your senses, that you may be the better judge. If there be any in this assembly, any dear friend of Caesar's, to him I say that Brutus' love to Caesar was no less than his. If then that friend demand why Brutus rose against Caesar, this is my answer: not that I loved Caesar less, but that I loved Rome more. Had you rather Caesar were living, and die all slaves, than that Caesar were dead, to live all freemen? As Caesar loved me, I weep for him; as he was fortunate, I rejoice at it; as he was valiant, I honour him; but as he was ambitious, I slew him. There is tears for his love; joy for his fortune; honour for his valour; and death for his ambition. Who is here so base that would be a bondman? If any, speak; for him have I offended. Who is here so rude that would not be a Roman? If any, speak; for him have I offended. Who is here so vile that will not love his country? If any, speak; for him have I offended.   [*Julius Caesar*, III.ii]

[*b*]
Of all the causes which conspire to blind
Man's erring judgment, and misguide the mind,

What the weak head with strongest bias rules,
is PRIDE, the never-failing vice of fools.
Whatever Nature has in worth denied,
She gives in large recruits of needless pride;
For as in bodies, thus in souls we find
What wants in blood and spirits, swell'd with wind:
Pride, where wit fails, steps in to our defence,
And fills up all the mighty void of sense.
If once right reason drives that cloud away,
Truth breaks upon us with resistless day.
Trust not yourself; but your defects to know,
Make use of every friend – and every foe.

[Pope, *An Essay on Criticism*, II]

Notes

1 This chapter is an expansion of the latter part of my essay 'Linguistics and the Figures of Rhetoric', in *Essays on Style and Language*, ed. R. G. FOWLER, London, 1966, 135–56.

2 *Pickwick Papers*, Chapter 33.

3 See P. L. GARVIN, trans., *A Prague School Reader on Esthetics, Literary Structure and Style*, Washington D.C., 1958, esp. B. HAVRÁNEK, 'The Functional Differentiation of the Standard Language', 1–18; and J. MUKAŘOVSKÝ, 'Standard Language and Poetic Language', 18ff.

4 'Foregrounding' is Garvin's translation (see n. 3) of the Czech term *aktualisace*.

5 MUKAŘOVSKÝ, *op. cit.*, 23.

6 J. LENNON, *John Lennon in His Own Write*, London, 1964, 66.

7 See R. WELLEK, 'The Main Trends of Twentieth Century Criticism', in *Concepts of Criticism*, ed. S. G. NICHOLS, New Haven, 1963. Also B. LEE, 'The New Criticism and the Language of Poetry', in FOWLER, *op. cit.*, 29–30.

8 W. Y. TINDALL, *A Reader's Guide to Dylan Thomas*, London, 1962, 117.

9 See G. N. LEECH, '"This Bread I Break": Language and Interpretation', *Review of English Literature*, 6.2 (1965), 66–75. Linguistic analysis and interpretation here correspond partially to what Richards calls the 'technical part' and the 'critical part' respectively of literary exegesis. See I. A. RICHARDS, *Principles of Literary Criticism*, London, 1925, 23–24. Also B. LEE, *loc. cit.*

10 An excellent linguistic account of parallelism is to be found in R. JAKOBSON, 'Grammatical Parallelism and its Russian Facet', *Language* 42, 2 (1966), 399–429.

11 We must here leave aside controversial matters of phonological analysis, especially matters of segmentation (where does a syllable or rhythm unit begin and end?). On the concepts of phoneme, syllable, and stress consult A. C. GIMSON, *An Introduction to the Pronunciation of English*, London, 1962, esp. 42–56, 234–239. On

the specific matter of syllable division, see J. D. O'CONNOR and J. L. M. TRIM, 'Vowel, Consonant and Syllable – a Phonological Definition', *Word*, 9, 2 (1953), 103–22, esp. 115–22.

12   This hierarchic approach to phonology is essentially that of M. A. K. HALLIDAY and associates. See M. A. K. HALLIDAY, A. MCINTOSH, and P. STREVENS, *The Linguistic Sciences and Language Teaching*, London, 1964, 42–7.

13   'Poetic Diction', *The Journals and Papers of Gerard Manley Hopkins*, ed. H. HOUSE and G. STOREY, London, 1959, 84; quoted in R. JAKOBSON, 'Grammatical Parallelism and its Russian Facet', 399–429.

14   JAKOBSON, *op. cit.*, 423.

15   J. G. HERDER, *Vom Geist der Ebräischen Poesie*, Dessau, 1782, 23; quoted in JAKOBSON, *op. cit.*, 423.

16   The musical analogy of poetic parallelism is developed in R. AUSTERLITZ, 'Parallelismus', in *Poetics*, Polska Akademia Nauk, Warsaw and The Hague, c. 1961, 439–444.

17   Discussed under the heading of 'coupling' in S. R. LEVIN, *Linguistic Structures and Poetry*, The Hague, 1962, 30–41.

Five

Verbal Repetition

The subject of parallelism was introduced in the last chapter, but much remains to be said if justice is to be done to its overriding importance in the structure and significance of works of literature. In this and the following chapters, I shall place parallelism in the context of a broad class of repetitive effects which were called 'schemes' (or 'figures of speech' in a more specific sense than is usual today) in traditional handbooks of rhetoric. Even after that, the aspect of parallelism which concerns versification will still await consideration. The particular theme of these chapters will be repetition, not in the abstract sense of recurrence of structure – the sense mainly under focus in §4.3 – but in the more direct sense of actual physical, acoustic repetition: in a word, the ECHOIC aspect of literary language.

But first we must draw a purely linguistic distinction. Obtrusive irregularity (poetic deviation) and obtrusive regularity (parallelism) account for most of what is characteristic of poetic language; but they do not both occur with equal frequency at the different levels of linguistic organization. Returning to the main levels drawn in figs. [c] and [d] (pages 37–8), we discover that foregrounded regularity is on the whole a feature of phonology (or graphology) and surface grammatical structure. This is only natural, since when we talk of deep grammatical structure and semantics, we are not involved in the directly perceivable pattern of a sentence, but rather in the underlying choices of meaning and presentation. On the other hand, obtrusive irregularity (linguistic deviation) is only of primary importance, as we saw in §3.2, when located in the areas of deep structure and semantics; i.e. in the right-hand half of fig. [c]. The two types of foregrounding therefore have complementary spheres of importance.

To refer to these spheres of importance, instead of 'left-hand half of fig. [c]' and 'right-hand half of fig. [c]', I propose to use the plain terms EXPRESSION and CONTENT respectively. Expression thus includes phonology and surface grammatical structure, whereas content includes semantics and deep grammatical structure. The two overlap in the lexicon. Now we may recapitulate the point made in the last paragraph more succinctly: foregrounded regularity predominates in linguistic expression, and foregrounded irregularity in linguistic content.

5.1 SCHEMES AND TROPES

The contrast between expression and content, with their associated types of foregrounding, has been made because of its connection with a traditional distinction between two classes of rhetorical figure, SCHEMES and TROPES. Unfortunately, the line between these two categories, as with many other rhetorical classifications, has always been vaguely and inconsistently drawn. Schemes, roughly, have included figures such as alliteration, anaphora, and chiasmus, and have been described as abnormal arrangements lending themselves to the forceful and harmonious presentation of ideas. Tropes, more radical in scope and more powerful in effect, have (again roughly) been identified as devices involving alteration of the normal meaning of an expression: they include metaphor, irony, and synecdoche. Some rhetoricians draw up a third category of 'figures of thought'. These are more concerned with the psychological strategy of developing a theme than with the actual choice of language, and so lie outside our province.

As the traditional classification, with its mixture of pragmatic and descriptive criteria, has fallen into general disuse, I see no harm in resurrecting the division between the schemes and tropes, and reinterpreting it on a more strictly linguistic basis. Schemes have to do with expression, and tropes with content: this much is traditional. But more particularly, I shall associate each term with the kind of linguistic foregrounding predominant in its half of the language process; i.e. I shall define them as follows:

SCHEMES: foregrounded repetitions of expression.
TROPES: foregrounded irregularities of content.

(My reasons for calling schemes 'repetitions' rather than 'regularities' will become clear in §5.2 below.)

The categories so defined account for much, but by no means all, of special linguistic effects in poetry. They do not, for example, include deviations of graphology, of register, or of historical period, as discussed in Chapter 3. Part of the trouble with the traditional classification was the rhetorician's tendency to try and make it as exhaustive as possible: to force every conceivable figure into one category or the other. Thus hyperbaton (arrangement of words, etc., out of their usual order) might find itself classified either as a scheme (being a matter of expression) or as a trope (being a kind of linguistic irregularity). Actually it lies outside the boundaries of both categories as they have been drawn here. Nevertheless, the present definitions cover in all essentials the categories as traditionally conceived.

A further point has to be made about schemes and tropes as I have defined them. We identify them at different levels: i.e. a scheme may be identified as a phonological, a graphological, or a formal (i.e. grammatical and/or lexical) pattern; likewise, a trope may be identified as a formal or a semantic deviation. But these identifications are not so distinct as they may seem, because there is a great deal of interdependence between the levels. Note the truth of the following observations:

1. Formal repetition often presupposes phonological repetition.
2. Formal deviation often presupposes semantic deviation.

To see the correctness of (1), one need merely reflect that to repeat a word is to repeat the sounds of which it is composed. The following extract contains, on a formal level, the repetition of the word *farewell*; on the phonological level the actual *sound* of the word *farewell* is echoed at irregular intervals, and itself constitutes a kind of phonological foregrounding. We listen to it as to the tolling of a bell, an audible signal of Othello's surrender of wordly pleasure and achievement:

> O, now for ever
> Farewell the tranquil mind! farewell content!
> Farewell the plumed troop and the big wars
> That make ambition virtue! O, farewell!
> Farewell the neighing steed and the shrill trump,
> The spirit-stirring drum, the ear-piercing fife,
> The royal banner, and all quality,
> Pride, pomp and circumstance of glorious war!
>   [III.iii]

Certain nineteenth-century poets, amongst them Gerard Manley Hopkins, have a tendency to use exact verbal repetition, which goes hand in hand with a tendency to 'orchestrate' their poetry with various kinds of phonological echo – consonance, alliteration, assonance, etc:

> My aspens dear, whose airy cages *quelled*,
> *Quelled* or *quenched* in *leaves* the *leaping* sun,
> All *felled*, *felled*, are all *felled*.

These opening lines of Hopkins's 'Binsey Poplars' exemplify both features, and show that in effect, they are one. The lexical repetitions of *quelled* and *felled* are part of the general symphony of phonological schemes. But notice that the relationship does not hold in the opposite direction: the initial repetitions of sound in '*qu*enched ... *qu*elled' and '*leaves ... leaping*' have nothing to do with any formal, lexical correspondences.

Illustrating statement (2) above, that formal deviation often presupposes semantic deviation, properly lies outside my present concern. However, so that the full symmetry of the relationship between schemes and tropes can be appreciated, we may return briefly to our familiar examples of 'a grief ago', and observe that this trope can be described from two points of view. On the formal level, it is an example of an incompatible juxtaposition of syntactic elements: a noun which is not a noun of time in the construction '... *ago*'. On the semantic level it is an example of the type of meaning transference generally called METONYMY (see §9.1.3). Again the relationship is not necessarily reciprocal, as it is not in the following extract:

> Sceptre and crown must tumble down
> And in the dust be equal made
> With the poor crooked scythe and spade.
> > [James Shirley, *The Contention of Ajax and Ullyses*, III]

The words *scythe* and *spade* here will normally be interpreted metonymically, as representing the abstract (or perhaps collective) notion of 'peasantry', even though there is no syntactic or lexical deviation to signal this unusual interpretation.

5.2 FORMAL REPETITIONS

Language allows for a great abundance of types of lexical and grammatical repetition, and my task now is to illustrate this variety of schemes, at the same time considering what artistic purposes they can serve. As abstract patterns of purely syntactic parallelism were exemplified at some length in §§4.3.3 and 4.3.4, I shall focus attention in this chapter on formal schemes which, like that of Othello's 'farewell' speech, contain verbal iterations, and hence repetitions of sound. My first point, however, is that not all repetitions of this kind take place within the framework of a parallelism: there is also a type of irregular repetition, or FREE REPETITION, which nevertheless strikes the reader as having a deliberate rhetorical effect. My definition of 'schemes' is wide enough to include both parallelism and this free repetition.

The passage from Othello quoted in §5.1 is actually on the border between these two categories. It starts off with a regular pattern consisting in the recurrence of the structure *Farewell* X, where X is a noun phrase. In a more general notation for symbolizing types of parallelism, we may let *a* stand for the unvarying element *farewell*, and b_1, b_2, b_3, etc. for the parallel noun phrases. The layout below follows the units of the parallelism, rather than the lines of verse:

Farewell the tranquil mind!	$a\ b_1$
farewell content!	$a\ b_2$
Farewell the plumed troop and the big wars /	
That make ambition virtue!	$a\ b_3$
O, farewell! /	$...a$
Farewell the neighing steed and the shrill trump	$a\ b_4$

After the third repetition, the pattern undergoes an interruption, and 'O farewell' is interjected without a following noun phrase. It is the bare reiteration of the word *farewell* that connects this exclamation to what precedes and follows it, not the regular pattern of parallelism, which is lost at this point. Most people will agree that the disturbance of the pattern, far from being a blemish, breaks up the formality of the speech, and makes it more like a genuine expression of strong feeling.

Rhetorical tradition has handed down a large number of technical names for different kinds of verbal repetition. In what follows I shall mention some of these terms, and, I hope, clarify their meanings within the general framework of linguistic foregrounding. But it will be as well to remind the reader of my comments on rhetorical nomenclature in the Introduction (§0.2): knowing the actual names is of minimal importance compared with understanding the realities they denote.

5.2.1 *Free Verbal Repetition*

Free repetition of form means the *exact* copying of some previous part of a text (whether word, phrase, or even sentence), since of course, if there were merely a partial repetition, this would amount to a parallelism. Traditional rhetoric distinguished two categories of free repetition: that of immediate repetition, or EPIZEUXIS (e.g. 'Come away, come away, death'), and that of intermittent repetition, or PLOCE (pronounced /plousi/). The second term was especially associated with the pregnant repetition of an item in different senses, as when the dying John of Gaunt puns on his own name:

> O, how that name befits my composition!
> Old *Gaunt*, indeed; and *gaunt* in being old.
> [*Richard II*, II.i]

Immediate repetition is predominant in the following extract from the Authorized Version of the Bible [Samuel 2], a passage in which David laments the death of his son:

> O my son Absalom, my son, my son Absalom! Would God I had died for thee, O Absalom, my son, my son!

In a similar vein, but in a very different style, the irregular reiteration of the name *Lycidas*, together with other repetitions, seems to contribute to the elegiac pomp of Milton's poem of that name:

> For *Lycidas* is *dead, dead* ere his prime,
> Young *Lycidas*, and hath not left his peer.
> Who would not *sing* for *Lycidas*? he know
> Himself to *sing*, and build the lofty rhyme.

The superfluity of expression in these passages runs counter to one strongly held tenet of poetic composition: that to compress, to say much in little, is the means to poetic intensity, and the mark of great poetry. And yet, if we turn to the ordinary emotive use of language, we see that repetition is a fundamental if primitive device of intensification. To call it a 'device', indeed, is to mislead, for repetition is almost involuntary to a person in a state of extreme emotional excitation. A tragi-comic realization of this in drama is Shylock's outburst over the elopement of his daughter:

> My daughter! O my ducats! O my daughter!
> Fled with a Christian! O my Christian ducats!
> [*The Merchant of Venice*, II.viii]

The powerful effect of repetition in David's lament, as in Milton's lament over Lycidas, seems to lie in the implication that the grief is too great for expression in few words: so deep a sorrow requires manifold utterance. Not that sorrow is the only emotion capable of expression in this way; few poetic rhapsodies can match the naked vigour of the Song of Deborah and Barak, another piece of Old Testament lyricism:

> At her feet he bowed, he fell, he lay down: at her feet he bowed, he fell;
> where he bowed, there he fell down dead.   [Judges 5]

The fierce exultation conveyed by this verse in its context is almost entirely due to its repetitiveness. The murder of Sisera, it seems to say, must be lovingly dwelt upon, so that every drop of joy can be squeezed out of it.

Although repetition sometimes indicates poverty of linguistic resource, it can, as we see, have its own kind of eloquence. By underlining rather than elaborating the message, it presents a simple emotion with force. It may further suggest a suppressed intensity of feeling – an imprisoned feeling, as it were, for which there is no outlet but a repeated hammering at the confining walls of language. In a way, saying the same thing over and over is a reflection on the inadequacy of language to express what you have to express 'in one go'.

An apparent haphazardness or disorderliness in the manner of repetition, as in the examples above, can also suggest spontaneity and exuberance. This disorderliness is, indeed, a necessary characteristic of free repetition, and a respect in which it contrasts with the formality and ceremoniousness of parallelism.

5.2.2 *Types of Verbal Parallelism*

The figures of speech we have now to consider take the form of exact verbal repetitions in equivalent positions. The commonest place for such repetitions is at the beginning of the relevant unit of text, like the repetition of *farewell* in Othello's speech. What is meant by 'relevant unit of text' varies from one case to another. It may be a grammatical unit, such as a clause or sentence, or a sequence of grammatical units, for example a noun phrase followed by a prepositional phrase. It may on the other hand be a prosodic unit – a line or stanza of verse; or a dramatic unit – a speech. Furthermore, it may simultaneously lie within two or more of these categories. The exact nature of the unit is irrelevant; what is important, if this is to constitute a parallelism, is that the repetition should be felt to occur at the beginning of equivalent pieces of language, within which there is an invariant part (the verbal repetition itself) and a variant part (the rest of the unit).

In both the well-known quotations that follow, different criteria coincide in isolating the parallel segments, or phases of the pattern. In [a], the repetition comes at the beginning of a dramatic speech, which also happens to consist of a single sentence. In [b], it constitutes the opening line of a stanza which is also a sequence of two sentences:

[*a*]

LORENZO: ..., *in such a night*
Troilus methinks mounted the Troyan walls,
And sighed his soul toward the Grecian tents,
Where Cressid lay that night.

JESSICA: *In such a night*
Did Thisbe fearfully o'ertrip the dew.
And saw the lion's shadow ere himself,
And ran dismayed away.

LORENZO: *In such a night*
Stood Dido with a willow in her hand
Upon the wild sea-banks, and waft her love
To come again to Carthage.

JESSICA: *In such a night*
Medea gathered the enchanted herbs
That did renew old Æson.
[*The Merchant of Venice*, V.i]

[*b*]

O *what can ail thee, knight-at-arms,*
   Alone and palely loitering?
The sedge has wither'd from the lake,
   And no birds sing.

O *what can ail thee, knight-at-arms,*
   So haggard and so woebegone?
The squirrel's granary is full,
   And the harvest's done.
[Keats, *La Belle Dame Sans Merci*]

Despite dissimilarities of structural detail, both these examples can be represented by the single formula $(a...)(a...)$, etc., with a symbolizing again the constant element, and brackets enclosing sections of text which in some structural sense can be taken as equivalent. By the 'etc.' I mean to convey that the parallelism may contain two, or more than two equivalent units.

In the rhetorical manuals of the Middle Ages and the Renaissance, verbal parallelisms were carefully distinguished according to their position.[1]

For example, the term ANAPHORA was applied to initial repetitions of the kind just illustrated. (In modern times, 'anaphora' has been applied to verbal repetition in general.) Despite a tendency towards pedantry and arbitrariness in these rhetorical distinctions, it would be wrong to dismiss them as of merely historical interest, for the features they analyse belong to poetry of all ages. This has been convincingly illustrated in a recent study of the wealth of verbal schemes in the poetry of T. S. Eliot.[2] Here are some of the figures of verbal parallelism apart from anaphora:

EPISTROPHE. Final repetition; the opposite of anaphora.

Formula: $(\ldots a)(\ldots a)$, etc.

Example:

Those who sharpen the tooth of the dog, *meaning*
Death
Those who glitter with the glory of the hummingbird, *meaning*
Death
Those who sit in the stye of contentment, *meaning*
Death
Those who suffer the ecstasy of the animals, *meaning*
Death
[T. S. Eliot, *Marina*]

SYMPLOCE. Initial combined with final repetition; i.e. anaphora and epistrophe together.

Formula: $(a \ldots b)(a \ldots b)$, etc.

Example:

I will recruit for myself and you *as I go*;
I will scatter myself among men and women *as I go*.
[Walt Whitman, *Song of the Open Road*]

(Another example is that given for epistrophe above.)

ANADIPLOSIS. The last part of one unit is repeated at the beginning of the next.

Formula: $(\ldots a)(a \ldots)$

Example:

The same that oft-times hath
Charm'd magic casements, opening on the foam
Of perilous seas, in faery lands *forlorn*.

Forlorn! the very word is like a bell
To toll me back from thee to my sole self!
[Keats, *Ode to a Nightingale*]

6—L.G.E.P.

EPANALEPSIS. The final part of each unit of the pattern repeats the initial part.

Formula: $(a \ldots a)(b \ldots b)$, etc.

Example:

> With *ruin* upon *ruin*, *rout* on *rout*,
> Confusion worse confounded.
> [*Paradise Lost*, II]

ANTISTROPHE. The repetition of items in a reverse order.

Formula (roughly): $(\ldots a \ldots b \ldots)(\ldots b \ldots a \ldots)$

Example:

> What's *Hecuba* to *him* or *he* to *Hecuba*
> That he should weep for her?
> [*Hamlet*, II.ii]

In almost all the examples of verbal parallelism given so far, the repetition of individual words is accompanied by some degree of repetition of syntactic structure. In the illustration of symploce, for instance, the sequence Main Clause + Temporal Clause is copied from the first line to the second. In that of epanalepsis, the sequence Noun + Prepositional Phrase is repeated. Indeed, so closely are verbal and syntactic parallelism interconnected that the attempt to deal with the one in isolation from the other, as in the conventional treatment of these schemes, is a slightly artificial undertaking. Anaphora, epistrophe, etc., should always be related where possible, to a context of syntactic parallelism.

I append to the above list two contrasting examples of repetition within the structure of the word; these are the morphological counterparts of anaphora and epistrophe.

POLYPTOTON. The repetition of a word with varying grammatical inflections.

Example:

> And *singing* still dost *soar*, and *soaring* ever *singest*.
> [Shelley, *To a Skylark*]

HOMOIOTELEUTON: The repetition of the same derivational or inflectional ending on different words.

Example:

> – Not for these I raise
> The song of thanks and praise;

But for those obstinate question*ings*
Of sense and outward things,
Fall*ings* from us, vanish*ings*,
Blank misgiv*ings* of a creature
Moving about in worlds not realized . . .
[Wordsworth, *Ode: Intimations of Immortality*]

Having been subjected to a certain amount of rhetorical terminology in this chapter, the reader may well feel that the practice of enumerating and naming figures of speech is an overrated pastime. This feeling is a far from new one, having been expressed by Quintilian, the greatest rhetorician of Imperial Rome, and many since him. However, whereas criticism of rhetorical tradition has tended to concentrate on its pedantic insistence on nice distinctions, I should like to focus attention at this point on its logical defects as a framework for analysis: not only are the distinctions made often unsystematic, but more fundamentally, the whole concept of *listing* types of repetition, or types of foregrounding generally, is a misconceived one.

For example, the rhetorical catalogue generally provides for initial and final verbal repetition, but makes no allowance for repetition in the middle of successive units. Though less prominent than the other two, this type is common enough, and is illustrated by the sequence '*that rubs its*' in the following pair of lines from Eliot's *The Love Song of J. Alfred Prufrock*:

The yellow fog *that rubs its* back upon *the window-panes,*
The yellow smoke *that rubs its* muzzle *on the window-panes*

This is an example of a fairly strong verbal parallelism, in which symploce (initial and final repetition) is combined with medial repetition, the pattern is represented by the formula $(a\ldots b\ldots c)(a\ldots b\ldots c)$. Of course, it would be possible to devise even more complicated examples, in which more than three (even an indefinitely large number of) sets of items would be repeated in successive structures. Thus if one followed the example set by 'symploce' of coining a new term for every combination of figures of repetition, the list would never be complete. There are other ways, too, in which the listing of foregrounded effects, if pursued consistently, would have to continue *ad infinitum*. What is required, rather than a catalogue of types of repetition, is a recognition of the different dimensions of structure on which schematic patterns may vary. This in turn presupposes a proper linguistic analysis, and study of different degrees of patterning on lines which have been hinted at in §4.3.2.

5.2.3 *The Functions of Verbal Parallelism*

In considering the functions of verbal parallelism in poetry, we have to take account of ways in which it is both like and unlike free verbal repetition (§5.2.1). The repetition of individual words here, as in free repetition, is a form of superfluity or redundancy of expression. Indeed, in most cases language provides a means of avoiding the repetition, either by substituting a 'proxy' word such as a pronoun, or by reorganizing the syntax, often with the help of co-ordination, so as to omit the repeated sequence altogether. The following, for example, is a more economical, though probably less effective, recasting of the passage of Whitman I used to exemplify symploce: 'As I go, I will recruit for myself and you, and scatter myself among men and women.' Nothing is changed here, except for the position of 'as I go' and the elimination of the repetitions of 'I will' and 'as I go'. Even the redundancies of the more complex repetitive pattern quoted from Eliot's *Prufrock* can be deleted, with the aid of that most useful abbreviatory device, the adverb *respectively*: 'The yellow fog and smoke that rub their back and muzzle (respectively) on the window-panes'. Let me hasten to point out that the concept of 'redundancy' is applied here only to the cognitive meaning of the passage. It is excruciatingly clear that the abridged version destroys most, if not all, of the artistic value of its original, and that the reiterated parts are far from dispensable to the total process of poetic communication.

The argument in defence of repetition in verbal parallelism can take the same course as that in defence of free repetition. Man needs to express himself superabundantly on matters which affect him deeply. The affinity, in this case, is not to the 'spontaneous overflow of powerful feelings', as with free repetition, but rather to those subterranean rivers of corporate belief and sentiment which find their expression in the iterative procedures of ritual. The Elizabethan divine Richard Hooker justified the repetitiveness of church ritual on the ground that the 'length thereof is a thing which the gravity and weight of such actions doth require'.[3] A similar argument might be advanced on behalf of the prolixity of epic poetry, and, on a very different scale, in defence of the use of measured verbal repetitions in poetry. A close analogy with ritual, actually with liturgical language, is discernible in some of the lengthier verbal parallelisms of poetry; for example, in the dialogue between Lorenzo and Jessica quoted in the previous section (§5.2.2). Here the alternation of parallel speeches reminds one of the antiphonal exchanges of church observance, and suggests that the participants are engaged in a litany of love – a ceremonial conjuration of the great lovers of the past.

Verbal parallelism resembles free verbal repetition in that it is *physically sensible* – i.e. audible to the listener, and visible to the reader. This means that the parallelism sets up a special relation between expression and content: the outer form of the message not only expresses underlying meaning, but imitates its structure. That we can actually see and hear the 'shape' of the ideas expressed is particularly evident in a pronounced parallelism, such as that of the Beatitudes:

> *Blessed are* the poor in spirit: *for* theirs is the kingdom of heaven.
> *Blessed are* they that mourn: *for* they shall be comforted.
> *Blessed are* the meek: *for* they shall inherit the earth . . .
> [Matthew 5]

Even if we have no knowledge of the language being used, we still have, as it were, a ground-plan of what is being said. To test this, the three verses quoted above are now quoted as they appear in a translation of the New Testament into Swahili:[4]

> *Wa kheri* walio maskini was roho: *maana* ufalme wa mbinguni ni wao.
> *Wa kheri* wenye huzuni: *maana* hawo watafarajika.
> *Wa kheri* wenye upole: *maana* hawo watairithi inchi.

The same alternating pattern of anaphora $(a\ldots)(b\ldots)(a\ldots)(b\ldots)$, etc. can be detected in both the English and the Swahili translations.

In this sense, verbal parallelism says the same thing twice over: the expression hammers home the content. To this quality of 'sound imitating sense' it owes its declamatory force, the power of emphasis which makes it a stock device of political oratory and of emotionally heightened language generally. I think that this quality also explains the annoyance one feels when verbal parallelism is overdone – i.e. is used more lavishly than is justified by the weightiness of the content. Such a feeling tends to arise in a modern audience when it encounters the heavy-footed Senecan rhetoric of some Elizabethan tragedies:

> He spake me fair, this other gave me strokes:
> He promised life, this other threatened death:
> He won my love, this other conquered me:
> And sooth to say, I yield myself to both.

This ornate passage from Kyd's *Spanish Tragedy* [I.ii] has neither more nor less parallelism than the Beatitudes. But it belongs to a relatively commonplace piece of dialogue, in which the emotions are not strongly engaged, and is therefore felt to have little artistic justification.

That gratuitous patterning of this kind was felt to be ridiculous even during the Elizabethan period is suggested by Shakespeare's parody of sententious dialogue in the conversations of Nathaniel and Holofernes, priest and pedant, in *Love's Labour's Lost*:

> NATH: I praise God for you sir: your reasons at dinner have been sharp and sententious; pleasant without scurrility, witty without affection, audacious without impudency, learned without opinion, and strange without heresy. I did converse this *quondam* day with a companion of the King's, who is intituled, nominated, or called, Don Adriano de Armado.

> HOLO: *Novi hominem tanquam te:* his humour is lofty, his discourse peremptory, his tongue filed, his eye ambitious, his gait majestical, and his general behaviour vain, ridiculous, and thrasonical.   [V.i]

Nevertheless, in judging such matters, we clearly have to take account of the different standards of different periods. We live at a time when poetic heightening for its own sake, i.e. the contrived distancing of poetic language from 'ordinary' language, tends to be avoided by poets and condemned by critics. Our demand for a justification of parallelism is stronger than that of other ages.

Examples for discussion

Distinguish different types of scheme in the following, with special attention to verbal repetitions. Consider the importance of schemes in the general appreciation of each example:

[a] *The Lady's Prudent Answer to her Love*
(A reply to the more famous ballad 'Come Live with me and be My Love.')

If all the world and Love were young
And truth in every shepherd's tongue,
These pretty pleasures might me move,
To live with thee and be thy love.
    These pretty pleasures, &c.

Time drives the flocks from field to fold
When rivers rage and rocks grow cold
And Philomel becometh dumb –
The rest complains of care to come.
   And Philomel, &c.

The flowers do fade, and wanton fields
To wayward winter reckoning yields;
A honey tongue, and heart of gall
Is fancy's spring, but sorrow's fall.
   A honey tongue, &c.

Thy gowns, thy shoes, thy beds of roses,
Thy cap, thy kirtle, and thy posies
Soon break, soon wither, soon forgotten,
In folly ripe, in reason rotten.
   Soon break, &c.

Thy belt of straw and ivy buds,
Thy coral clasps and amber studs,
All these in me no means can move
To come to thee, and be thy love.
   All these, &c.

If youth could last, and love still breed,
Had joys no date, nor age no need,
Then these delights my mind might move
To live with thee and be thy Love.
   Then these delights, &c.
           [Sir Walter Ralegh]

[b]
   We are the hollow men
   We are the stuffed men
   Leaning together
   Headpiece filled with straw. Alas!
   Our dried voices, when
   We whisper together
   Are quiet and meaningless
   As wind in dry grass
   Or rats' feet over broken glass
   In our dry cellar
   Shape without form, shade without colour,
   Paralysed force, gesture without motion;

   Those who have crossed
   With direct eyes, to death's other Kingdom

Remember us – if at all – not as lost
Violent souls, but only
As the hollow men
The stuffed men.

[T. S. Eliot, *The Hollow Men*, i]

[*c*]

He lifted his head from his drinking, as cattle do,
And looked at me vaguely, as drinking cattle do,
And flickered his two-forked tongue from his lips, and mused a moment,
And stooped and drank a little more,
Being earth-brown, earth-golden from the burning bowels of the earth
On the day of Sicilian July, with Etna smoking.

The voice of my education said to me
He must be killed,
For in Sicily the black, black snakes are innocent, the gold are venomous.

And voices in me said, If you were a man
You would take a stick and break him now, and finish him off.
But I must confess how I liked him,
How glad I was he had come like a guest in quiet, to drink at my water-trough
And depart peaceful, pacified, thankless,
Into the burning bowels of this earth.

Was it cowardice, that I dared not kill him?
Was it perversity, that I longed to talk to him?
Was it humility, to feel so honoured?
I felt so honoured.

[D. H. Lawrence, *Snake*]

Notes

1   See, for example, the summary of medieval poetic (Geoffrey de Vinsauf) in J. W.
    H. ATKINS, *English Literary Criticism: The Medieval Phase*, Cambridge, 1943, 201–2;
    also the figures of repetition listed in G. PUTTENHAM, *The Arte of Poesie*, ed. G. D.
    WILLCOCK and A. WALKER, Cambridge, 1936, 198–202.

2   K. WRIGHT, 'Rhetorical Repetition in T. S. Eliot', *A Review of English Literature*,
    6.2 (1965), 93–100.

3   R. HOOKER, *Ecclesiastical Polity*, ed. KEBLE, Oxford, 1888, ii, 145; quoted in I. A.
    GORDON, *The Movement of English Prose*, London, 1966, 82.

4   *The New Testament* translated into Swahili (Zanzibar dialect), British and Foreign
    Bible Society, London, 1942.

Six

Patterns of Sound

Phonological schemes, like formal ones, consist either of free repetition or of parallelism. In view of the limitation to echoic effects announced at the beginning of the last chapter, I shall concern myself now with patternings of phonemes (of individual vowels and consonants) rather than with rhythmic patternings of syllables. The subject of metre is best left to the next chapter, when we turn to the subject of versification generally.

6.1 SOUND PATTERNS WITHIN SYLLABLES

Let us start with a brief survey of the kinds of parallelism which can theoretically exist between two syllables.[1] Recall that the general structural formula for the English syllable is $C^{0-3} V C^{0-4}$ – i.e. a cluster of up to three consonants followed by a vowel nucleus followed by a cluster of up to four consonants. (For reasons which will become evident in §6.2 it is useful to say that a syllable which contains no consonants at the beginning or end has a 'null' consonant cluster in that position.) Now, parallelism exists wherever there is a partial, not full, correspondence between pieces of text. There is no parallelism if all three structural parts of the syllable vary at once, nor is there if, on the other hand, all three parts stay the same. This leaves us, on the present level of analysis, the following six possible ways in which either one or two of the structural parts may vary. (The unvarying parts are in **bold face**; C symbolizes a consonant cluster, not a single consonant):

[a]	**C** V C	**great**/**grow**	**send**/**sit**	('alliteration')
[b]	C **V** C	great/**fail**	send/**bell**	(ASSONANCE)
[c]	C V **C**	great/**meat**	send/**hand**	(CONSONANCE)
[d]	**C V** C	**great**/**grazed**	**send**/**sell**	(REVERSE RHYME)
[e]	**C** V **C**	**great**/**groat**	**send**/**sound**	(PARARHYME)
[f]	C **V C**	great/**bait**	send/**end**	('rhyme')

The first and last of these types, which are directly complementary to one another, are also the most important. I have put their labels, 'rhyme' and 'alliteration' in quotation marks, because a rather different interpretation of these words is more usual than the present one (see §6.2). For the fourth possibility, I know of no recognized term, and therefore suggest 'reverse rhyme'. This type of echo occurs twice in a line of Hopkins already quoted in Chapter 5: 'Quelled or quenched in leaves the leaping sun'. The fifth type, pararhyme, has occasionally been used instead of rhyme as a line-ending in verse structure, and with particular success by Wilfred Owen:

> It seemed that out of battle I escaped
> Down some profound dull tunnel, long since scooped
> Through granites which titanic wars had groined.
> Yet also there encumbered sleepers groaned,
> Too fast in thought or death to be bestirred.
> Then as I probed them, one sprang up, and stared
> With piteous recognition in fixed eyes,
> Lifting distressful hands as if to bless.
> And by his smile, I knew that sullen hall,
> By his dead smile I knew we stood in Hell.
> [Strange Meeting]

Incidentally, types [a], [b], [e], and [f] above were all systematically and regularly used in the medieval Icelandic dróttkvætt verse.

We have here looked at parallelisms between syllables on one particular level, i.e. in terms of the phonemic make-up of the three constituents C V C; but other kinds of parallelism are possible. Consonant clusters can be related in terms of partial, not full identity. There is, for example, a semi-alliteration between good and glad, in that both begin with /g/, although the initial clusters /g/ and /gl/ are not identical. There is also a semi-consonance between eyes and bless (the two words which interrupt the pattern of pararhyme in the above passage from Strange Meeting), because although the final consonantal sounds are different (viz. /z/ and /s/), they differ in only one particular, in that /z/ is a voiced consonant like /d/, /g/, etc., whereas /s/ is voiceless, like /t/, /k/, etc. In other words, there can be foregrounding of certain classes of sound, such as sibilants, nasals, back vowels, etc., as well as of individual sounds and sound clusters.

6.2 SOUND PATTERNS IN RELATION TO STRESS

In the last section I put forward a definition of rhyme and alliteration based on the individual syllable. But more commonly, these terms relate to the rhythmic measure, i.e., the unit of rhythmic patterning, which extends from the onset of one stressed syllable to the onset of the next (see §§4.3.1, 7.1). In fact, this is always so when rhyme and alliteration are considered as features of versification. In the alliterative prosody of Anglo-Saxon poetry, the alliterations which help to make up the required pattern of verse occur on stressed syllables only. This is also the form alliteration generally takes in later poetry, as exemplified by Coleridge's line 'the furrow followed free' discussed in §4.3.1, and by Shakespeare's parody of excessive alliteration in *A Midsummer Night's Dream*:

> Whereát with *blá*de, with *bló*ody *blá*meful *blá*de,
> He *brá*vely *bró*ached his *bó*iling *bló*ody *bré*ast.
>   [V.i]

It may be noted incidentally, that the occurrence of no initial consonant in successive stressed syllables, as in Tennyson's '*I* am the *heir* of *all* the *ages*' (*Locksley Hall*), is itself normally considered a pattern of alliteration, and was so considered in Old English alliterative verse. This accords with my treatment of such syllables as having a 'zero' consonant cluster: i.e. it counts as a positive correspondence between consonant clusters.

Similarly rhyme, as a basic component of verse form, is a correspondence between rhythmic measures rather than syllables. It is true that because of metrical and other considerations monosyllabic rhymes are in the majority. But we know well enough that there is the possibility of two-syllable ('feminine') rhymes, such as *butter/splutter*; even of polysyllabic rhymes like *civility/mobility*, *stationary/inflationary*. Thus, to redefine alliteration and rhyme in their most widely used senses, we first divide the rhythmic measure into two parts: *A* (the initial consonant cluster) and *B* (the whole of what follows *A*, prior to the onset of the next stressed syllable).

fig. [ʃ]

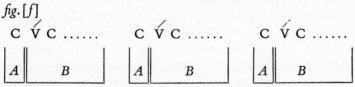

Alliteration is then the parallelism which consists in keeping *A* constant while *B* varies, whereas rhyme is the parallelism which consists in keeping *B* constant while *A* varies.

It may seem that this account of rhyme and alliteration has been making heavy weather of what seems, after all, to be a relatively simple matter. I would claim that, on the contrary, the superficial arbitrariness of the ordinary descriptions of these concepts has been elucidated by showing how they make sense in terms of the general concept of parallelism. Consider the rather involved definition of rhyme in the *Concise Oxford Dictionary*: 'Identity of sound between words or verse-lines extending from the end to the last fully accented vowel and not further'. The proviso 'and not further' is crucial, for if the identity were extended to the initial consonant cluster of the stressed syllable, this would no longer be a case of parallelism, but of one measure completely duplicating another. Various types and degrees of 'imperfect rhyme' have been accepted in English verse – particularly in light verse, where virtuosity in solving, or roughly solving, difficult problems of rhyme is a source of entertainment in itself: *table/miserable*; *scullion/bullion*; *pretty/bet I*; etc. But significantly, the complete identity of two measures, as in *greed/agreed*, *lava/palaver*, *unnerve us/nervous*, etc., is not even accepted as an approximate rhyme according to the conventions of English verse. *Sale/ale* and similar examples, on the other hand, count as rhymes, because *ale*, according to the point of view put forward here, has a 'null' initial consonant cluster, which contrasts positively with the /s/ of *sale*.

It should be clear now that alliteration and rhyme in English are not to be defined with reference to words. When we speak of words rhyming, what we mean, strictly speaking, is that the final measure of one word rhymes with that of the other. A rhyme need not, of course, be confined within the boundaries of a single word, as is shown by such examples as *linnet/in it*, *save you/gave you*; nor does an initial consonantal contrast between words, and correspondence from then on, as in *deceive* and *receive*, guarantee a rhyme. Similarly with alliteration: it is the main stressed syllable of a word which generally carries the alliteration, not necessarily its initial syllable. *Long* alliterates with *unlovely* in Tennyson's 'Here in the long unlovely street' [*In Memoriam*, vii].

Another misconception (fostered, in fact, by the name 'alliteration') is that these schemes are based on spelling rather than on pronunciation. In so far as the spelling system is phonemic, the phonological correspondences are indeed reflected in writing; but where spelling and pronunciation diverge, alliteration and rhyme follow the latter: *great* rhymes with *mate*, not with *meat*; *city* alliterates with *sat*, not with *cat*. If *great* is put in correspondence with *meat* in a poem, this counts only as an EYE-RHYME, a category of near-rhyme sometimes tolerated as a licence, but not to be confused with a 'true rhyme'. However, it must be continually borne in mind, when reading poetry of past centuries, that what is only an eye-rhyme to us may have been a 'true rhyme' to the poet. When Pope, for example, rhymes *line* and *join*, this is because they were commonly pronounced alike in his day.

6.3 'MUSIC' IN POETRY

It was suggested earlier that parallelism is the aspect of poetic language which most obviously relates it to music. If this is so, then surely the comparison with music is especially applicable to the various parallelisms of sound we have dealt with in the past two sections. Exactly what a person means when he says that a piece of poetry is 'musical' eludes analysis. But it is very likely that alliteration, assonance, consonance, and other sound echoes play an important part in it. These effects need not be in the forefront of attention to be successful: indeed, they are often most successful when least obtrusive. We see this if we examine a piece of poetry with good musical qualities, such as the opening part of Coleridge's *Kubla Khan*:

> In Xanadu did Kubla Khan
> A stately pleasure-dome decree:
> Where Alph, the sacred river, ran
> Through caverns measureless to man
>   Down to a sunless sea.

Various observations can be made about the patterning of sound in these lines, apart from that of its verse structure, which we will take for granted. In the first place, the rhyming word of every line is linked by alliteration (of syllables or measures) to one of the words closely preceding it: '*K*ubla *K*han', '*d*ome *d*ecree', '*r*iver, *r*an', '*m*easureless to *m*an', '*s*unless *s*ea'. Secondly, there is an internal rhyme (i.e. as opposed to the end-rhymes prescribed by the verse pattern) between *pleasure-* and *measure-*, despite the two-line gap between them. Thirdly, the first line of the poem contains a symmetrical pattern of assonances on stressed syllables: /æ/ /u/ /u/ /æ/. (Here I assume that *Khan* is pronounced like *can*, as is required by its rhyme with *ran* and *man*; if, on the other hand, it is pronounced with the long back vowel of *car*, the pattern is less regular, but can still be stated in terms of the *similarity*, rather than *identity* of the first and last vowels.) Fourthly, there is an intermittent consonance of /n/ in the latter half of the extract: *ran*, *caverns*, *man*, *down*, *sunless*. These clinical comments, and others which could be made on the same lines, do not amount to an explanation of the euphony of the passage; but they do show that considerable musical artistry (conscious or unconscious) may be hidden in poetry which, although musically satisfying, does not seem to strive after phonological effects.

These auxiliary musical effects, in contrast to the even patterning of versification, do not generally set up equivalence relationships of the kind associated with formal parallelism. There is a fitful, disorderly air about them which associates them with what I have termed 'free repetition'. Here, however, 'free repetition' must be understood rather differently from the way in which it was applied to formal repetition. In prosody, there is a hierarchic structure of parallelisms: of metrical feet, lines, and stanzas, such that a whole poem can be segmented exhaustively into these units. But occasional effects such as assonance are generally unsystematic, in that there are irregular gaps between corresponding pieces of sound. Whereas there is parallelism on the immediate level of the syllable or rhythmic measure, there is no parallelism within a larger context, such that the text is felt to be divided into equivalent sections. We have noted elsewhere (§4.3.2) the difficulty of deciding whether a certain repetition is foregrounded or not; but here is an additional way in which schemes 'shade off' into their background: variation in the width of the gap between initial occurrence and repetition. For example, we may agree in recognizing the rhyme of *measure-* and *pleasure-* in the opening lines of Kubla Khan. But what if these two segments were separated not just by two lines, but by three, four, five, ten lines, etc.? Would a rhyme still be felt to exist?

If we pursue this line of thought a little further, we come to view free sound repetition in terms of deviations from an assumed norm of frequencies of phonemes and phoneme combinations. In Dylan Thomas's short poem *This Bread I Break* (Examples for Discussion 3 [b] below, pp. 101–2)[2] all but five of a hundred words are monosyllabic. This exceptional density of monosyllables goes with an exceptional density of consonants, since monosyllables tend to have a high proportion of consonants to vowels. Consequently, the poem has a rather slow-moving, consonant-congested movement. Combined with this general density of consonants, is a particular density of plosive consonants (otherwise called 'stop consonants'), i.e. /p/, /t/, /k/, /b/, /d/, or /g/, in final consonant clusters. In fact, over half of the stressed vowels in the poem are followed by post-vocalic plosives: *bread, break, oat, drink, snap,* etc. Plosives are those consonants articulated by a sudden damming up and sudden release of the stream of air from the lungs. Thus to the general bunching of consonants they add a particular texture of sound: a pervasive abruptness; a flinty, unyielding hardness.

This is probably the opposite of the kind of effect usually evoked by the phrase 'the music of poetry', but there is no reason why we should reserve the term 'musical' for the sonority of Milton or the mellifluence of Tennyson. After all, music is Stravinsky and Schoenberg, as well as Beethoven and Brahms.

6.4. THE INTERPRETATION OF SOUND PATTERNS

The question of what and how a sound pattern communicates is one of the most mysterious aspects of literary appreciation. First, let us accept that to a great extent, the 'music' of phonological schemes, however difficult that quality may be to analyse, is its own justification. One does not feel cheated because the alliterations of 'measureless to man', 'sunless sea', etc. do not seem to have any external significance – for example, any imitative effect. On the other hand, there are ways in which external considerations may add point to the patterning of sound, and two of them are now to be considered: 'chiming' and onomatopoeia.

6.4.1 *'Chiming'*

The alliteration of 'mice and men', discussed in §4.3.4, is an example of 'chiming', the device of (in Empson's words) connecting 'two words by similarity of sound so that you are made to think of their possible connections'.[3] Here are three Shakespearean examples of such a phonetic bond between words: an alliterative bond in the first case, and one of pararhyme in the second and third:

So *foul* and *fair* a day I have not seen
[*Macbeth*, I.iii]
(Macbeth's first words in the play, echoing the portentous 'Fair is foul and foul is fair' of the three witches.)

Big Mars seems bankrupt in their *beg*gar'd host
[*Henry V*, IV.ii]

(A French Lord's contemptuous description of the English army on the morning of Agincourt.)

What thou wouldst *highly*,
That wouldst thou *holily*
[*Macbeth*, I.v]
(Lady Macbeth on her husband.)

I leave it to the reader to consider the implications of these connections. It is worthwhile pointing out, however, that the phonological bond is most striking when, as in these cases, it is between words which are grammatically paired but which contrast in reference and in associations.

6.4.2 *Onomatopoeia*

A very different kind of reinforcement takes the form of a resemblance between what a piece of language sounds like, and what it refers to. This is ONOMATOPOEIA, in a broad sense of that often loosely used word.

As the imitative aspect of language is often misunderstood, it is best to begin with some elementary remarks about it. Firstly, contrary to popular feelings about words, the relation between sound and reference is arbitrary: there is no necessary similarity between these two facets of language. There is nothing essentially 'doggy' about the sound of the word *dog*, nor is there anything 'piggy' about the sound /pig/, although our habitual association of the sound with the animal may persuade us that there is. This is confirmed by the lack of phonetic resemblance between different words having the same reference – for example, between these two words and their French equivalents *chien* and *cochon*. Secondly, it is true that a comparatively small number of words, in English as in other languages, are onomatopoeic: *buzz, clatter, whisper, cuckoo*, etc. But even in these cases, the correlation between sound and reference is only partial and indirect: although English *whisper* and French *chuchoter* are both felt to be onomatopoeic, there is scarcely any phonetic likeness between them.

In poetry, as we have noted, people tend to be on the look-out for reinforcements for schematic patterns. They are therefore sensitive to suggestive qualities of sound which pass unnoticed in other kinds of discourse. However, a configuration of sounds suggests a particular type of reference only if that reference is in any case invoked by the meaning. John Crowe Ransom has a witty illustration of this point:[4] only two slight changes of pronunciation, he notes, can turn Tennyson's evocative phrase 'the murmuring of innumerable bees' [*The Princess*, VII] into 'the murdering of innumerable beeves' – a phrase from which the pleasant suggestion of humming on a sultry summer afternoon is utterly banished.

What seems to me the correct perspective with regard to onomatopoeia is provided with admirable clarity by Shapiro and Beum in *A Prosody Handbook*[5]:

In the first place, certain sounds – the voiceless *s*, for example – possess a *range of potential* suggestibility, rather than a fixed or single capability. Thus a prominence of *ss* is capable of suggesting certain classes of sounds (rustling, hissing, sighing, whispering) but not other classes (booing, humming, hammering, or groaning).

In the second place, this power of suggesting natural sounds or other qualities is relatively *weak* – too weak to operate unsupported by meaning – and because of its range, is only *latent*. The semantic content of words has to activate and focus this imitative potential. If the semantic content does not do this, then the collocations of sounds are in most cases neutral.

6.4.3 *Varieties of Onomatopoeia*

'Onomatopoeia' can be understood in a number of different ways.[6] In its narrowest and most literal sense, it refers to the purely mimetic power of language – its ability to imitate other (mostly non-linguistic) sounds. In the opening lines of Spenser's *Prothalamion*, the italicized sibilants represent, in this literal way, the sound of the wind:

Calm was the day, and through the trembling air
    Sweet-breathing Zephyru*s* did *s*oftly play.

Like /s/ and /z/, the sighing of the wind is a fricative sound, produced by the passage of air through gaps or past obstructions; there is consequently a resemblance on a fundamental physical level. An example of a similar kind is Keats's line:

Thou watche*st* the la*st* oo*z*ing*s* hour*s* by hour*s*

where the consonances of /st/ and /z/ are perhaps felt to mimic the sound of apples being squeezed in the cider-press – a kind of prolonged squishiness.

But on a wider and rather more abstract interpretation, the phonological patterns of these two examples can be taken to represent not just the *sound* of what they describe, but the activity as a whole. The connection is made not via the ear alone, but through the little understood pathways of empathy and synaesthesia. Spenser's sibilants depict the wind by providing a phonetic correlate of its continuing, fluctuating motion: something we can feel and see (for example, in the fluttering of leaves on a tree), as well as hear. Similarly, Keats's line dwells not just on the sound of squashing, but on the general *idea* of squashing – the slow application of pressure to pulpy, crushable matter. The tactile element of this is perhaps more important than its auditory element. A very different effect, for which a similar

explanation may be offered, is the pervading 'brittleness' of sound, discussed in §6.3 above, of Dylan Thomas's 'This Bread I Break' (Examples for
Discussion 3[b] below). The sudden cut-off effect of the post-vocalic plosives
echoes the theme of 'breaking' which runs through the poem, and which
is manifest in the four-times repeated item *break/broke* itself, and in the final
word *snap*. Although this relationship might be put on a purely mimetic
level, as an imitation of the actual sound made when a hard object is
broken, in fact the more abstract property of abruptness, which might be
perceived in terms of any of the five senses, is most relevant to the analogy.
In cases like these, we may say (adapting Mrs Nowottny's phrase) that the
sound 'enacts the sense',[7] rather than merely echoes it.

On a third, even more abstract and mysterious plane of suggestion,
onomatopoeic effects are attributable to the general 'colour' of sounds on
such dimensions 'hardness'/'softness', 'thinness'/'sonority'.[8] Although
judgment of whether a sound is 'hard' or 'soft', etc. is ultimately subjective, it seems that there is enough general agreement on such associations
to form the basis of a general system or 'language' of sound symbolism.
Moreover, this language is apparently common to different literatures.
The association between the consonant /l/ and the impression of 'softness',
for instance, has been traced in the poetry of several languages by Ullmann,[9] who cites the following lines by Keats as an English example:

> Wild thyme and valley-lilies whiter still
> Than Leda's love, and cresses from the rill.
>   [*Endymion*, I]

It is, in fact, possible to list classes of English consonants impressionistically
on a scale of increasing hardness:

1. liquids and nasals: /l/, /r/, /n/, /ŋ/ (as in 'thing').
2. fricatives and aspirates: /v/, /ð/ (as in 'there'), /f/, /s/, etc.
3. affricates: /ʧ/ (as in 'church'), /ʤ/ (as in 'judge').
4. plosives: /b/, /d/, /g/, /p/, /t/, /k/.

Such a scale helps us to see why the opening of Tennyson's Œnone ushers
in the image of a bland, idyllic landscape:

> There lies a vale in Ida, lovelier
> Than all the valleys of Inoian hills.[10]

All the consonants of these lines, with the exception of the /d/ of *Ida*, belong
to the 'soft' end of the scale. Moreover, every single consonant is a member of the voiced, rather than voiceless category: voiced consonants (/v/,

/ð/, /z/, etc.) have a more relaxed articulation than their voiceless counter-parts (/f/, /θ/, /s/, etc.), and so the presence of voice is another factor which tends to suggest softness. The same applies to the placing of plosives be-tween vowels, as in *Ida*, where the *d* is less vigorously articulated than it would have been if the name had been 'Dia'. The peculiar richness of sound texture in the passage comes out of the interlacing of several kinds of phonological repetition: the repetition of /l/, of /v/, of /n/, and of the diphthong /ai/ in *lies*, *Ida*, and *Ionian*.

This can be compared with another Tennysonian example, contrasting in subject matter, but rather similar in onomatopoeic effect:

So all day long the noise of battle rolled
[*The Passing of Arthur*]

The verb *rolled* here signifies a deep, booming noise, as of the rolling of a drum or the rumbling of distant thunder; and this interpretation is rein-forced onomatopoeically, by the muffled, booming sound of the line. The connection is difficult to trace in terms of plain mimicry, but can be estab-lished on the more abstract level of sound symbolism, where we note the prominence of 'soft' consonants and 'sonorous' vowels. 'Sonority' may be associated with the two vowel features of *openness* and *backness*, especi-ally in combination; i.e. it is, subjectively speaking, a quality of vowels which tend to be pronounced with a wide passage between the tongue and the roof of the mouth, and with the back of the tongue higher than the front. The 'sonorous' vowels are those which tend to be written with an *o* or an *a* (although English spelling is not a reliable guide on this point): in Tennyson's line, the vowels of *all*, and *long*, and the opening parts of the diphthongs of *so*, *noise*, and *rolled* all fit into this category. As for 'softness', we may observe that all the consonants of the line, with the exception of the initial /s/ and the /t/ of *battle*, are voiced; and that the liquid and nasal consonants /l/, /ŋ/, /n/, and /r/ are more numerous than any other kind.

The theme of 'sound enacting sense' can be extended to other fields apart from phonemic repetition. It is well known, for instance, that metre can be used mimetically, to suggest sluggish movement, galloping, etc. In his book *Articulate Energy*,[11] Donald Davie also makes us aware of various ways in which the syntax of a poem may enact, dramatize, or otherwise symbolically represent its content. The imitative function of language is not restricted to phonology, therefore, but belongs to the apparatus of ex-pression as a whole. Poems may even be visually emblematic of their con-tent, as is George Herbert's *Easter Wings*, each stanza of which in print actually has the shape of a pair of wings. To pursue this theme any further, however, is beyond the purpose of this chapter.

We may conclude this discussion of onomatopoeia with a warning: it is easy to yield to the vague suggestiveness of sounds, and to write enthusiastically, if loosely, about 'joyful peals of labials and liquids', 'the splendid gloom of repeated /u/s', 'the pastoral charm of the /a/s and /o/s', etc. Such remarks, whatever their value in recording the subjective impressions of the writer, must not be confused with well-based appeals to linguistic evidence. All too often imaginative reactions to the meanings of words are projected on to the sounds of which they are composed. We must be careful, therefore, to distinguish between the generally agreed symbolic range of a sound, and its associative value as apprehended by a particular reader in a particular linguistic context.

Examples for discussion

1. Identify and classify patterns of sound repetition [a] in the 'The Lady's Prudent Answer to her Love' (Examples for Discussion, Chapter 5, pp. 86–7); and [b] in the following poem. What, if any, is the artistic justification for these schemes?

> Bird of the bitter bright grey golden morn
>   Scarce risen upon the dusk of dolorous years,
> First of us all and sweetest singer born
>   Whose far shrill note the world of new men hears
>   Cleave the cold shuddering shade as twilight clears;
> When song new-born put off the old world's attire
> And felt its tune on her changed lips expire,
>   Writ foremost on the roll of them that came
> Fresh girt for service of the latter lyre,
>   Villon, our sad bad glad mad brother's name!
>   [From Swinburne, *A Ballad of François Villon*]

2. Examine the following pieces of poetry in the light of the view (expounded in §6.3) that patterns of sound repetition (alliteration, assonance, etc.) play an important part in the euphony, or musical quality of poetry:

[a]
>   Thus with the year
> Seasons return; but not to me returns
> Day, or the sweet approach of ev'n or morn,

Or sight of vernal bloom, or summer's rose,
Or flocks, or herds, or human face divine.
[*Paradise Lost*, III]

[*b*]   Song

A widow bird sate mourning for her love
    Upon a wintry bough;
The frozen wind crept on above,
    The freezing stream below.

There was no leaf upon the forest bare,
    No flower upon the ground,
And little motion in the air
    Except the mill-wheel's sound.
       [Shelley, *Charles The First*]

3. Discuss the nature and artistic function of phonological and formal schemes in these two poems, placing them within the total interpretation of each:

[*a*]   *Bantams in Pine Woods*

Chieftain Iffucan of Azcan in caftan
Of tan with henna hackles halt!

Damned universal cock, as if the sun
Was blackamoor to bear your blazing tail.

Fat! Fat! Fat! Fat! I am the personal.
Your world is you. I am my world.

You ten-foot poet among inchlings. Fat!
Begone! An inchling bristles in these pines,

Bristles, and points their Appalachian tangs,
And fears not portly Azcan nor his hoos.
       [Wallace Stevens]

[*b*]   *This Bread I Break*

This bread I break was once the oat,
This wine upon a foreign tree
Plunged in its fruit;
Man in the day or wind at night
Laid the crops low, broke the grape's joy.

Once in this wind the summer blood
Knocked in the flesh that decked the vine,
Once in this bread
The oat was merry in the wind;
Man broke the sun, pulled the wind down.

This flesh you break, this blood you let
Make desolation in the vein,
Were oat and grape
Born of the sensual root and sap;
My wine you drink, my bread you snap.
                    [Dylan Thomas]

Notes

1 A thorough classification of phonemic repetitions is provided by D. I. MASSON,
   'Sound-repetition Terms', in *Poetics*, Polska Akademia Nauk, Warsaw and The
   Hague, *c.* 1961, 189–99.

2 See G. N. LEECH, '"This Bread I Break": Language and Interpretation', in *A Review of English Literature*, 6.2 (1965), 66–75.

3 W. EMPSON, *Seven Types of Ambiguity*, 2nd edn., London, 1947, 12; quoted by
   W. NOWOTTNY (*The Language Poets Use*, London, 1962, 5).

4 J. C. RANSOM, *The World's Body*, New York, 1938, 95–7; quoted in R. WELLEK and
   A. WARREN, *The Theory of Literature*, London, 1949, 163.

5 K. SHAPIRO and R. BEUM, *A Prosody Handbook*, New York, 1965, 14–15.

6 Cf. the discussion of different kinds of onomatopoeia in NOWOTTNY, *op. cit.*, 3–4.
   I am much indebted to Mrs Nowottny's book for both ideas and examples on
   this topic.

7 NOWOTTNY, *op. cit.*, 116.

8 Cf. SHAPIRO and BEUM, *op. cit.*, 9–17.

9 S. ULLMANN, *Language and Style*, Oxford, 1964, 70–1.

10 Cf. NOWOTTNY, *op. cit.*, 4.

11 D. DAVIE, *Articulate Energy*, London, 1955.

Seven

Metre

Prosody (the study of versification) is an area which, like grammar and rhetoric, has suffered from scholars' disillusionment with traditional theory, and their failure to replace it with an agreed alternative. Harvey Gross is a spokesman of current perplexity on this subject when he says at the beginning of his book *Sound and Form in Modern Poetry*: 'The prosodist attempting the hazards of modern poetry finds his way blocked by the beasts of confusion. Like Dante he wavers at the very outset of his journey. He finds four beasts: no general agreement on what *prosody* means and what subject matter properly belongs to it; no apparent dominant metrical convention such as obtained in the centuries previous to this one; no accepted theory about how prosody functions in a poem; and no critical agreement about the scansion of the English meters.'[1] Certainly matters are not so clear-cut as they were when the rules of Latin scansion were religiously applied to English verse, on the mistaken assumption that the accentual rhythm of English could be handled in the same terms as the quantitative rhythm of Latin. This is an age which has learnt to question official dogmas rather than to accept them – in the case of prosody, with good reason. And yet out of the doubt of recent years there has emerged a certain amount of agreement on the nature of verse structure.

7.1 RHYTHM AND METRE

It has become widely accepted, for instance, that versification is a question of the interplay between two planes of structure: the ideally regular, quasi-mathematical pattern called METRE, and the actual rhythm the language insists on, sometimes called the 'PROSE RHYTHM'.[2] The difference between the two, as imaginatively felt by the poet himself, is expressed by W. B. Yeats (*A General Introduction for my Work*) as follows: 'If I repeat the first line of *Paradise Lost* so as to emphasize its five feet, I am among the folk-singers – "Of mán's first dísobédience ánd the frúit", but speak it as I should I cross it with another emphasis, that of passionate prose – "Of mán's fírst disobédience and the frúit"; . . . the folk song is still there, but a ghostly voice, an unvariable possibility, an unconscious norm.' Actually, Yeats is not comparing 'prose rhythm' with metre directly in this passage, but rather with a type of rendition – that of the folk-singer – which reproduces the metrical regularity at the expense of 'prose rhythm'. However, there is no better way of describing the metrical pattern than by the image of a 'ghostly voice' in the background.

A third factor is sometimes distinguished: that of the PERFORMANCE of a particular recitation. This is clearly extraneous to the poem, for the poem is what is given on the printed page, in abstraction from any special inflections, modulations, etc., which a performer might read into it, just as the play *Hamlet* exists independently of actual performances and actual theatrical productions.[3] But performance is related to 'prose rhythm' in the following way. 'Prose rhythm' is not any one particular way of saying a piece of poetry, but rather the potentiality of performance according to the rules of English rhythm. Two different Mark Antony's might render the line 'If yóu have téars, prepáre to shéd them nów' either as just marked, or with a different placing on the first stress thus: 'Íf you have téars, prepáre to shéd them nów'. Either would be permissible according to the rules of normal English pronunciation. Thus performance may be regarded as a particular choice from the aggregate of possible pronunciations in keeping with the normal rhythm of spoken English.

The distinction between metre and rhythm (the qualification of '*prose* rhythm' is unnecessary, and perhaps misleading) suggests a clear strategy for investigating the pattern of English verse. According to the principle 'divide and rule', we may consider in turn [a] the rhythm of English speech, [b] the metrics of English verse tradition, and [c] the relation between the two. We also need to examine the relation between verse form and other aspects of linguistic structure. Naturally one chapter devoted to such a large area of study can only deal with each topic in brief outline: metrics is a complicated subject which has filled many volumes.

7.2 THE RHYTHM OF ENGLISH

Underlying any talk of 'rhythm' is the notion of a regular periodic beat; and the very fact that we apply this term to language means that some analogy is drawn between a property of language, and the ticking of a clock, the beat of a heart, the step of a walker, and other regularly recurrent happenings in time. In phonological discussion, the grandiose term ISOCHRONISM ('equal-time-ness') is attached to this simple principle. To attribute the isochronic principle to a language is to suppose that on some level of analysis, an utterance in that language can be split into segments which are *in some sense* of equal duration. In certain languages, such as French, this segment is the syllable. In others, such as English, it is a unit which is usually larger than the syllable, and which contains one stressed syllable, marking the recurrent beat, and optionally, a number of unstressed syllables. This is the unit that I have previously called the (rhythmic) MEASURE. Thus English and French are representatives of two classes of language, the 'stress-timed' and the 'syllable-timed' respectively.[4]

I have emphasized the qualification '*in some sense* of equal duration', because the rhythm of language is not isochronic in terms of crude physical measurement. Rather, the equality is psychological, and lies in the way in which the ear interprets the recurrence of stress in connected speech. Here there is a helpful analogy between speech and music. A piece of music is never performed in public with the mechanical rhythm of the metronome, and yet despite various variations in tempo, some obvious and deliberate, some scarcely perceptible, rhythmicality is still felt to be a basic principle of the music and its performance. The gap between strict metronomic rhythm and loose 'psychological' rhythm also exists in language, where there are even more factors to interfere with the ideal of isochronism. For example, the duration of the measure (corresponding to the musical bar) tends to be squashed or stretched according to the number of unstressed syllables that are inserted between one stress and the next, and according to the complexity of those syllables. In this, a speaker of English is rather like a would-be virtuoso who slows down when he comes to difficult, fast-moving passages of semi-quavers, and accelerates on reaching easy successions of crochets and minims. Although some people reject the principle of isochronism because of the lack of objective support for it, I shall treat it here as a reasonable postulate without which a meaningful analysis of rhythm cannot be made. What we call 'stress', by the way, cannot be merely reduced to the single physical factor of loudness: pitch and length also have a part to play. Stress is an abstract, linguistic concept, not a purely acoustic one.

7.2.1 *The Measure: the Unit of Rhythm*

As the rhythm of English is based on a roughly equal lapse of time between one stressed syllable and another, it is convenient, taking the comparison with music further, to think of an utterance as divided into 'bars' or (as I have already called them) MEASURES, each of which begins with a stressed syllable, corresponding to the musical downbeat. A number of unstressed syllables, varying from nil to about four, can occur between one stressed syllable and the next, and the duration of any individual syllable depends largely upon the number of other syllables in the same measure. If we assign the value of a crochet to each measure, then a measure of three syllables can be approximately represented by a triplet of quavers, a measure of four syllables by four semi-quavers, etc. This method of rhythmic analysis,[5] which is not to be considered a method of 'scansion' as usually understood, is illustrated in these two passages of rhythmically free poetry:

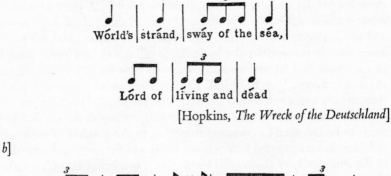

a]

World's | stránd, | swáy of the | séa,

Lórd of | líving and | déad

[Hopkins, *The Wreck of the Deutschland*]

b]

I would | sée them | thére, my | móther and my | síster

Wándering and | méeting in the | gárden's | quíet

[Henry Reed, *Chrysothemis*]

These notations give only one possible rendering of each line, the one which seems most natural to me in a fairly slow delivery. (All examples of rhythmic analysis in this chapter show only one of the possible performances of the lines in question.)

7.2.2 *Which Syllables are Stressed?*

To analyse a passage into measures in this way, we need to be able to judge which syllables are normally stressed. Although there are plenty of exceptions, it is a useful general rule that proper nouns and lexical words (most nouns, verbs, adjectives, and adverbs) bear stress in connected speech, whereas grammatical words (prepositions, auxiliaries, articles, pronouns, etc.), particularly monosyllabic grammatical words, usually do not. In reading aloud the sentence 'John is the manager', we scarcely have any choice about where to place the stresses: they fall naturally in two places – viz. on *John* and the first syllable of *manager*. The rhythm is therefore ♩♩♩ | ♩♩♩. Now if the sentence is rearranged to read 'The manager is John', the stresses still fall on *manager* and *John*, but the rhythm is radically changed to something like ♪ | ♫♫ | ♩. In each case, the grammatical words *is* and *the* remain unstressed. Thus the placing of stress in English is strongly conditioned, though not absolutely determined, by grammar and lexicon.

Some polysyllabic lexical words, like *trépidátion* and *cóunterféiter*, have two stresses; and if the word is uttered in isolation or at the end of a sentence, one of these stresses takes precedence over the other in bearing the nucleus of the intonation pattern: *trépiDÁtion*, *CÓUNterféiter*. In certain treatments of the subject, this extra prominence is described as an extra degree of stress. However, for the purpose of metrics, we can ignore it, and be content to regard *trepidation* and *counterfeiter* as rhythmically alike.

Words which normally have no stress can be stressed for some special purpose; to my knowledge, Hopkins is the only major English poet to mark special stresses in his text; for example 'Yes I cán tell such a key' (*The Leaden Echo and the Golden Echo*). Elsewhere, one generally refrains from reading into a poem unusual stresses of this kind, unless the context clearly demands it.

The system of musical notation as so far developed gives only a rough picture of the rhythmic values of syllables. It is possible to add various refinements, of which two are considered in the following two sections.

7.2.3 *Pauses*

In music, pauses are marked by rests of various lengths (𝄽 𝄾 𝄿 etc.), and it is easy to adapt this notation to the purpose of recording rhythmic values in poetry. Pauses are often felt necessary at the end of larger syntactic units – sentences, clauses, and some phrases – in fact, at the boundaries of intonation units. Allowance must be made both for pauses in the middle or at the end of a measure, and for pauses at the beginning of a measure, standing in place of a stressed syllable. Such 'silent stresses' (∧) can occur within a line of poetry, at a point where the traditional prosodist would mark a caesura:[6]

Éyeless in | Gáza | ∧ at the | míll with | sláves

[Milton, *Samson Agonistes*]

A | thíng of | béauty | ∧ is a | jóy for | éver

[Keats, *Endymion*, I]

Because it preserves the five-stress pattern of the pentameter, this reading is probably to be preferred to one in which the pause is omitted, and the number of stresses reduced to four: 'Éyeless in Gáza at the míll with sláves'.

7.2.4 *Syllable Length*

It is clear from examples given so far that syllables within the same measure do not all have to have the same length. In writing a three-syllable measure ♫♩, for instance, we may slightly misrepresent a rhythm which is closer to ♩.♫ or ♫♩. (In symbolizing three-syllable measures, I shall omit the triplet-sign from now on.) Ezra Pound notes in his *A.B.C. of Reading* that syllables have 'original weights and durations', as well as 'weights and durations that seem naturally imposed on them by other syllable groups around them'.[7] We may translate this observation into terms suitable for the present discussion as follows: one syllable may be longer than another [a] because it is in a measure containing fewer syllables, or [b] because of its internal structure in terms of vowels and consonants. Some vowel nuclei, including all diphthongs, tend to be long (as in *bite, bait, beat, bought*) whereas others tend to be short (*bit, bet, bat, but*). Moreover, the type of final consonant influences the length of the vowel: *beat* is shorter than *bead*, *bead* than *bees*, etc. If there is more than one final consonant, this again contributes to the length of the syllable: *bend* is longer, in relative terms, than *bed* or *Ben*. All these factors show that syllables vary in intrinsic length, as well as in the length imposed on them by the rhythmic beat. The duration of a measure is not equally divided, therefore, but is apportioned amongst its syllables according to their relative weights. Consider, for example, the rhythmic difference between the words *boldly*, *second*, and *comfort*, when spoken in isolation (each constituting a complete measure). The proportional lengths of the syllables can be represented, with tolerable accuracy, as ♩ ♪, ♪♪, and ♫; that is, as long+short, short+long, and equal+equal.[8]

Syntax, too, has an important bearing on syllable quantity. It seems to be a general principle that an unstressed syllable is especially short if it more closely relates, in syntax, to the stressed syllable following it. This means that unstressed prefixes, and words like *the*, *a* and *is*, tend to be pronounced quickly in comparison with unstressed suffixes. We may call the syntactically forward-looking unstressed syllables 'leading syllables', and the backward-looking syllables 'trailing syllables'.

A convincing illustration of this contrast is found in the two phrases 'some addresses' and 'summer dresses',[9] which are identical in pronunciation except for a difference of rhythm, in slow delivery at least, due to the different position of the word-boundary. The *a-* of *addresses* is a leading syllable, whereas the *-er* of *summer* is a trailing syllable; for this reason the first two syllables of 'some addresses' are long+short, whereas those of 'summer dresses' are equal+equal.

Some nursery rhymes, because of their extreme mechanical regularity of rhythm, are useful as illustrations of the metrical effect of syntax[10]:

Bóys and gírls cóme óut to pláy,

The móon doth shíne as bríght as dáy.

As shown by the slur lines, each unstressed syllable in this couplet is syntactically grouped with the following, not the preceding stress. Each unstressed syllable, therefore, is a 'leading' syllable, and recitation naturally follows the jerky long+short rhythm of (1):

(1) ♩ ♪|♩ ♪|♩ ♪|♩ (2) ♫ |♫ |♫ |♫

'Peter Peter pumpkin-eater' on the other hand has only trailing syllables, and illustrates the even rhythm of (2).

Such obvious repetitions of the same rhythmic pattern are rarely found in serious poetry, where subtler effects are obtained from the various possibilities of slight rhythmic variation. However, it is interesting to see how the movement of the following brief elegy hinges on a contrast between the rhythms illustrated by (1) and (2):

Úndernéath this sáble héarse

Líes the súbject of áll vérse:

Sýdney's síster, Pémbroke's móther:

Déath, ere thóu hast sláin anóther,

Fáir and léarn'd, and góod as shé,

Tíme shall thrów a dárt at thée.

[attrib. William Browne, *Elegy on the Countess of Pembroke*]

Winifred Nowottny, in her detailed analysis of this poem,[11] observes that for all its apparent simplicity, it generates a remarkable intensity of feeling; a power which 'comes from the sudden reversal of attitude that occurs at the word "Death", the violent explosion of life, passion, compliment, and affirmation'. She also notes the importance of the rhythm in achieving this effect; how the turning point at the beginning of the fourth line is marked by a change in rhythmic movement, as if the poet were fighting against the weight of the tomb, as expressed by the solemn elegiac movement of the first three lines.

This rhythmic *volte-face*, on examination, proves to be a change from the predominance of trailing syllables in the first three lines (particularly of the third line, which has the exact rhythm of (2) on Page 109) to a virtual monopoly of leading syllables in the last three lines. In terms of effect, it is a change from the smooth funereal 'slow-march' of the first half to the jerky, animated rhythm of the second half of the poem.

Whilst the time factor is relatively constant from one measure to the next, we see that latitude in the length of syllables *within* the measure provides scope for the poet to enrich the emotive range of his poetry.

7.3 METRE AND THE LINE OF VERSE

The kind of metre which has dominated English prosody for the past six centuries is strictly known as 'accentual syllabic'; that is, it is a pattern of regularity both in the number of syllables and in the number of stresses. It is to be distinguished from the purely 'accentual metre' of Anglo-Saxon poetry, in which the number of syllables, but not the number of accents per line, is variable; and also from the purely 'syllabic metre' of (say) French verse, in which the number of syllables per line is constant, but not the number of accents.

7.3.1 *English Metre as Rhythmic Parallelism*

Stripped of all subtleties, conventional English metre is nothing more than rhythmic parallelism: a patterning of the succession of stressed and unstressed syllables with greater regularity than is necessary for spoken English in general. (Notice that this is parallelism, not complete repetition, because although the rhythm is repeated, the actual sounds, of course, are not.) One type of metrical parallelism consists in the strict alternation of stressed and unstressed syllables, as in these last two lines of Milton's *L'Allegro*:

These de | lights if | thou canst | give,

Mirth, with | thee I | mean to | live.

We can go further, and point out that English verse is a hierarchical edifice of parallelisms, of which parallel segments of rhythm are the building bricks. The patterns of rhythm organize themselves into lines, which in turn enter into further structures of parallelism: couplets, stanzas, etc. Verse form, with its layers of structure, imitates the hierarchical organization of language itself into units of phonology, of grammar, etc. The difference between them, obviously enough, is that the constraints of verse form are adopted by the poet of his own free will, as a matter of convention, whereas the unit-by-unit grammatical and phonological organization of English is inescapable and unalterable, except by abandonment of the language itself as a system of communication.

If for the moment we consider the measure to be the basic unit of metrical parallelism, as distinct from the 'foot' of traditional scansion, we may set up four general types of metre, based on measures consisting respectively of one, two, three, and four syllables:

fig. [*g*]

One syllable:	One	year	floods	rose
Two syllables:	Mirth with	thee I	mean to	live
Three syllables:	La- dy- bird,	La- dy- bird,	fly a- way	home
Four syllables:	female of the	species is more	deadly than the	male

In theory, it would also be possible to construct a line of verse in which each measure contained five syllables, but I am not aware that such a metre has ever been seriously attempted. Even the first and last of the above four types are unusual, simply because one-syllable and four-syllable measures are less common in connected speech than those with two or three syllables, so that it is difficult to sustain such patterns for long. The disyllabic and trisyllabic metres are by far the most common, and are the only types which traditional English prosody generally acknowledges. Notice how the impression of speed increases with the number of syllables per measure. Trisyllabic metres are commonly thought lively and suitable for light-hearted subjects. The four-syllabic 'pæonic' metre favoured by Kipling calls for a brisk, cantering tempo of recitation. It is scarcely conceivable that such a metre would be chosen for a solemn poem on (say) a religious subject.

7.3.2 *The 'Foot' of Traditional Prosody*

It is clear that the measure, which (like the bar in music) invariably begins with an accent, is not to be confused with the FOOT of traditional prosody, which may begin either with a stressed or unstressed syllable. The main types of foot generally allowed to play a significant part in English verse are:

IAMB	× /	ANAPAEST	× × /
TROCHEE	/ ×	DACTYL	/ × ×

The 'foot' is actually the unit or span of stressed and unstressed syllables which is repeated to form a metrical pattern. This may or may not coincide with the measure, or unit of rhythm. In a regular iambic pentameter, the basic repeated pattern of syllables is the sequence × ╱, or the iambic foot:

The | ploughman | homeward | plods his | weary | way
×   ╱   ×   ╱   ×   ╱   ×   ╱ ×   ╱

Here the measures, separated by vertical lines, are clearly distinguishable from the feet, marked by horizontal brackets. In a regular trochaic penta-meter, on the other hand, the feet and measures coincide:

| ╱ × | ╱ × | ╱ × | ╱ × | ╱ × |

However, it is a notorious failing of traditional prosody that the distinction between 'rising rhythm' (iambs, anapaests) and 'falling rhythm' (trochees, dactyls) cannot be reasonably drawn when both the initial and final syllable of a line are stressed, or when both are unstressed:

(1) ╱ × ╱ × ╱ × ╱ × ╱

(2) × ╱ × ╱ × ╱ × ╱ × ╱ ×

Both these types of pattern, which are extremely common in English poetry, could be scanned equally well in terms of iambic or trochaic metre. Analysing into measures, we know there is only one way of distributing the bar-lines: namely, by placing one before each stressed syllable. But analysing into feet, we have to commit ourselves arbitrarily in favour of iambs or trochees.

The measure is therefore a more reliable concept than the foot in English prosody. The importance of the foot lies mainly in its historical position in the body of theory which poets through the centuries have learnt, and have more or less consciously applied in their poetry. This theoretical apparatus originated in a misapplication of classical metrics to the rhythm of English, and there is reason to feel that despite its longstanding hold over English versification, it has never become fully assimilated. When we turn away from the learned tradition, towards the 'folk prosody' of nursery rhymes and popular songs, the metrical foot becomes a patently unsuitable tool of analysis. Harvey Gross uses the example of *Old Mother Hubbard* in this con-nection[12]:

Old Mother Hubbard	| ╱ × × | ╱ ×
Went to the cupboard	| ╱ × × | ╱ ×
To give her poor doggy a bone.	× | ╱ × × | ╱ × × | ╱ | ∧
When she got there	| ╱ × × | ╱
The cupboard was bare	× | ╱ × × | ╱
And so the poor doggy had none.	× | ╱ × × | ╱ × × | ╱ | ∧

8—L.G.E.P.

The important metrical fact about this rhyme is that it is written in three-time throughout, all measures internal to a line having three syllables. But operating with traditional feet, one would feel obliged to scan lines 1, 2, and 4 in terms of 'falling rhythm' (dactyls and trochees) and lines 3, 5, and 6 in terms of 'rising rhythm' (iambs and anapaests), and thus obscure the regularity of the pattern. Here, and in countless other cases, traditional scansion forces one to over-analyse, by introducing distinctions which are irrelevant to the metre.

7.3.3 *The Line of Verse*

To live up to its label 'accentual-syllabic', conventional English verse has to be capable of division not only into regular numbers of unstressed syllables per stressed syllable, but into regular numbers of stresses or accents per line. This second layer of analysis is acknowledged in the designations MONOMETER, DIMETER, TRIMETER, TETRAMETER, PENTAMETER, HEXAMETER, for lines containing one to six stresses respectively.

We now need to consider how to identify and define a line of poetry – for to function as a phonological unit of verse, the line must be distinguishable on some grounds other than mere typography. As David Abercrombie points out,[13] a line is delimited by 'various devices which may be called line-end markers, and there seem to be three of these in use in English verse'. The three he specifies are the following, which may be used individually or in combination:

[a] rhyme, or some other sound scheme.
[b] a silent final stress.
[c] a monosyllabic measure, not used anywhere else, coinciding with the last syllable of the line (see fig. [g] on p. 112).

If one or more of these markers are present in a poem, even though it may be printed or recited as if it were prose, a person confronted with it for the first time should be able to recognize the line divisions. The most interesting of them, from the metrical point of view, is the silent stress (∧), which sometimes has an entire silent measure to itself:

| Ding | dong | bell | / | Pussy's | in the | well |
| / | / | / | ∧ | / ✗ | / ✗ | / |

and sometimes shares a measure with the anacrusis (initial unstressed syllable or syllables) of the following line:

| There | was a | crooked | man | / Who | walked a | crooked | mile |
| ✗ | / ✗ | / ✗ | / | ∧ ✗ | / ✗ | / ✗ | / |

The silent stress is most clearly perceived in these examples if one taps rhythmically in time with the stressed syllables, noting how an extra beat naturally fills in the time between one line and the next.

7.3.4 *Some Numerical Aspects of Metre*

Following Abercrombie further,[14] we may observe that silent stresses normally intrude themselves at the end of lines with an odd number of accents, but not at the end of those with an even number. Trimeters and pentameters, for example, have a silent stress, but not tetrameters. If, therefore, we add the silent stress on to the number of vocalized stresses in each line, we reach the conclusion that all metres, even those apparently odd, are actually based on an even number of stresses per line. A pentameter can be regarded as a hexameter with one stress silent, and so on. The double measure (corresponding to the traditional 'dipode') is a basic unit of metre.

To test this, read through the following extracts, and note how a pause seems to be required between trimeters or between pentameters, but not between dimeters or between tetrameters. Again, tapping in time with the stressed syllables may aid the perception of silent stresses.

Dimeter: | Óne more Un|fórtunate

| Wéary of | bréath,

| Ráshly im|pórtunate,

| Góne to her | déath!

[T. Hood, *The Bridge of Sighs*]

Trimeter: I am | mónarch of | áll I sur|véy, | ∧

My | ríght there is | nóne to dis|púte; | ∧

From the | céntre all | róund to the | séa | ∧

I am | lórd of the | fówl and the | brúte. | ∧

[Cowper, *Verses supposed to be written by Alexander Selkirk*]

Tetrameter: But | háil, thou | góddess | ságe and | hóly,
　　　　　 | Háil, di|vínest | Mélan|chóly!
　　　　　　　　　　[Milton, *Il Penseroso*]

Pentameter: The | plóughman | hómeward | plóds his | wéary | wáy, |∧
　　　　 And | léaves the | wórld to | dárkness |∧ and to | me. |∧
　　　　　　　　　　　　　　[Gray, *Elegy*]

Recognizing the existence of silent stresses can help us to appreciate further connections between verse and music. Just as the simpler song and dance forms of music tend to break down into four-bar, eight-bar, and sixteen-bar sections, so many verse forms are constructed out of the basic rhythm units by multiples of two. Each of the three popular metrical patterns set out below has the symmetrical structure of a square, being composed of four sections of four measures each. These sections do not in every case correspond to verse lines, which are separately indicated (by the symbol ₁):

[a]　| ╱ × × | ╱ ×₁ | ╱ × × | ╱ ×₁
　　× | ╱ × × | ╱ × × | ╱₁ | ∧
　　| ╱ × × | ╱₁ × | ╱ × × | ╱₁
　　× | ╱ × × | ╱ × × | ╱₁ | ∧

[b]　× | ╱ × × | ╱ × × | ╱ (×)₁ | ∧
　　× | ╱ × × | ╱ × × | ╱ (×)₁ | ∧
　　× | ╱ × × | ╱₁ × | ╱ × × | ╱₁
　　× | ╱ × × | ╱ × × | ╱ (×)₁ | ∧

[c]　× | ╱ × | ╱ × | ╱ × | ╱₁
　　× | ╱ × | ╱ × | ╱ (×)₁ | ∧
　　× | ╱ × | ╱ × | ╱ × | ╱₁
　　× | ╱ × | ╱ × | ╱ (×)₁ | ∧

If, as I hope, the reader has been able to decipher these formulae without too much difficulty, they may well be recognized as [a] the metre of *Old Mother Hubbard*, [b] the limerick metre, and [c] the popular ballad metre of *The Ancient Mariner* and many other poems. This way of displaying the metrical pattern shows a regularity obscured by the normal line-by-line arrangement. In more sophisticated stanza forms, this mathematical symmetry of pattern is generally less marked, but it may be part of the set of expectations we bring to English verse.

Whilst on the subject of duality, we may notice that there is a curious ambivalence between single measures and double measures, which is parallel to the ambivalence of two-time and four-time in musical time-signatures. It is easy to interpret the same piece of poetry as consisting of either two measures of two syllables, or one measure of four syllables; which interpretation suggests itself most strongly is largely controlled by the speed of delivery. Kipling's four-syllable (pæonic) metre, as we saw earlier, requires recitation at a rather fast, cantering speed:

An' the | dáwn comes up like | thúnder outer | Chína 'crost the | Báy!

[*Mandalay*]

If the speed is slowed down, however, intermediate stresses make themselves felt on the third syllable of each foot, causing the listener to reinterpret the passage in two-syllable measures. This should cause no wonder, since it is a well-known fact of English rhythm that the slower the speed at which an utterance is spoken, the greater the proportion of stressed to unstressed syllables. Yet the dominance of alternate stresses in the Kipling line is still felt, so that there is a case for analysing it both in terms of double measures and single measures, marked by greater (⟋) and lesser (╱) degrees of stress:

An' the | dáwn comes | úp like | thúnder | óuter | Chína | 'cróst the | Báy!

It also seems to be a characteristic of English rhythm that when a measure contains three unstressed syllables, one of these, usually the middle one, tends to receive a subordinate 'incipient' stress, which may be represented by the grave accent (╲). Thus the other Kipling line quoted in this chapter might be most accurately transcribed:

For the | fémale òf the | spécies ìs more | déadly thàn the | mále.

Here the words *for*, *of*, *is*, and *than* are somehow more prominent than their immediate neighbours, even though they belong to the class of words which are normally unstressed, and even though three of them may (even in this context) be pronounced with reduced forms containing the neutral vowel 'schwa': /fə/, /əv/, /ðən/. Yet the difference between this and the preceding example seems to be one of degree rather than kind.

The equivocality of stress values, which is here due to the overriding pattern of rhythm rather than to the inherent weights of syllables, probably explains why it is possible to treat unstressed syllables as if they were stressed for the purposes of scansion in lines such as those quoted in §7.2.3:

Éyeless in Gáza àt the míll with sláves

This rendering, in which the word *at* is assigned 'incipient' stress and pro-
moted *ad hoc* to the rhythmic status of a stressed syllable, is more realistic in
a reasonably fast performance than the rendering with a silent medial stress
given earlier, which belongs more to a slow and deliberate style of delivery:

Éyeless in Gáza ∧ at the míll with sláves.

Such is the instability of the rhythmic structure of English, that it is difficult to reduce its description to a 'yes-or-no' analysis. We have to acknowledge that the ambivalence of division into single measures or double-
measures sometimes suggests conflicting accounts of the same line of verse.
But it cannot be denied that the concepts of 'single measure' and 'double-
measure' are in themselves useful, if not indispensable to a satisfactory and
comprehensive explanation of English metre.

7.3.5 *Accentual Metre*

Accentual metre, sometimes called 'strong stress' metre, is the type of
metre based on an equal number of stresses per line, without respect to the
exact number of syllables per stress. It is of some importance in the history
of English prosody, being the metre of the earliest poetry recorded in our
language. Although in the thirteenth and fourteenth centuries it was replaced by the continental accentual-syllabic metric as the main prosodic
foundation of English poetry, it has survived in popular verse (ballads,
nursery rhymes, etc.), and has enjoyed a revival at the hands of twentieth-
century poets like Eliot and Auden. Hopkins's 'sprung rhythm' is also a
variant of accentual metre.

In theory, accentual verse may exploit the full possibilities of rhythmic
structure from one-syllable measures to four- and five-syllable measures.
But often in practice one-syllable and four-syllable measures are rare (except at the end of lines, where the former are naturally acceptable), yielding
an irregular vacillation between duple and triple time. This is the case, for
example, with many late nineteenth- and early twentieth-century poems,
of which this of Hardy is an example:

He énters, and múte on the édge of the cháir
Sits a thín-faced lády, a stránger thére,

A týpe of decáyed gentílitỳ;
And by sóme small sígns he wéll can gúess
That she cómes to him álmost bréakfastléss.
                [*In the Study*]

Such a metre may be regarded as a restricted form of accentual metre, or,
perhaps more plausibly in its historical context, as a relaxation of the
accentual-syllabic conventions, to permit free variation between two-
syllable and three-syllable measures.

The accentual metre of Anglo-Saxon alliterative poetry is illustrated in
the following passage from *Beowulf*:

Strǽt wæs stán-fah,   stíg wísode
gúmum ætgǽdere.   Gúð-byrne scán,
héard, hónd-locen,   hríng-iren scír
sóng in séarwum.[15]

Every line is divided into two half-lines, each containing two stresses. Here
again there are restrictions of various kinds on the number and position of
unstressed syllables: according to the most widely-held view of Anglo-
Saxon prosody, the rhythm of each half-line was drawn from a limited set
of patterns, including (for example) / / × ×, but not × × / /.[16]

7.4 THE INTERACTION OF RHYTHM AND VERSE FORM

Yeats was right to describe the 'ghostly voice' of metre as 'an unconscious
norm'. Just as poetic language deviates, in other spheres, from norms operating within the language as a whole, so within poetic language itself,
verse form, and especially metre, constitutes a secondary norm, an expected standard from which deviation is possible. In poetry, that is, a
particular verse pattern (say, blank verse), although foregrounded against
the background of everyday 'prose rhythm', is itself taken as a background
against which further foregrounding may take place.

7.4.1 *Defeated Expectancy*

Any noticeable deviation from a verse convention, as a disturbance of the
pattern which the reader or listener has been conditioned to expect, produces an effect of DEFEATED EXPECTANCY. A flippant illustration of this

effect is provided by the following piece of verse, which, although it scans like a limerick, contains none of the usual rhymes on which a limerick depends for much of its point:

> There was an old man from Dunoon,
> Who always ate soup with a fork;
>> For he said, 'As I eat
>> Neither fish, fowl, nor flesh,
> I should finish my dinner too quick'.

The temporary sense of disorientation, almost of shock, caused by deviation from a verse pattern may have a clear artistic purpose, as in the sudden interposition of a two-syllable line in this speech by Othello:

> O, that the slave had forty thousand lives!
> One is too poor, too weak for my revenge.
> Now do I see 'tis true. Look here, Iago;
> All my fond love thus do I blow to heaven:
> 'Tis gone.
> Arise, black vengeance, from thy hollow cell!
> Yield up, O love, thy crown and hearted throne
> To tyrannous hate! Swell, bosom, with thy fraught,
> For 'tis of aspics' tongues!

> [Othello, III.iii]

On a practical level, it allows time, assuming a strict apportionment of six measures per iambic pentameter, for the speaker's symbolic gesture to be carried out. But in addition, the prominence given to the words ''Tis gone' by this check in the movement of the verse adds force to the gesture, and draws attention to it as a landmark introducing a new and terrible phase of Othello's psychological development.

The power of defeated expectancy as a poetic device depends, naturally enough, on the rigidity of the verse form as it is established in the reader's mind. A truncated line of blank verse such as that just quoted would be less obtrusive in one of the Elizabethan or Jacobean plays in which metrical conventions are handled with greater laxity than in *Othello*. There is a great deal of difference, in principle and in effect, between occasionally violating a well-defined verse pattern, and gently stretching the pattern, so that it tolerates a greater degree of variation. The latter process applies to the loose tetrameters of Hardy quoted in §7.3.5.

7.4.2 *Metrical Variation*

As with other kinds of linguistic deviation, it is necessary to distinguish un-predictable licences of versification from 'routine licences' which are themselves allowed by prosodic convention. In the first of these categories belongs METRICAL VARIATION, or acceptable deviation from the metrical norm in terms of the distribution of stressed and unstressed syllables.

Metrical variation can be conveniently studied in this passage from Canto I of Pope's *The Rape of the Lock*:

Of thése am Í, who thỳ protéction cláim,   105
A wátchful spríte, and Áriel ìs my náme.
Láte, as I ránged the crýstal wílds of áir,
In the cléar mírror òf thy rúling stár
I sáw, alás! some dréad evént impénd,
Ére to the máin this mórning sún descénd;   110
But héaven revéals not whát, or hów, or whére:
Wárn'd by the sýlph, óh, píous máid, bewáre!

Perhaps the most frequent of all deviations from the perfect iambic pattern (× / × / × / × / × /) is the reversal of the stressed and unstressed syllable of a foot, especially at the beginning of a line. This is seen in lines 107 ('Late, as I ranged . . .') and 112 ('Warn'd by the sylph . . .'), both of which begin with the configuration / × × / instead of × / × /. A similar, but less common irregularity is the reversal of the order of successive syllables which belong to different feet, as at the beginning of line 108, where the stress values of the second and third syllables are exchanged: 'In the clear mirror . . .' (× × / / × is the most natural pronunciation).

Almost as important as the rearrangement of stress and unstress is another kind of variation: the substitution of a stressed for an unstressed syllable, or *vice versa*. There is an example of the introduction of an extra stress in the last line of the passage, if the word *oh* is pronounced, as one supposes it normally would be, as a stressed syllable. The rhythmic pattern of the line, so rendered, goes: / × × / / / × / × /. A replacement in the other direction is likely in lines 105, 106, and 108, where *thy*, *is*, and *of*, words normally without stress, are placed in a position of metrical stress. Such substitutions seem to violate the metrical design more drastically than re-arrangements. The reason for this is that they alter the number of stresses per line, break up the pattern of an even number of stresses, and so disturb the musical continuity of the verse. The introduction of an extra stress holds back the movement because it introduces an extra measure; whereas the subtraction of a stress has the opposite effect of hurrying the line on. Line 108, for instance, can be read as a four-measure line ××//××××/×/, or, in musical notation:

| In the | clear | mirror of thy | ruling | star |

However, I have suggested in the course of this chapter two other ways in which such a line may be rendered. The one is to insert a silent stress just before the unexpectedly unstressed syllable (× × / / × ∧ × × / × /), and the other is to substitute a subordinate stress, marked (/) above, for the normal lack of stress.

The addition of 'uncounted' unstressed syllables, especially where two short syllables come together, is a further allowed licence, illustrated in the *-i-* of *Ariel* (line 106) and the second syllable of *heaven* (line 111). This type of variation may not be evident in performance, as it is often possible to slur over the extra syllable in fast pronunciation; *Ariel* can be pronounced as only two syllables, and *heaven* possibly as only one.

Metrical variation involves the conflict between two sets of expectations: the expectations of normal English speech rhythm, and the expectations of conformity to the metrical design. In recitation, we may insist that the metre yield entirely to 'prose rhythm', or we may strike a compromise, by speaking the lines in a somewhat poetic manner, with a special verse rhythm; or we may even sacrifice 'prose rhythm' entirely to metre, reciting in the artificial manner of Yeats's folk-singer. However the poem is performed, a tension between the two standards remains in the text, and is a fruitful source of rhetorical emphasis, onomatopoeia, and other artistic effects. Metrical variation need not, however, have any function apart from making the task of metrical composition less confining, and providing relief from the monotony which would arise from a too rigid adherence to the metrical pattern.

7.5 GRAMMAR AND METRE

The interplay between verse and other strata of linguistic patterning is such a vast subject, that here I can do little more than indicate the vastness of it, and touch upon one subject of particular importance and interest: the relation between grammatical units and metrical units.

Verse can interact with linguistic patterning on many different levels.

To give a complete account of this interaction, we should have to consider separately the different levels of linguistic organization – phonology, grammar, graphology, etc. – in relation to verse structure. We should also have to give attention to other foregrounded patterns, such as formal parallelisms. Furthermore, we should need to examine the *manner* of interaction between patterns. Briefly, one linguistic pattern may either be congruent with another, or may cut across it.[17] As it is usual for linguistic patterns to coincide rather than to be at odds with one another, the second circumstance is the more interesting one. Here is a pronounced instance of syntax and verbal parallelism cutting across the line-divisions of verse:

> I wish a greater knowledge, than t'attain
> The knowledge of myself: a greater gain
> Than to augment myself: a greater treasure
> Than to enjoy myself: a greater pleasure
> Than to content myself.

> [Francis Quarles, *Christ and Ourselves*]

This can be contrasted with the congruity of formal pattern and verse pattern displayed in most examples of verbal parallelism quoted in §5.2.2 above.

7.5.1 *Enjambment*

We have seen (§7.2.4) the significance of the relationship between syntactic units and rhythmic measures. There is even more to be said about the relationship between syntactic units and verse lines. Commonly a distinction is drawn between 'end-stopped lines', in which the last syllable coincides with an important grammatical break, and 'run-on lines' in which there is no congruity of this kind. For the second case, in which there is a grammatical overflow from one line to the next, we may use the term ENJAMBMENT, which, however, by rights refers more especially to a grammatical overlap between couplets. Of the two relationships, congruity is treated as the normal, and enjambment as the marked, or abnormal, state of affairs. Enjambment is therefore like metrical variation in setting up a tension between the expected pattern and the pattern actually occurring. A parallel in music is provided by syncopation, the playing off of the expected rhythm against a rhythm caused by the displacement of accent. Another musical analogy is frequently used: that of counterpoint, the independent movement of two melodic parts.

It is not merely the tendency for patterns to reinforce rather than resist one another that makes the end-stopped line the norm. Enjambment is most frequently discussed in connection with heroic couplets and blank verse; and, as we saw in §7.2.4, the pentameter, if it is metrically regular, ends with a silent stress. A pause (a deliberate silence), however, is appropriate only at a grammatical boundary of some importance. Thus enjambment in a pentameter creates a conflict between the metrical system, which demands a pause, and the grammatical system, which resists one:

> His legs bestrid the ocean: his rear'd arm
> Crested the world: his voice was propertied
> As all the tuned spheres, and that to friends;
> But when he meant to quail and shake the orb,
> He was as rattling thunder. For his bounty,
> There was no winter in't; an autumn 'twas
> That grew the more by reaping; his delights
> Were dolphin-like: they show'd his back above
> The element they lived in: in his livery
> Walk'd crowns and crownets; realms and islands were
> As plates dropp'd from his pocket.
>
> [*Antony and Cleopatra*, V.ii]

We would be tempted to laugh at a schoolboy Cleopatra who read these lines in the metrically regular way, with a silent stress at the end of each. Instead, we assume that a skilful reader will in this, as in most other respects, obey the dictates of 'prose rhythm'. However, the metre receives some compensation for the loss of a stress. It is unusual not to have a major grammatical break (e.g. between clauses) every few words, so that where enjambment occurs, such breaks are almost bound to occur either in the preceding line, or in the following line, or in both. These breaks require pauses, making up for the silent stress omitted at the end of the line. One disturbance of the metrical movement therefore tends to rectify the other: a reader is held up by an unmetrical break before the end of one line, but makes up for it by a headlong swoop into the next.

When enjambment becomes more than an occasional device, it becomes almost impossible for a listener to follow the line-divisions of blank verse without a text in front of him. The disorientation is complete if the hallucination of an end-stopped line is created where actually none exists. For example, the clause 'an autumn 'twas / That grew the more by reaping', which is 'straddled' between two lines, would have made an acceptable pentameter. Such ghost lines are not infrequent in Shakespeare's later dramatic blank verse.[18]

As Roger Fowler points out,[19] enjambment is really a matter of degree – of the degree of grammatical cohesion between the end of one line and the beginning of the next. The solidity of the bond can be roughly measured by asking what is the smallest grammatical unit to which the end of the one line and the start of the next belong? A hierarchy of four grammatical units, word, phrase, clause, and sentence suffice for the purpose.[20] The most extreme form of enjambment occurs when both are part of the same word: Thomas Campion's 'Ever perfect, ever in them-/Selves eternal' [Rose-cheek'd Laura, Come] is an example. A less extreme form of cohesion occurs when both are part of the same phrase, though not of the same word: 'my sons/Invincible' [Paradise Lost, VI].[21] The most common and least startling form of enjambment is that in which the end of one line and the beginning of the following one belong to different phrases, but are part of the same clause (for example, when the line-division occurs between subject and predicate). There are several examples of this in Cleopatra's speech: one is 'his delights / Were dolphin-like'.

We may describe enjambment as the placing of a line boundary where a deliberate pause, according to grammatical and phonological considerations, would be abnormal; that is, at a point where a break between intonation patterns is not ordinarily permitted.[22] Such a break most frequently coincides with a clause boundary or sentence boundary. There are some places within the clause, however, at which an intonation break is appropriate; for instance, after an initial adverbial phrase like Cleopatra's 'For his bounty, there was no winter in't'. This does not, then, count as enjambment according to the definition I have just given. As punctuation marks generally indicate places where a pause is allowable, the identification of enjambment by the absence of end-punctuation is a rule-of-thumb good enough for most purposes.

7.5.2 The 'Verse Paragraph'

One of the important functions of enjambment is its role in building up expansive structures known as VERSE PARAGRAPHS. This term has been applied to successions of blank verse lines which seem cemented into one long, monumental unit of expression. To the skilful construction of verse paragraphs is attributed much of the epic grandeur of Milton's blank verse. In describing these structures, it is difficult to avoid architectural meta-

phors: one thinks of a multitude of assorted stone blocks interlocking to
form a mighty edifice.

The verse paragraph is neither a unit of syntax nor a unit of verse: it is
rather a structure which arises from the interrelation of the two. To see
this, let us examine a famous passage in which Milton writes of his own
blindness, from the beginning of Book III of *Paradise Lost*:

> Yet not the more
> Cease I to wander where the Muses haunt
> Clear spring, or shady grove, or sunny hill,
> Smit with the love of sacred song; but chief
> Thee, Sion! and the flowery brooks beneath, 30
> That wash thy hallowed feet, and warbling flow,
> Nightly I visit, nor sometimes forget
> Those other two equalled with me in fate,
> So were I equalled with them in renown,
> Blind Thamyris, and blind Mæonides,
> And Tiresias, and Phineus, prophets old:
> Then feed on thoughts, that voluntary move
> Harmonious numbers; as the wakeful bird
> Sings darkling, and in shadiest covert hid
> Tunes her nocturnal note. 40

The essence of the verse paragraph is an avoidance of finality. But what
does 'finality' mean? In prose there are various degrees of syntactic finality
(end of phrase, end of clause, etc.), leading up to the absolute finality of the
end of a sentence. In verse there is also the metrical finality of a line-division. In blank verse, a point of complete rest is only reached when a sentence boundary and a line boundary coincide. If either occurs without the
other, some structural expectation is still unfulfilled; the reader has, as it
were, arrived at a halting-place, not a destination. Perhaps we may refer to
the various kinds of medial stopping place as 'points of arrest', reserving
the term 'point of release' for the ultimate point of rest: the coincidence of
line-end and sentence-end.[23] The verse paragraph can then be seen as the
piece of language intervening between one point of rest and another.

What is remarkable about Milton's style of blank verse is first of all the
length of his verse paragraphs – indeed, rarely outside Miltonic blank
verse does the unit extend far enough to make the term 'paragraph' applicable. The piece quoted is evidently only an excision from the middle of one
of these units of expression, for although it constitutes a complete sentence,
it begins and ends at a point of metrical incompleteness – i.e. in the middle

of a line. It is also worth noting how Milton deprives the reader of the comfort of relaxing at intermediate stopping places. This is partly brought about by the frequency of enjambment (in this passage, lines 26, 27, 29, etc.), with its corollary, the placement of heavy breaks in the middle of the line. Thus when the metre bids the reader pause, the syntax urges him on, and *vice versa*.

Another factor is the Latin syntax of the periodic sentence, protracted by parentheses, lists, and involved structures of dependence. A particular contribution to the onward-thrusting movement of the language is the way in which anticipatory structure sets up syntactic expectations which are kept in suspense over a long stretch of verse. For example, 'Thee, Sion! ...' at the beginning of line 30 above requires completion by a transitive verb which is not supplied until the third word of line 32: 'Nightly I visit'. A more striking illustration comes at the very beginning of *Paradise Lost*, quoted below. Thus three factors – medial sentence boundaries, enjambment, and periodic syntax – combine to provide the tension, the unstaying forward impetus of Milton's blank verse, and (to revert to the architectural simile) make up the cement with which these massive linguistic structures are held together.

Often in Milton's blank verse, as in that of the later Shakespeare, enjambment is so frequent that the line-divisions can scarcely be followed by the ear unaided by the eye. Yet the blank verse mould, I feel, must be continually felt beneath the overlapping syntax: otherwise one misses the effect of criss-crossing patterns, the counterpoint in which lies so much of the power of this kind of verse. Without a feeling for the underlying pentameter scheme, moreover, one fails to appreciate the relaxation of a resolved conflict when the poem at length is brought to a 'point of release'. This profoundly satisfying effect can be likened to that produced by the perfect cadence at the end of a Bach fugue. Sometimes, as in the first twenty-six lines of *Paradise Lost*, the release of tension is enhanced by an uncharacteristic sequence of end-stopped lines, the last of which, in addition, is (also uncharacteristically) a regular pentameter free of metrical variation:

Of man's first disobedience, and the fruit
Of that forbidden tree, whose mortal taste
Brought death into the world, and all our woe,
    .   .   .
                    ... What in me is dark,
Illumine! what is low, raise and support!

That to the heighth of this great argument
I may assert eternal Providence,
And justify the ways of God to men.

It is clearly wrong to talk of this as a return to the 'norm' in any statistical sense of that word, for there are more run-on lines than end-stopped lines at the beginning of *Paradise Lost*. Indeed, here the concept of norm and deviation as applied to verse pattern is turned on its head: the irregularity becomes the rule, and the reversion to end-stopped lines becomes telling in contrast.

I may seem to have devoted more attention to an individual poet's style here than is justified. But of course, the Miltonic manner, far from being restricted to Milton, is a wide-ranging influence in English poetry.[24] Besides, this brief study of Milton has revealed deeper applications of notions like deviation, variation, and defeated expectancy: applications not limited to Milton and those who wittingly or unwittingly come under his influence. It would be instructive, for example, to investigate enjambment and resolution in the work of a poet like T. S. Eliot, who expressly repudiates the Miltonic manner.

For discussion

Study in detail the versification of any piece of poetry, by undertaking:

[a] a rhythmic analysis, with alternatives where necessary, in terms of measures with stressed and unstressed syllables, pauses, etc. (Musical notation can be applied to selected passages.)
[b] an account of verse form: measures or feet, lines, stanzas, etc.
[c] an account of the relation between [a] and [b].
[d] an account of the relation between verse form and grammar.

Examples suitable for this purpose are Chapter 3, 2[a], [b], and [c] (pp. 53–4); Chapter 4, 2[b] (pp. 70–1); Chapter 6, 2[a], [b], 3[a], [b] (pp. 100–102).

Notes

1   H. GROSS, *Sound and Form in Modern Poetry*, Ann Arbor, 1964, 3.
2   See the survey of some modern opinions in R. FOWLER, '"Prose Rhythm" and

Metre', *Essays on Style and Language*, ed. R. FOWLER, London, 1966, 82–3; also his 'Structural Metrics', *Linguistics*, 27 (1966), 49–64. In this development Eastern European prosodists have anticipated the thinking of scholars in the West. See the discussion of the Russian 'formalists' in R. WELLEK and A. WARREN, *Theory of Literature*, London, 1949, 173–4. A most thorough and interesting theoretical and practical study of metre is S. CHATMAN, *A Theory of Meter*, The Hague, 1965. Many of the points made in this chapter are to be found in Chaps. 2 and 5 of Chatman's book.

3 See, for example, R. WELLEK and A. WARREN, *op. cit.*, 171, referred to by R. FOWLER, *op. cit.*, 82–3.

4 The distinction between stress-timing and syllable-timing has been made by Daniel Jones, David Abercrombie, and many other phoneticians. See M. A. K. HALLIDAY, A. MCINTOSH, and P. STREVENS, *The Linguistic Sciences and Language Teaching*, London, 1964, 71–2. I call the unit of rhythm a 'measure' rather than a 'foot', to distinguish it from the 'foot' of traditional prosody (see §7.3.2).

5 'Musical scansion' has a long and rather unfortunate history, beginning with S. LANIER, *The Science of English Verse*, New York, 1880. More recently, phoneticians have placed the parallel between musical rhythm and speech rhythm on a sounder basis. See W. JASSEM, *Intonation of Conversational English*, Wroclaw, 1952, 41; D. ABERCROMBIE, 'A Phonetician's View of Verse Structure', in *Studies in Phonetics and Linguistics*, London, 1965, 16–25.

6 On silent stress, see ABERCROMBIE, *loc. cit.*; HALLIDAY, MCINTOSH, and STREVENS, *loc. cit.*

7 E. POUND, *A.B.C. of Reading*, London, 1951, 198–9.

8 See D. ABERCROMBIE, 'Syllable Quantity and Enclitics in English', *op. cit.*, 26–34.

9 W. JASSEM (*op. cit.*, 38) is the author of this example.

10 On the practical and illustrative value of nursery rhymes for students of English rhythm, see J. D. O'CONNOR, 'Fluency Drills', *English Language Teaching*, 6, 3 (1952), 90–1.

11 W. NOWOTTNY, *The Language Poets Use*, London, 1962, 108–11.

12 GROSS, *op. cit.*, 90–1. However, I would disagree with Gross's explanation of this as a blend of accentual and accentual-syllabic metre. (Gross's version of the rhyme, and that with which I am most familiar, has *dog* instead of *doggy*. When it was quoted in class, however, my students insisted on the emendment to *doggy*, which they took to be the authentic version. This increases the regularity of the metre, and so makes the illustration more convincing.)

13 D. ABERCROMBIE, 'A Phonetician's View of Verse Structure', 25. The scope and wording of Abercrombie's categories have been slightly altered to fit them into the present discussion.

14 *Ibid.*, 23.

15 Translation by J. R. CLARK HALL: 'The road was paved, the path guided the men together ... each corslet glittered, hard and linked by hand, the gleaming rings of iron clinked in their harness' (*Beowulf and the Finnesburg Fragment*, rev. edn, London, 1950, 36).

16 The orthodox system of metrical analysis for Old English poetry is readably summarized in J. R. R. TOLKIEN, 'Prefatory Remarks II: On Metre', in CLARK HALL, *op. cit.*, xxviii–xliii. A persuasive application of 'musical scansion' to Old English poetry is that of J. C. POPE, *The Rhythm of Beowulf*, New Haven, 1942.

17 A revealing study of these two relationships between metre and formal patterns (both grammatical and lexical) in Old English poetry and elsewhere is found in R. QUIRK, 'Poetic Language and Old English Metre', Chap. 1 of his *Essays on the English Language*, London, 1968.

18 F. KERMODE (Introduction to *The Tempest*, Arden ed., London, 1958, xvii) uses the phrase 'straddled lines', quoted by FOWLER, *op. cit.*, 90.

19 R. FOWLER, *op. cit.*, 88.

20 On a hierarchy of units in grammar, see HALLIDAY, MCINTOSH, and STREVENS, *op. cit.*, 25.

21 This example is from FOWLER, *op. cit.*, 89; the preceding one I owe to Michael Randle.

22 On the correspondence between units of intonation ('tone-groups') and units of grammar, see HALLIDAY, MCINTOSH, and STREVENS, *op. cit.*, 51. A more detailed and technical study of this problem is to be found in A. MCINTOSH and M. A. K. HALLIDAY, *Patterns of Language*, London, 1966, 111–33.

23 'Arrest' and 'release' are used in roughly these senses by J. MCH. SINCLAIR, 'Taking a Poem to Pieces', in *Essays on Style and Language*, ed. R. FOWLER, 72.

24 Two valuable studies of Milton's verse technique and language are S. E. SPROTT, *Milton's Art of Prosody*, Oxford, 1953: and C. RICKS, *Milton's Grand Style*, Oxford, 1963.

Eight

The Irrational in Poetry

As the last three chapters have been devoted to the study of schemes, to balance the picture, we must in the next three chapters turn to the study of tropes, which were described in §5.1 as 'foregrounded irregularities of content'. We may be content to look upon these, in plain language, as linguistic effects involving something odd in the cognitive meaning of a word, a phrase, etc. To the chronically literal-minded, poetry is a variety of nonsense; the difference between gibberish and metaphorical truth may depend on the leap the imagination is prepared to take in order to render meaningful what is apparently absurd. There are different kinds of absurdity, which rhetoric and logic distinguish by such labels as 'paradox' and 'oxymoron'. Further, the notion of 'irregularity of content' may be extended to include vacuity or redundancy of meaning, as in pleonasm, tautology, and circumlocution.

8.1 A LOGICAL VIEW OF MEANING

To lay the foundation of an enquiry into metaphor and similar devices, we have first to consider, very briefly, some general questions of semantics, without any special reference to literature. Remember (§3.1.3) that we reserve the term 'meaning' for the narrow sense of 'cognitive information', preferring 'significance' when we need to talk generally about what a piece of language communicates. For the present, our attitude to meaning will be closer to that of the logician than to that of the literary critic.

8.1.1 *Some Types of Semantic Oddity*

In the linguistic exchanges of everyday life we expect some cognitive information to be explicitly passed from one participant to another; it may be information about the internal state of the speaker ('I feel hungry') or about the objective world ('Yes, it's nearly nine o'clock') or about how a person, activity, etc., is evaluated ('An excellent book!'); but nevertheless, information. Because of our expectation that language should communicate in this fashion, we cannot help being struck by the bizarreness of sentences such as 'Is your wife married?' or 'He climbed up the surface of the lake', or 'They played a duet for violin, 'cello, and piano', in which this normal information-bearing function of language seems to be disturbed or frustrated.

In illustrating the most important kinds of semantic oddity, I shall restrict myself to simple relations of meaning between small groups of English words.

PLEONASM: An expression which is semantically redundant in that it merely repeats the meaning contained elsewhere, in what precedes or follows it: 'my female grandmother'; 'a false lie'; 'a philatelist who collects stamps'.

OXYMORON: The yoking together of two expressions which are semantically incompatible, so that in combination they can have no conceivable literal reference to reality: 'my male grandmother'; 'a true lie'; 'a philatelist who doesn't collect stamps'.

TAUTOLOGY: A statement which is vacuous, because self-evidently true: 'My grandmother is female'; 'That lie is false'; 'Philatelists collect stamps'. (Tautologies tell us nothing about the world, but may well tell us something about the language: e.g. what the word *philatelist* means.)

PARADOX ('Contradiction'): A statement which is absurd, because self-evidently false: 'My grandmother is male'; 'That lie is true'; 'Philatelists don't collect stamps'.

PERIPHRASIS ('Circumlocution'): An expression which is of unnecessary length, in that the meaning it conveys could have been expressed more briefly, e.g. by a single word: 'My female grandparent' (= 'my grandmother'); 'He makes untrue statements' (= 'He tells lies'); 'A dog of no definable breed' (= 'mongrel').

The first four types divide naturally into 'inanities' which convey no information in the cognitive sense (pleonasm and tautology) and 'absurdities' which convey self-conflicting information (oxymoron and paradox). As we see from the parallel examples, pleonasm is complementary to oxymoron, and tautology to paradox. The fifth category, periphrasis, does not

really fit into either class, but it is more like an 'inanity' than an 'absurdity', because it involves superfluity of expression.

To these a sixth type of exceptional importance must be added: it is the
kind of absurdity, mentioned in §3.1.2, which results from making a 'mistake' of selection: i.e. putting an element into a context which it does not
fit. Examples are seen in the following sentences:

1. Water has eaten kindness.
2. These cabbages read bottles.
3. Is the music too green?
4. That man is underneath my idea again.

To say exactly what is wrong with the first two sentences, we point out
that each verb in English is restricted as to what kind of subject can precede, and what kind of complement can follow it. The transitive verb, *eat*,
understood literally, only makes sense if preceded by a subject denoting
some kind of animal, and when followed by an object denoting some concrete object or substance. Neither *water* nor *kindness*, in the given sentence,
fulfils these respective conditions. Likewise *read* requires a human subject
and an object denoting some 'readable' entity, such as a book, a language,
or a letter. Examples (3) and (4) show variations on the same theme: in (3)
it is the subject *music* and the attributive colour adjective *green* which are
incompatible; in (4), the preposition *underneath* needs to be followed by a
nominal expression indicating something with spatial dimension, unlike
the abstraction 'my idea'. Plainly this kind of literal senselessness is at the
root of much figurative language. Imaginatively, for example, we may
find it possible to associate colour and sound so as to make 'green music' a
valid expression. In linguistics there is disagreement on whether these conditions of selection are part of syntax or part of semantics. I prefer to
treat them as semantic, since their effect is best described in terms of
meaning.

It might be questioned whether there are any grounds for separating the
violation of selection restrictions from paradox and oxymoron, which also,
after all, consist in selecting an expression at variance with its context. But
in the case of oxymoron and paradox, the incompatibility is of a stronger
sort: the expressions actually denote irreconcilable opposites. For example,
in 'my male grandmother', the meaning of *grandmother* contains the
element 'female', which is directly contrary to the 'male' of the qualifying
adjective. In 'green music' on the other hand, there is no such direct clash
of meaning. The difference is brought out in the following diagram, in
which contrasting elements of meaning are represented by plusses and

minuses: + Concrete for 'concrete' and − Concrete for 'non-concrete'
(= 'abstract'), etc.

fig. [*h*]

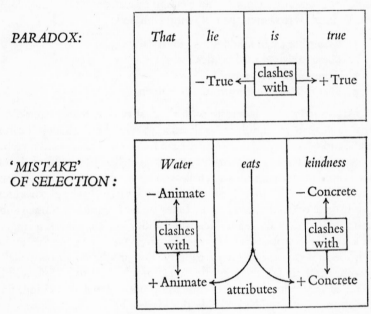

In the case of 'Water eats kindness', the elements 'animate' and 'concrete'
are not really part of the meaning of *eats*: we must rather say that they are
attributed by the word *eats* to the other, neighbouring words.

8.1.2 *Definition and Description*

Before we come to the utilization of the irrational in poetry, one more
point of general theory must be clarified. This is the distinction, in semantics, between meaning and reference, or (to change the emphasis slightly)
between DEFINITION and DESCRIPTION. What would be our response, if
someone asked us to give a definition of (say) the noun *father*; and how
would it differ from our response when asked to *describe what fathers are
like*? Definition calls for succinctness, a minimum periphrasis for the word
in question, showing its connection in meaning to other items in the same
language: a reasonable definition would be 'one's male parent'. In *describ-*

ing fathers, on the other hand, we would probably give details of the characteristic age and behaviour of fathers; their attitudes towards their children; their position in society; their legal rights and duties; and so forth. Whereas definition tells what we know about the language (or rather one aspect of the language – the meaning of words), description tells what we know about the objects, activities, etc. language can refer to – and this can include anything whatsoever we know about the world at large. Description includes definition, but it also includes a great deal of other information. The one is the function of the encyclopaedia, the other of the dictionary.

The acceptance of this distinction, despite the difficulty of applying it in some cases, leads us to recognize two kinds of absurdity: one contradicting something we know about meaning, the other contradicting our general factual knowledge of the universe. Examples of the former, that is, of linguistic or logical absurdity, are 'a female father', 'I am my father's father', 'my father isn't a parent', etc., which are shown to be ridiculous by what we know about the meaning of *father* in relation to other, connected words, like *son, parent, male,* and *mother.* Similarly, 'He is his father's son' is a logical tautology, which is nevertheless a popular saying, being specially interpreted to mean 'He has inherited his father's character'. On the other hand, it is only on the basis of our factual biological knowledge that we judge 'David Copperfield's mother never met his father' to be sheer nonsense, but not 'David Copperfield never met his father'. Further examples of statements which are odd for factual rather than linguistic reasons are: 'My father is four years old'; 'Tom was very angry with his naughty father, and sent him to bed without any supper'; 'He loathed her like a father'; 'After washing the children's clothes, Father laid the table and put on a clean dress ready for Mother's return from work'.

At this point we must slightly revise the formulations of §8.1.1: it is not the expression, but rather an interpretation of the expression, that is dismissed as absurd or vacuous. Confronted with a sentence like 'My father is four years old', we work according to the hypothesis that people do not normally make idiotic remarks; that is, according to what I earlier called 'the principle that human nature abhors a vacuum of sense'. Hence when a puzzling sentence contains an established ambiguity, we may after some hesitation arrive at a less obvious interpretation which is more acceptable than that which first occurred to us. 'Married bachelors', for instance, although an oxymoron according to its most prominent interpretation, is sensible if we take 'bachelors' in the sense of 'holders of university degrees'. When the search for a reasonable interpretation yields no clear ambiguity, the principle that 'human nature abhors a vacuum of sense' often leads us to hit on a 'nonce-interpretation' which, like the 'nonce-formations' discussed in §3.2.1, is devised for this specific occasion. For example, it is possible to make up a non-paradoxical reading of 'That truth is a lie' by imagining quotation marks enclosing the word *truth*, which is then taken ironically to mean 'what you/they/somebody else calls a "truth"'. As I indicated in §2.4, however, the difference between an established interpretation and a 'nonce-interpretation' is by no means clear-cut: there is no neat dividing line between literal and figurative meaning.

It has to be emphasized that any kind of absurdity, whether logical or factual, can rule out a particular literal interpretation, and cause the reader to search for a figurative one.

Some books are to be tasted, others to be swallowed, and some few to be chewed and digested.

We are scarcely aware, when reading Bacon's aphorism from *Of Studies*, that we have unconsciously rejected the literal, physical meanings of *tasted*, *swallowed*, *chewed*, and *digested*. Yet there is nothing in the definitions of these words which excludes their occurrence in the context. Indeed, that books should be eaten is not even a factual impossibility: it is merely the factual implausibility of that literal interpretation, together with the linguistic context, that causes us to think of mental, rather than physical consumption.

The importance of situation in the choice between different linguistically possible interpretations cannot be stressed too much. We can easily envisage some unlikely context, say a dialogue between bookworms in a child's story, in which 'I have just eaten a book' can be taken literally. On the other hand, for most perfectly acceptable sentences, it is possible to devise a context in which that sentence would be ridiculous, because it would be resting on patently false presuppositions. 'What a lovely evening!' would be ridiculous if uttered during a snowstorm at 2 o'clock in the afternoon. This 'contextual absurdity' comes to the fore in sarcasm and irony (see §10.2.1).

8.2 REDUNDANCY IN POETRY

In noting the applications of the various kinds of semantic redundancy in poetry, we may start with devices of lesser importance – those involving redundancy.

8.2.1 *Pleonasm*

In circumstances of functional communication, pleonasm, even more than other forms of semantic redundancy, is regarded as a fault of style. Generations of rhetoricians and composition teachers have frowned on solecisms like 'The reason is because . . .' and 'a villainous scoundrel'. Yet pleonasm has humorous uses, as in the following passage in which Touchstone harangues a peasant:

> . . . abandon the society of this female; or, clown, thou perishest; or, to thy better understanding, diest; or, to wit, I kill thee, make thee away, translate thy life into death![1]   [*As You Like It*, V.i]

For the serious poetic use of pleonasm, which is rather rare, we turn to the Old Testament. The passage quoted earlier from the Song of Deborah and Barak (§5.2.1) is a particularly striking example; another one is this verse from Ecclesiastes:

> I praised the dead which are already dead more than the living which are yet alive.   [4: 2]

The semantic parallelism characteristic of the Psalms is also a form of pleonasm. For hints on the function of this kind of redundancy, we may return to the discussion of repetitiveness in §§5.2.1 and 5.2.3.

In more recent times, when poets have aimed at tautness of expression as opposed to prolixity, pleonasm has been censured in poetry, as in other fields of communication.

> Away! – there need no *words* nor *terms* precise,
> The paltry jargon of the marble mart.
> > [Byron, *Childe Harold's Pilgrimage*, IV, 50][2]

The padding out of a line of verse by such means as the conjunction of quasi-synonyms *words* and *terms* in this passage is usually considered a culpable form of redundancy.

8.2.2 *Tautology*

Like pleonasm, tautology is a device of limited usefulness in literature. *Hamlet* is one of the few literary works in which I have noticed its calculated use. When Hamlet is questioned by his companions on what he has learnt from the Ghost, he replies, after some prevarication,

> There's ne'er a villain dwelling in all Denmark
> But he's an arrant knave.

To which Horatio, the paragon of good sense, replies:

There needs no ghost, my lord, come from the grave
To tell us this.
[*Hamlet*, I.v]

Hamlet's statement, if not a complete tautology, is something so close to it as to reveal no information worth having. His use of this cryptic response matches the popular use of tautology in the remark 'I know what I know', which by its very vacuity of sense conveys the information that the speaker means to keep his knowledge secret. This use of tautology is ironical: the cloak of idiocy hides the speaker's true thoughts and feelings. It is in this respect different from the genuine idiocy of Polonius's comment

For to define true madness,
What is't but to be nothing else but mad?
[II.ii]

Yet even this, from the dramatist's point of view, has an ulterior motive: the depiction of a combination of foolishness and pedantry in Polonius's character. Thus the lack of cognitive content does not necessarily go with a lack of significance; in fact, the vacuity of tautology can be an indirect means of conveying information about character and state of mind.

8.2.3 *Periphrasis*

Periphrasis is far more common in poetry than pleonasm and tautology, although it has some resemblance to them in that it involves saying more than is warranted by the amount of meaning communicated. The principle of economy of expression discourages the use of periphrasis in most communicative situations. It is difficult to find a general explanation of its popularity in poetry, but no doubt part of the matter is the purely technical value of periphrasis as a routine licence in any lengthy poem taxing to a versifier's ingenuity. Particularly in epic poetry, it is a convenience for the poet to have various ways of referring to the same thing, especially if that thing is of key significance in the poem. One thinks of the many synonyms for 'sea', 'battle', and 'warrior', in the Old English epic *Beowulf*. According to the requirements of metre, the Anglo-Saxon poet often makes use of longer, periphrastic expressions, such as *gomen-wudu* ('game-wood') for 'harp'; *hilde-setl* ('battle-seat') for 'saddle'. Especially characteristic of early Germanic poetry are KENNINGS, or periphrastic compounds which incorporate metaphors, like *swan-rad* ('swan's riding-place', = 'sea') and *mere-hengest* ('sea-horse', = 'ship)'. An interesting parallel in later literature (dramatic, not epic) is the variety of periphrases for 'crown' in Shakespeare's history plays: 'this golden rigol' (= 'ring' or 'circle'), 'this inclusive verge of golden metal', 'the circle of my glory', 'the imperial metal circling now my head', 'this golden round', 'the round and top of sovereignty'. Such designations, whether in *Beowulf* or Shakespeare, must be attributed not merely to metrical convenience and 'elegant variation' for the avoidance of monotony, but to the poet's desire to elaborate a thematically important concept, by throwing the emphasis now on one, now on another of its facets, thus deepening its symbolic and emotive significance. Groom, from whom the list of Shakespearean periphrases is taken,[3] suggests that 'the notion of royalty and its appurtenances was so august that the word "crown" was often too poor for the occasion, and a phrase had to be invented'.[4]

The connection between periphrasis and dignity of expression is an important one, especially evident in eighteenth-century poetic diction. In the nature poetry of that period, it was common, as we have seen in §1.2.3, for aspects of nature to be denoted by phrases such as *woolly care* ('sheep'), *busy nations* ('bees'), *feather'd choirs* ('birds'), no doubt partly because the dignity of poetry was conceived to be incompatible with such common-or-garden words as *birds* and *bees*. A more positive justification of this periphrastic heightening has been offered by Tillotson,[5] who suggests that it expressed the eighteenth-century scientific perception of order in creation, by assigning each species, each element, etc., a general title ('nation', etc.) and a particular epithet which singles out a salient property of the species – for birds, tunefulness or featheredness; for bees, industry; etc.

The reverse side of this linguistic propriety shows itself outside poetic language in euphemism – an alternative, often roundabout mode of expression used in preference to a blunter, less delicate one. Euphemistic periphrases abound in areas of social taboo: 'the smallest room', 'gone to his last rest', 'in the family way' are examples. They are not entirely absent from poetry: Victorian nicety in referring to childbirth seems to be reflected in this description from Tennyson's *The Marriage of Geraint*:[6]

> another gift of the high God
> Which, maybe, shall have learn'd to lisp you thanks.

More to the taste of the present age is an anti-euphemistic vein which shows itself when a taboo subject is described by means of a jokingly indelicate periphrasis, often a figurative one: *kick the bucket* for 'die', etc.

This appears to spring from a complementary, and equally deep-rooted tendency in the human mind: the urge to overcome one's fear by turning its object into a matter of familiarity and fun. A literary example is Mercutio's railing acceptance of his death-wound in *Romeo and Juliet* [III.i]: 'A plague o' both your houses! They have *made worm's meat of* me'.

We do less than justice to periphrasis if we think of it as the substitution of a longer synonym, or semantically equivalent expression, for a shorter one. Poetic periphrases are almost always descriptions, rather than definitions; and descriptions – particularly figurative descriptions – can give a heightened imaginative appreciation of the object described. No one would ever claim that another periphrasis from *Romeo and Juliet* –

> Night's candles are burnt out, and jocund day
> Stands tiptoe on the misty mountain tops ...
>   [III.v]

could be replaced without severe loss by the simple declaration 'Morning is come'.

8.3 ABSURDITY IN POETRY

Next we turn to oxymoron and paradox: two types of absurdity which entail irreconcilable elements of meaning or reference.

8.3.1 *Oxymoron*

The way in which we arrive at an interpretation of oxymoron is enacted in slow motion for us at the opening of the revels in Act 5, Scene 1 of *A Midsummer Night's Dream*. Duke Theseus reads through the programme of entertainment:

> *A tedious brief scene of young Pyramus,*
> *And his love Thisbe; very tragical mirth.*

and comments:

> Merry and tragical! tedious and brief!
> That is, hot ice and wondrous strange snow.
> How shall we find the concord of this discord?

The Master of the Revels, Philostrate, explains:

A play there is, my lord, some ten words long,
Which is as brief as I have known a play;
But by ten words, my Lord, it is too long,
Which makes it tedious: for in all the play
There is not one word apt, one player fitted:
And tragical, my noble lord, it is;
For Pyramus therein doth kill himself:
Which when I saw rehears'd, I must confess,
Made mine eyes water; but more merry tears
The passion of loud laughter never shed.

Theseus's question 'How shall we find the concord of this discord?' and Philostrate's reply represent the puzzle and the solution: two stages of a process which is generally so automatic that we are not aware of its taking place. The solution can take one of two forms. Firstly, the apparent irreconcilables may be found to be in this instance, contrary to expectation, compatible; as when Philostrate tells why brevity and tediousness, on the face of its mutually exclusive properties, are reconciled in Peter Quince's play. Second, an ambiguity may be discovered or invented, allowing the interpreter to by-pass the absurd interpretation. This occurs when Philostrate reveals a hidden ambiguity in the word *tragical*, which can be used in the technical sense of 'play which ends in death'; or in a looser sense of an entertainment, etc., which provokes a solemn response. Philostrate points out that the first sense does not necessarily entail the second.

Although wresting a line from its context deprives the reader of many clues to interpretation, it is an interesting exercise to ask oneself to interpret the following examples of oxymoron, and then to analyse the result:

1. Parting is such *sweet sorrow*
        [*Romeo and Juliet*, II.ii]
2. Thou art to me a *delicious torment*
        [Emerson, 'Friendship', *Essays*]
3. To live a life half-dead, a *living death*
        [Milton, *Samson Agonistes*]
4. And love's the *noblest frailty* of the mind
        [Dryden, *The Indian Emperor*, II.ii]

Examples (1) and (2) testify to humanity's ability to experience pleasure mingled with pain: a type of apparent absurdity which has the classical precedent of Catullus' well-known paradox 'Odi et amo' ('I hate and I love'). We probably interpret them as 'a mixture of sweetness and sorrow', 'a mixture of delight and torment', although it could be argued that it is the mysterious merging of contrary emotions that is imaginatively realized in such expressions rather than their coexistence.

Milton's oxymoron 'a living death', referring to Samson's blindness, can be resolved by construing *death*, by metaphorical extension, as 'a condition which seems like death'.

Dryden's 'noblest frailty' is not so much a logical absurdity as a contradiction of accepted values. Nobility is associated with strength, and ignobility with weakness. Hence 'noblest frailty' argues a reassessment of our moral assumptions, by telling us that nobility and weakness are compatible. Another possible interpretation would be to construe 'frailty' as emotional vulnerability rather than moral weakness.

8.3.2 *Paradox*

Much the same comments apply to paradox. The following examples will provide a basis for discussion:

> War is peace. Freedom is slavery. Ignorance is strength.
> [George Orwell, *1984*, I.i]

> For I,
> Except you enthral me, never shall be free,
> Nor ever chaste, except you ravish me.
> [Donne, *Holy Sonnets*, XIV]

> But he that hides a dark soul, and foul thoughts,
> Benighted walks under the midday sun.
> [Milton, *Comus*]

Orwell's slogans reflect the nightmare society he created in *1984*, and particularly the ability of its organizers to make its citizens believe the opposite of the truth. This equation of antonyms, perhaps the simplest and boldest form of paradox, can be made meaningful if we understand one term in a sense which is not incompatible with the other: 'Freedom of body' and 'slavery of mind', for example. Perhaps the authors of Newspeak would prefer us to interpret each slogan in a manner similar to that earlier suggested for 'That truth is a lie'; i.e. 'What you think is war is actually peace'; 'What you think is freedom is actually slavery', etc.

Likewise 'benighted' and 'under the midday sun', in the example from

Comus, have to be taken in non-equivalent senses, namely that of literal, physical sunshine, and that of metaphorical, spiritual darkness.

Donne's address to the Deity in the second example is a striking illustration of the religious use of paradox. That submission to God means freedom from the bond of sin is a commonplace of Christian thought. The notion of God as a bridegroom or a lover is more audacious, but scarcely more original. Tradition therefore predisposes us, without further context, to accept enthral and ravish in metaphorical senses. What gives particular force to the clash of meaning here is the way in which these verbs throw emphasis on the violence of God's taking possession of the soul.

Love and religion, two themes of universal and profound poetic significance, lend themselves especially to treatment by semantic contradictions. The 'delicious torment' of the lover, the 'fair cruelty' of the mistress, the 'sweet sorrow' of their parting, all bear witness to the powerful conflicts of emotion aroused by the experience of sexual love. Religion presents us with such enigmas as death in life and life in death:

> I die, yet depart not,
>   I am bound, yet soar free;
> Thou art and thou art not
>   And ever shalt be!

> [Robert Buchanan, 1841–1901, *The City of Dreams*]

There is a mystical feeling, in both these areas of inner experience, that truth eludes the puny force of unaided human reason. Reality lies beyond the literal, commonsense view of life as systematized in ordinary usage, and therefore the poet, to reach it, must violate the categories of his language.

8.4 BEYOND REASON AND CREDIBILITY

I have dealt in some detail with two types of linguistic absurdity (the third type mentioned, violation of selection restrictions, will be more fully illustrated in the next chapter), and may now finish with some general remarks on the element of absurdity and illogicality in poetry. So important does this element seem to be that a recent literary theorist, Wayne Shumaker, has devoted a book to the subject, attempting to trace by its means the primitive psychological and anthropological sources of literature.[7] A modern poet, Robin Skelton,[8] has commented on the incredibility or marvellousness of events and worlds projected by the poetic imagination. He points out, for example, the 'miracle' of fire burning under water described in the following stanza:

In what distant deeps or skies
Burnt the fire of thine eyes?
On what wings dare he aspire?
What the hand dare seize the fire?

[Blake, 'The Tyger', *Songs of Experience*]

In this respect the poet seems to aspire some way towards the condition of the religious mystic: the state in which the relation between 'reality' and 'imagination' is reversed, the imaginary becoming more real than the apparent. This is implied in Wallace Stevens's remark that 'metaphor creates a new reality from which the original appears to be unreal'.[9] When we come to anatomize metaphor in the next chapter, we shall not lose sight of this mysterious actuality of the metaphorical experience.

Examples for discussion

Discuss the irrational element of poetry with detailed reference to the following:

1. I travel'd thro' a land of men,
   A land of men and women too,
   And heard and saw such dreadful things
   As cold earth-wanderers never knew.

   For there the babe is born in joy
   That was begotten in dire woe;
   Just as we reap in joy the fruit
   Which we in bitter tears did sow.

   And if the babe is born a boy
   He's given to a woman old,
   Who nails him down upon a rock,
   Catches his shrieks in cups of gold.

   She binds iron thorns around his head,
   She pierces both his hands and feet,
   She cuts his heart out at his side
   To make it feel both cold and heat.

Her fingers number every nerve,
Just as a miser counts his gold;
She lives upon his shrieks and cries,
And she grows young as he grows old.

Till he becomes a bleeding youth,
And she becomes a virgin bright;
Then he rends up his manacles
And binds her down for his delight.

He plants himself in all her nerves,
Just as a husbandman his mould;
And she becomes his dwelling-place
And garden fruitful seventy-fold.

[Blake, from 'The Mental Traveller', *Songs of Experience*]

2.   *Metaphors of a Magnifico*
Twenty men crossing a bridge,
Into a village,
Are twenty men crossing twenty bridges,
Into twenty villages,
Or one man
Crossing a single bridge into a village.

This is an old song
That will not declare itself . . .

Twenty men crossing a bridge,
Into a village,
Are
Twenty men crossing a bridge
Into a village.

That will not declare itself,
Yet is certain as meaning . . .

The boots of the men clump
On the boards of the bridge.
The first white wall of the village
Rises through the fruit-trees.
Of what was it I was thinking?
So the meaning escapes.

The first white wall of the village . . .
The fruit trees . . .

[Wallace Stevens]

3.   *Pyramus and Thisbe*
   Two, by themselves, each other, love and fear
   Slain, cruel friends, by parting have join'd here.
                    [Donne, *Epigrams*]

Notes

1 The example is from S. ULLMANN, *Semantics: An Introduction to the Science of Meaning*, Oxford, 1962, 144.
2 Cf. ULLMANN, *op. cit.*, 154.
3 B. GROOM, *The Diction of Poetry from Spenser to Bridges*, Toronto, 1955, 34.
4 *Ibid.*, 34.
5 G. TILLOTSON, 'Eighteenth Century Poetic Diction', *Essays and Studies*, 25 (1939), 77–80.
6 Cf. GROOM, *op. cit.*, 216.
7 W. SHUMAKER, *Literature and the Irrational*, Englewood Cliffs, N.J., 1960.
8 R. SKELTON, *Poetry* (Teach Yourself Books), London, 1963, 61.
9 W. STEVENS, 'Adagia', *Opus Posthumous*, New York, 1957, 169.

Nine

Figurative Language

We have seen that the process of coming to terms with figurative language divides itself into two stages: the rejection of an orthodox, but (in the given instance) unacceptable interpretation, and the discovery of an unorthodox, figurative interpretation. Some of the traditional trope labels, like 'oxymoron', refer to a type of meaningless expression which confronts the reader in the first stage of the process, whereas others, like 'metaphor', refer to a mode of interpretation; that is, to the second stage. Thus it is quite possible for oxymoron and metaphor to be involved in the same act of comprehension: for an oxymoron, that is, to be interpreted metaphorically. 'A human elephant', for instance, permits two metaphorical interpretations: [a] 'A human being like an elephant' (in clumsiness, length of memory, etc.) and [b] 'an elephant like a human being' (in behaviour, understanding, etc.). As the last chapter was devoted to the explanation of terms like 'oxymoron', in this one we move on to terms like 'metaphor', which refer to modes of figurative interpretation.

It is as well to begin by reminding ourselves once more that literal and figurative usage, as was shown in §2.4, are two ends of a scale, rather than clear-cut categories. In the dictum 'Language is fossil poetry',[1] Emerson draws our attention to the fact that the expressive power of everyday language largely resides in countless 'dead' metaphors, which have become institutionalized in the multiple meanings of the dictionary. Countless other metaphors are in various stages of 'moribundity', so that it would be a misrepresentation to treat them either as completely commonplace or as utterly unorthodox. This makes the discussion of metaphor and related figures rather awkward. All the same, the literary metaphor *par excellence* is an image freshly created in the imagination of the poet, and perhaps we may be excused for concentrating on this extremity of the scale, and thinking of figurative and literal language in terms of black and white, and not of various shades of grey. In any case, so long as it is remembered that 'orthodox' and 'unorthodox' are relative terms, no harm will come of identifying the one with literal and the other with figurative meaning.

One further adjustment of our mental equipment may be necessary before we begin the pursuit of this ever-inviting, ever-elusive subject. When we talk of 'the metaphor of X' in a certain piece of language, we prejudge the issue of whether there is one or more than one acceptable interpretation. In 'the human elephant' we have just seen a particularly clear instance of an absurdity which has two figurative 'solutions'. Although in practice we rarely notice them, because our attention is fixed upon the one interpretation which seems to be relevant, such ambiguities are of unsuspected frequency. One has to allow, then, for the exercise of the reader's subjective judgment, consciously or unconsciously, in selection from a number of rival figurative readings.

On the other hand, there is the opposite danger of suggesting that figurative interpretation is a vague hit-or-miss affair. If it were largely a matter of chance, two people would rarely agree on how to understand a line of poetry, and a poet would find it impossible to communicate, except in the most haphazard way, with his public. The truth lies somewhere between this extremity and the view that metaphors, metonyms, etc., are unambiguously 'there' in the text. Critics are rarely at a loss for alternative interpretations over which to argue, especially in the work of 'difficult' poets who leave relatively few clues for interpretation; and yet most people would agree that within certain limits a poet can convey his intended meaning to his reader.

9.1 TRANSFERENCE OF MEANING

One of the reasons why figurative interpretation is not completely random is that language contains RULES OF TRANSFERENCE, or particular mechanisms for deriving one meaning of a word from another.[2] A general formula which fits all rules of transference is this:

> 'The figurative sense F may replace the literal sense L if F is related to L in such-and-such a way.'

A simple example is the rule which allows one to use a word denoting such-and-such a place in the sense 'the people in such-and-such a place'; the following sentences illustrate this rule:

> The whole village rejoiced.
> (= All the people in the village rejoiced.)

Washington has reacted cautiously to the latest peace proposals.
(= The people in Washington . . ., i.e. The people in Washington who run the American government . . .)
Our road is very friendly.
(= The people in our road are very friendly.)

The relation between figurative and literal senses can be represented by the formula F='the people in L'. The above statements are ridiculous on a literal plane, because they attribute the behaviour of human beings to places, which are inanimate. In a description of a rural celebration of Eucharist, Tennyson applies the same rule in a less hackneyed manner:

Or where the kneeling hamlet drains
The chalice of the grapes of God.
[*In Memoriam*, X]

Once more the figurative meaning becomes necessary because the literal meaning is absurd; hamlets, literally speaking, cannot kneel, so for 'the hamlet' we substitute, in sense, 'the inhabitants of the hamlet'.

Another rule of transference might be called the 'Quotation Rule'; it is the one we encountered in interpreting the paradox 'That truth is a lie' (§8.1.2). In that case, we made sense of an apparent absurdity by reading it as if part were enclosed in quotation marks. This is a common device of popular irony: 'He did it accidentally on purpose' is best construed as if quotation marks enclosed *accidentally*; the sense is then: 'He did it on purpose (although he claims to have done it accidentally)'. A literary parallel is Jane Austen's 'You have delighted us long enough', spoken by Mr Bennett [*Pride and Prejudice*, Chap. 18] to his daughter, who is overzealously entertaining the company with her mediocre musical talent. The superficial oddity of this remark lies in the qualifying of 'delighted' by 'long enough', which suggests paradoxically that after a certain period delighting no longer delights. (Compare W. S. Gilbert's 'Modified rapture!' from Act I of *The Mikado*.) As an irony, the import of Mr Bennett's assertion is: 'I use the word "delighted" because that is the word one conventionally uses of a young lady's performance at the pianoforte; however, by adding "long enough", I intimate that this performance has really been far from delightful.'

'The work(s) for the author' is a further standard example of transference of meaning: for example, when we say 'I love Bach' referring to the music, not the man; or 'I've been reading Dickens'. We apply these rules automatically in our daily speech, and are scarcely aware of their existence.

In literature they are used more daringly, just as the rules of word-formation (see §3.2.1) are applied beyond the usual restrictions.

9.1.1 *Synecdoche*

Particular names have become attached to certain rules of transference. The traditional figure of SYNECDOCHE is identified with a rule which applies the term for the part to the whole. This is of little literary interest, but is found in proverbs:

Many *hands* make light work.
Two *heads* are better than one.

Also in conventional expressions such as *sail* for 'ship'. A variant of this rule of synecdoche is found in the following:

When by thy scorn, O murd'ress, I am dead,
And that thou think'st thee free
From all solicitation from me,
Then shall my ghost come to thy bed,
And thee, feign'd vestal, in *worse arms* shall see . . .
[Donne, *The Apparition*]

where 'worse arms' requires the interpretation 'the arms of a worse person'.

The use of a particular term for a corresponding general term is also commonly treated by textbooks as synecdoche; for example, when a proper noun is handled as if it were a common noun: 'His true *Penelope* was Flaubert' [E. Pound, *Mauberley*, I]; 'A whale ship was my *Yale College* and my *Harvard*' [H. Melville, *Moby Dick*, Chap. 24].

A further illustration of the ambiguity of the term 'synecdoche' is its occasional use for the converse substitutions of the above two types: i.e. the term for the whole for the part, and the general term for the particular. Sometimes the latter is interpreted to mean 'abstract property for possessor of abstract property', as in 'Farewell, fair *cruelty*' [*Twelfth Night*, I.v].

9.1.2 *Metaphor*

METAPHOR is so central to our notion of poetic creation that it is often treated as a phenomenon in its own right, without reference to other kinds of transferred meaning. Yet I believe that it cannot be properly understood unless seen against the background of the various other mechanisms of figurative expression. In fact, metaphor is associated with a particular rule of transference, which we may simply call the 'Metaphoric Rule', and which we may formulate: F='like L'. That is, the figurative meaning F is derived from the literal meaning L in having the sense 'like L', or perhaps 'it is as if L'. We have already seen the twofold application of this rule to 'a human elephant'; but perhaps the simplest kind of metaphor to use as an illustration is that based on a clause structure with the verb *to be*:

> Life's but a walking shadow, a poor player
> That struts and frets his hour upon the stage,
> And then is heard no more: it is a tale
> Told by an idiot, full of sound and fury,
> Signifying nothing.
> [*Macbeth*, V.v]

At face value, this purports to be a series of definitions of *life*; but they are plainly not the definitions for that term we would expect to find in a dictionary. In the literal parts of our minds, we know well enough that life is *not* a walking shadow, *nor* a poor player, *nor* a tale told by an idiot. We therefore realize that either the one or the other, the *definiendum* or the definition, is to be taken in a figurative sense. With the aid of the metaphoric rule, we actually understand 'Life is a walking shadow' as 'Life is *like* a walking shadow', or 'Life is, *as it were*, a walking shadow'. In notional terms, 'life' is the TENOR of the metaphor – that which is actually under discussion – and the purported definition 'a walking shadow' is its VEHICLE – that is, the image or analogue in terms of which the tenor is represented.[3] Metaphor, in these terms, may be seen as a pretence – making believe that tenor and vehicle are identical. But as many writers have observed, the pretence often seems more serious and more real than the 'real' world of literal understanding. Macbeth's very words are appropriate (though not his sentiments): 'life' may seem to be a mere 'shadow' of the inner reality captured through metaphor. Nevertheless, from a linguistic point of view, the literal meaning is always basic, and the figurative meaning derived.

Naturally enough, metaphoric transference can only take place if some likeness is perceived between tenor and vehicle. This brings us to the third notional element of metaphor: the GROUND of the comparison.[4] Every metaphor is implicitly of the form 'X is like Y in respect of Z', where X is the tenor, Y the vehicle, and Z the ground. Reading 'human elephant' so that *elephant* is figurative, we most commonly take Z to be either clumsiness or long memory. In similes such as 'His face was as white as a sheet', tenor, vehicle, and ground are all explicitly mentioned.

9.1.3 *Metonymy*

Definitions of the figure METONYMY are often broad enough to include the preceding two tropes synecdoche and metaphor. *Webster's Third New International Dictionary*, for instance, calls it 'A figure of speech that consists in using the name of one thing for that of something else with which it is associated'. This covers all rules of transference, including that of metaphor, since similarity is a form of association. However, in practice metonymy is treated as a residual category including all varieties of transference of meaning apart from those separately classed as synecdoche or metaphor. Thus the first examples I gave of rules of transference in §9.1 are standard examples of metonymy: 'The whole village rejoiced'; 'I've been reading Dickens'; etc. *Webster* gives, as further examples from common usage, 'lands belonging to the *crown*' (concrete symbol representing abstract institution) and 'ogling the heavily mascaraed *skirt* at the next table' (article of clothing for person wearing it). One can very often give a literal paraphrase of a sentence containing metonymy simply by inserting one or two extra words: 'I've been reading *the works of* Dickens'.

In literature, metonymy is often overlooked because of the more powerful effect of metaphor, but is all the same extremely important. From Tennyson, who provided the 'kneeling hamlet' example of §9.1, are taken these further illustrations:

> the sinless years
> That breathed beneath the Syrian blue.
>> [*In Memoriam*, LI]

(A reference to the life of Christ; 'the sinless years' is approximately equivalent to 'the years lived by one who was sinless, and who breathed . . .')

> Led on the gray-hair'd wisdom of the east.
>> [*The Holy Grail*]

('gray-hair'd wisdom' = 'gray-hair'd possessors of wisdom', i.e. sages.)

> And all the pavement stream'd with massacre.
>> [*The Last Tournament*]

('with massacre' = 'with the blood of massacre'.)

Metonymy can be regarded as a kind of ellipsis: its obvious advantage in poetry is its conciseness. Yet as with metaphor and synecdoche, the expanded paraphrase seems to fail in capturing the immediacy of superimposed images, the vivid insight, which is characteristic of figurative expression. With 'sinless years' we feel that the perfection of Christ's life has somehow been transferred by contagion to the years through which he lived; with 'gray-hair'd wisdom' we somehow see wisdom and hoary-headedness merging into a single indivisible quality. The compressed allusive character of metonymy is well expressed in the following quotation by G. Esnault, which also perceptively sums up the relation between metonymy and metaphor: 'Metonymy does not open new paths like metaphorical intuition, but, taking too familiar paths in its stride, it shortens distances so as to facilitate the swift intuition of things already known.'[6]

9.2 ASPECTS OF METAPHOR

In a simile, the two things to be compared and (sometimes) the ground of the comparison are spelt out in succession: the comparison itself, too, is made explicit by means of such constructional elements as *like, as. . .as, more . . . than*. But in a metaphor, these three parts of the analogy have to be hypothesized from 'what is there' in the text. Moreover, the separation of tenor and vehicle is not usually so clear as in a definitional metaphor like 'Life's but a walking shadow'. This is why it is useful to have a technique for analysing metaphors, like that set out in the following section. It should be made clear that this is not a procedure for *discovering* a metaphor, or of finding out its significance – because of the subjective element of figurative interpretation, it would be vain to look for such a procedure. On the contrary, we must assume that we already understand the metaphor; our task is to analyse and to explain what we understand. For clarity's sake, the method of analysis will be set out as a sequence of directions to the reader.

9.2.1 *How to Analyse a Metaphor*

Let us take these three examples of metaphor for analysis:

[a] But ye loveres, that *bathen in* gladnesse
         [Chaucer, *Troilus and Criseyde*, I]

[b] Some time walking, not unseen,
      By hedge-row elms, on hillocks green,
      Right against the eastern *gate*,
      Where the great sun *begins his state*
           [Milton, *L'Allegro*]

[c] The sky *rejoices in* the morning's *birth*
         [Wordsworth, *Resolution and Independence*]

Stage I: SEPARATE LITERAL FROM FIGURATIVE USE

Decide which parts of the metaphoric expression are taken figuratively (they are in italics in the examples above); then separate them by setting them out on different lines. The jump from literal to figurative meaning, or *vice versa*, occurs at a point where literal interpretation is baffled, usually by a violation of selection restrictions. The lines as set out below are labelled 'L' (='literal') and 'F' (='figurative'). What appears on each line should on its own make literal sense – i.e. should not involve any absurdities.

[a] L: *But ye loveres, that*————*gladnesse*
     F: „ „ „ „ *bathen in*

[b] L: *the eastern*————*where the great sun begins*————
     F: „ „ *gate* „ „ „ — „ *his state*

[c] L: *The sky*————*the morning*————
     F: ————*rejoices in* ————*'s birth*

Ditto marks are placed beneath words which belong equally to the literal as to the figurative interpretation. In example [a], the lovers can literally bathe, just as they can literally experience gladness. Hence 'But ye lovers, that . . .' is merely an introductory context for 'bathen in gladnesse' – the dittos indicate that it is strictly not part of the metaphor. The blanks, on the other hand, signify textual gaps in the literal or in the figurative interpretation.

Stage II: CONSTRUCT TENOR AND VEHICLE, BY POSTULATING SEMANTIC ELEMENTS TO FILL IN THE GAPS OF THE LITERAL AND FIGURATIVE INTERPRETATIONS

Replace the blanks by a rough indication of what elements of meaning might reasonably fill the gaps. Both the top line and the bottom line should now make complete 'literal sense' on their own. The top line now represents the tenor ('*TEN*') and the bottom line the vehicle ('*VEH*') of the metaphor. This method shows clearly that tenor and vehicle, i.e. the things compared in the metaphor, are not usually identified with the literal or figurative senses of particular words: often one whole clause is placed in opposition to another. The tenor is the literal part of the expression with its reconstructed literal context, and the vehicle is the figurative part of the expression, together with *its* reconstructed context.

[a] TEN: *But ye loveres, that* ┆ [feel] ┆ *gladnesse*
     VEH: „ „ „ „ ┆ *bathen in* ┆ [water, etc]

[b]

TEN: *the eastern*	[part of the sky]	*where the great*	*sun*	*begins*	[its daily course]
VEH: „ „	*gate*	„ „ „	[king etc]	„	*his state*

[c]

TEN: *The sky*	[looks bright at]	*the morning's*	[beginning]
VEH: [animate]	*rejoices in*	[animate] *'s*	*birth*

As a general principle, make the 'gap-fillers' (the parts in square brackets) as unspecific as you reasonably can. Thus following '*bathen in*' in [a] any kind of liquid would be appropriate, although water is the most obvious choice. In [b], the figurative counterpart of '*sun*' might be a king, or some other kind of dignitary. In [c], the gap-filler 'animate' is used twice to fill out the vehicle, for there is no reason here to restrict the class of meanings allowed in these positions by the selection conditions of *rejoice*, which demands an animate subject, and *birth*, which demands an animate genitive complement. The tenor and vehicle should not be made any more precise than is warranted by rules of selection and appropriateness of context.

Another rule is: avoid if at all possible inserting a further figurative expression. To use figurative language in expounding tenor and vehicle is merely to multiply one's task by explaining one metaphor by another.

Stage III: STATE THE GROUND OF THE METAPHOR
The ground of a metaphor is more clearly seen once we have isolated tenor and vehicle. To find it, we simply ask the question: 'What similarity can be discerned between the top and bottom lines of the analysis?' How we answer this is very much a question of personal intuition; I therefore do not ask the reader to agree with the following suggestions, but merely to accept that they offer one possible analysis of each example.

[a] The lovers' attitude to gladness is that they wholeheartedly commit themselves to it. Gladness becomes their element – they see nothing beyond it. Their delight is simple, uncomplicated, untarnished by worry, like that of a person enjoying the water – the natural gift of God.

[b] There is an obvious resemblance between the sun and a king: we look up to both; both are powerful, being capable of giving and taking away life; both are glorious and of dazzling brightness (the one literally, the other metaphorically). The eastern quarter of the sky is like a gate because it is the sun's 'entrance' to the sky.

[c] Here are two separate comparisons; that between the brightness or clearness of the sky, and a person's rejoicing; and that between dawn and a birth. The second is the simpler: the connection is plainly that both are beginnings – dawn is the beginning of day, and birth the beginning of life. The first comparison rests on a commonplace metaphorical link between visual brightness and 'brightness' in the sense of cheerfulness, happiness, liveliness. On a less superficial level, these metaphors, which attribute life to inanimate things, are justified by Wordsworth's philosophy of nature.

9.2.2 Simile and Metaphor

Simile is an overt, and metaphor a covert comparison. This means that for each metaphor, we can devise a roughly corresponding simile, by writing out tenor and vehicle side by side, and indicating (by *like* or some other formal indicator) the similarity between them. 'The ship ploughs the waves', a stock classroom metaphor, may be translated into a simile as follows: 'The ship goes through the waves like a plough ploughing the land.' Example [c] above can be translated: 'The sky looks bright at dawn, like someone rejoicing in a birth.'

However, this equivalence, this translatability between metaphor and simile, should not obscure important differences between the two:

[a] A metaphor, as we noted earlier of metonymy, is generally more concise and immediate than the corresponding literal version, because of the superimposition, in the same piece of language, of tenor and vehicle.

[b] A simile, conversely, is generally more explicit than metaphor. 'That bathen in gladnesse', for instance, does not tell us exactly what gladness is compared to. Instead, there is a bundle of interrelated possibilities: the sea, a lake, water generally, some other liquid, etc. But in translating into simile, we have to make up our minds which of these is intended. The very circumstantiality of simile is a limitation, for the ability of metaphor to allude to an indefinite bundle of things which cannot be adequately summarized gives it its extraordinary power to 'open new paths' of expression.[7]

[c] Simile can specify the ground of the comparison: in 'I wandered lonely as a cloud', loneliness is stated as the property which the speaker and a cloud have in common. Also a simile can specify the *manner* of comparison, which may, for example, be a relationship of inequality, as well as equality: 'In number more than are the quivering leaves/Of Ida's forest' [*II Tamburlaine*, III. V]. It is more flexible, in this respect, than metaphor.[8]

[d] Metaphor, on the other hand, is inexplicit with regard to both the ground of comparison, and the things compared. This is not only a matter of indefiniteness, as noted in [b] above, but of ambiguity. Consider the line 'This sea that bares her bosom to the moon' [Wordsworth, *The World is too much with us*]. Taking 'bares her bosom' to be figurative, we construct the skeleton tenor 'This sea that does-something-or-other to the moon'. We then might theoretically entertain the following possible literal relationships between sea and moon:

1. The sea reflects-the-image-of the moon
2. The sea is-spread-out-underneath the moon
3. The sea is-made-visible-by the moon
4. The sea is-tidally-affected-by the moon
   etc.

Two factors help us to eliminate all but the most appropriate choices: one is context, and the other is the principle, which we unconsciously follow, of *making the tenor as similar to the vehicle as is feasible*; i.e. of maximizing the ground of the comparison. Both factors conspire to eliminate (4), which is utterly inappropriate; the second factor also eliminates (1). We are left, then, with an interpretation of 'bares her bosom' which is something like a blend of (2) and (3): roughly 'the sea which *lies stretched out and open to view by the light of* the moon'. Hence it is an important difference between simile and metaphor that in metaphor, because both ground and tenor are to some extent unknown, the determination of a ground may logically precede the determination of a tenor. In retrospect, we can now see why the three stages of analysis in §9.2.1 should not be confused with stages in the psychological process of understanding a metaphor: the ground should not be thought of as necessarily the last thing to be established.

Simile and metaphor have complementary virtues. Poets quite often take advantage of both by producing a hybrid comparison, in which simile and metaphor are combined. An example of such a blend is Wordsworth's

> The City now doth, like a garment, wear
> The beauty of the morning
>
> [*Sonnet composed upon Westminster Bridge*]

in which *wear* is used figuratively, whereas *garment* is introduced by a simile.[9]

9.2.3 *Notional Classes of Metaphor*[10]

It would be futile to attempt a full typology of metaphors according to the relation of meaning between literal and figurative senses. Nevertheless, certain types of semantic connection have been traditionally recognized as more important than others. They include:

[a] *The Concretive Metaphor*, which attributes concreteness or physical existence to an abstraction: 'the *pain* of separation', 'the *light* of learning', 'a vicious *circle*', '*room* for negotiation', etc.

[b] *The Animistic Metaphor*, which attributes animate characteristics to the inanimate: 'an *angry* sky', 'graves *yawned*', '*killing* half-an-hour', 'the *shoulder* of the hill', etc.

[c] *The Humanizing* ('*Anthropomorphic*') *Metaphor*, which attributes characteristics of humanity to what is not human: 'This *friendly* river', '*laughing* valleys', 'his appearance and manner *speak eloquently* for him'.

[d] *The Synaesthetic Metaphor*, which transfers meaning from one domain of sensory perception to another: '*warm* colour', '*dull* sound', '*loud* perfume', [Donne, *Elegy IV*], 'Till ev'n his beams *sing*, and my music *shine*' [Herbert, *Christmas*].[11]

Categories [a], [b], and [c] overlap, because humanity entails animacy, and animacy entails concreteness. The familiar poetic device of PERSONIFICATION, whereby an abstraction is figuratively represented as human (e.g. '*Authority* forgets a dying king', Tennyson, *The Passing of Arthur*) actually combines all three categories.

These categories reflect the tendency of metaphors to explain the more undifferentiated areas of human experience in terms of the more immediate. We make abstractions tangible by perceiving them in terms of the concrete, physical world; we grasp the nature of inanimate things more vividly by breathing life into them; the world of nature becomes more real to us when we project into it the qualities we recognize in ourselves. Metaphors in the reverse direction are less common, and have a flavour of singularity. Thus dehumanizing metaphors, which ascribe animal or inanimate properties to a human being, frequently have a ring of contempt:

You *blocks*, you *stones*, you worse than *senseless things*!

[*Julius Caesar*, I.i]

or of ironic disparagement:

> I found you as a *morsel, cold upon*
> *Dead Caesar's trencher.*
>
> [*Antony and Cleopatra*, III.xiii]

It is the difference between tenor and vehicle, rather than their similarity that comes to the attention in these cases.

9.2.4 *Extended Metaphor*

An EXTENDED METAPHOR is a metaphor which is developed by a number of different figurative expressions, extending perhaps over several lines of poetry. In the following, a whole series of literal absurdities is explained by the same comparison between a mental experience and a physical experience:

> I fled Him, down the nights and down the days;
> I fled Him, down the arches of the years;
> I fled Him, down the labyrinthine ways
> Of my own mind; and in the mist of tears
> I hid from Him, and under running laughter.
> Up vistaed hopes, I sped;
> And shot, precipitated
> Adown Titanic glooms of chasmed fears.
>
> [Francis Thompson, *The Hound of Heaven*]

This is the beginning of a poem which explores, in a striking way, the image of the love of God as an animal hunting the human soul. The whole of man's inner life then becomes translated in spatial terms: 'down the arches of the years' makes us see the succession of years as (perhaps) an arcade or a vaulted passage; 'under running laughter' makes laughter into a waterfall; hopes become hills and valleys fears in this topographical account of the human mind. The tenor and vehicle which are invoked by the first line are merely continued and elaborated in the lines that follow.

9.2.5 *Compound Metaphor and Mixed Metaphor*

The 'mixed metaphor', like the 'split infinitive', has been such a shibboleth of bad style, that we have to be careful not to confuse it with COMPOUND METAPHOR, a perfectly legitimate and frequently powerful device of poetic expression. A compound metaphor consists in the overlapping of two or more individual metaphors. It is by no means confined to highly concentrated and elliptical styles of poetic writing, but occurs even in passages of verse which are fairly easy to follow and understand, such as this extract in which Byron addresses himself to the ocean:

> Unchangeable, save to thy wild waves' play,
> Time writes no wrinkle in thine azure brow:
> Such as creation's dawn beheld, thou rollest now.
>
> [*Childe Harold's Pilgrimage*, IV]

In the second of these three lines, there are two 'humanizing' metaphors: the sea is personified in 'thine azure brow', and time in 'Time writes no wrinkle'. However, these two metaphors do not operate at the same level: at the level where we imagine the sea as a person, we do not conceive of time as literally writing wrinkles on this person's brow – that would indeed be an incongruous metaphor. Rather, *writes* is still figurative on the level where *brow* is literal. Hence we need to replace the standard two-layer analysis of metaphor into tenor and vehicle by a three-layer analysis, in which the middle layer, containing *wrinkle* and *brow*, is figurative with respect to the azure sea, and literal with respect to the writing of Time:

$$L_1 \quad Time \underline{\qquad\qquad\qquad\qquad} azure \underline{\qquad}$$
$$F_1/L_2 \; ,, \quad \underline{\qquad} no\ wrinkle\ on\ thine \underline{\qquad} brow$$
$$F_2 \underline{\qquad} writes \; ,, \; \underline{\qquad} \; ,, \; \underline{\qquad\qquad}$$

A rough Stage II of the analysis is:

TEN_1	Time	$\begin{bmatrix} \cdot & \text{causes no indentation} \\ & \text{to appear on the sea's} \end{bmatrix}$	azure	[surface]
VEH_1 } TEN_2 }	,,	$\begin{bmatrix} \text{causes-to-} \\ \text{appear} \end{bmatrix}$ no	wrinkle on thine	[?]	brow
VEH_2 [somebody]	writes	,, [lines] ,,	$\begin{bmatrix} \text{a piece of paper} \\ \text{stone, etc.} \end{bmatrix}$

Thus we have two tenors and two vehicles, but in the middle layer the tenor of one metaphor and the vehicle of another are collapsed into one. This analysis, however crude and tentative, shows how the two separate images co-exist: that of a brow without wrinkles, and that of a person writing on some kind of writing surface. There is no reason, apart from ease of comprehension, why compound metaphors containing four or even more layers of analysis should not be built up in this way.

Expressions that we condemn as mixed metaphors, on the other hand, occur when dead metaphors, which have lost their imaginative force, are brought incongruously together so that a conflict in their literal meanings, which normally go unnoticed, is forced upon our attention. Corpses so indecently exhumed have, needless to say, no place in serious poetry. Comically exaggerated examples are: 'The hand that rocked the cradle has kicked the bucket'; 'The boot is on the other kettle of fish'; 'The ship of state is at last getting down to brass tacks and putting its best foot forward in the teeth of adversity.'

Although in theory one would like compound metaphors and dead metaphors to be distinct, in practice one has to recognize that there is no clear-cut boundary between them, precisely because there is no clear-cut division between 'living' and 'dead' metaphors. To a modern reader, Hamlet's 'to take arms against a sea of troubles' may have something of the awkwardness of the mixed-metaphor, because 'to take (up) arms against' is a cliché expression for 'to oppose'.

9.2.6 *Symbolism and Allegory*

We have approached metaphor by way of absurdity: metaphor, that is, has been treated as one of the possible answers to an enigma posed by apparent nonsense. It is now time to modify this point of view, by acknowledging that literal absurdity is not the only path that can lead to a figurative interpretation. Christine Brooke-Rose, who makes this clear in her important book *A Grammar of Metaphor*,[12] notes how many proverbs are ambiguous as to literal or metaphorical interpretation. 'A rolling stone gathers no moss' and 'Empty vessels make the most sound' are both true, if trite, as literal propositions; as proverbs, however, we understand them to refer figuratively to human character.[13]

Miss Brooke-Rose uses the following extract to illustrate the same point in poetry:

Stop playing, poet! May a brother speak? . . .
But why such long prolusion and display,
Such turning and adjustment of the harp,
And taking it upon your breast, at length,
Only to speak dry words across its strings?

[Browning, ' *Transcendentalism*']

There was a time, she says, when poets actually played harps, so that this might be an imagined scene literally recounted by Browning. Moreover, the 'brother' might even be a literal brother, a sibling of the poet. But in fact we understand things differently. Browning, we assume, is talking about a brother-poet, viz. Browning himself as a fellow artist. We also take it that the poet's harp is not a literal harp, but his medium of artistic expression – his language. It is not a question of rejecting one interpretation as unacceptable, but rather of preferring one of two acceptable solutions to the other.

This optional extension, as it were, of the meaning from literal to figurative is what we associate with SYMBOLISM. Symbols in common use, such as 'lamp' = 'learning', 'star' = 'constancy', 'flame' = 'passion', are assigned their underlying meaning by custom and familiarity. There need not, therefore, be any linguistic indication of what the tenor is, or of why the term cannot be taken at its face value. The most interesting symbols, poetically, are metaphorical – i.e. X (the symbol) stands for Y because X *resembles* Y – but many of the more conventional ones are metonymic: for example, 'coffin' and 'skull' as the symbols of death.

It is difficult to say exactly how, when there is a choice between literal and figurative readings, one is preferred to the other. Sometimes convention is the operative factor, and sometimes context. The 'mental set' of the reader is also important. The adjustment we make, when we turn from reading, say, a newspaper to reading poetry (especially the poetry of certain poets), includes expecting symbolic interpretations to arise. There is furthermore some impingement of artistic judgment on interpretation, in that poets rely on the reader to select the aesthetically most acceptable solution. We shall return to this in §12.3.3.

Poets frequently adapt and develop their own symbols, instead of relying on traditional ones. These may be esoteric, like those of Yeats and Blake, or made transparent by the poet's exposition, like the symbol of 'grass' in this short poem by Carl Sandburg:

Grass

Pile the bodies high at Austerlitz and Waterloo.
Shovel them under and let me work –
    I am the grass; I cover all.

And pile them high at Gettysburg
And pile them high at Ypres and Verdun.
Shovel them under and let me work.
Two years, ten years, and passengers ask the conductor:

What place is this?
Where are we now?

I am the grass
Let me work.

Here, as in metaphor generally, the tenor is not precise, because not explicit. Is it merely forgetfulness of the past in general that is symbolized by the grass? Or is it forgetfulness of the pity and honour due to the dead? Or forgetfulness of hostility, of the horror of war, of the enormity of man's past deeds, of past glory? The poem does not answer these questions, but leaves them for the reader's judgment.

ALLEGORY stands in the same relation to an individual symbol as extended metaphor does to simple metaphor: in fact, an allegory might be described as a 'multiple symbol', in which a number of different symbols, with their individual interpretations, join together to make a total interpretation. So considered, an allegory on superficial interpretation may be a story (like *Pilgrim's Progress*) or a description (like the various portraits of Marvell's *The Gallery*). It partakes of the ambivalence and indeterminacy we have noted in ordinary symbolism. It may also contain within itself no overt linguistic indication of its underlying significance, being thus completely cut loose from the anchorage of literal interpretation. A naive reader may well take an allegory at its face value as a simple narrative. However, it is a convention of allegory that a hint of the tenor, the underlying sense, should be allowed to peep through, in the form of proper names like Dowel, Dobet, and Dobest [*Piers Plowman*]; Mr Great-heart, Vanity Fair, the Slough of Despond [*Pilgrim's Progress*]; the House of Holiness, the Bower of Bliss [*The Faerie Queene*].

The lack of overt linguistic clues for symbolic and allegorical interpretations should perhaps remind us that we have touched on a topic which goes beyond linguistics and beyond the scope of this book into the broader subject of the psychology of symbolism in all its forms. Symbols and allegories may be expressed by non-linguistic means – for example, in painting; and the principle of transferred meaning, which we began to look at in a purely linguistic light, is wide enough to embrace the whole area of artistic communication, whether in literature, music, or art.

Examples for discussion

Study the figurative element of the following poems, analysing metaphors into
tenor, vehicle, and ground in the manner set out in §9.2.1.

[a]   *The Rainy Summer*

There's much afoot in heaven and earth this year;
        The winds hunt up the sun, hunt up the moon,
Trouble the dubious dawn, hasten the drear
        Height of a threatening noon.

No breath of boughs, no breath of leaves, of fronds
        May linger or grow warm; the trees are loud;
The forest, rooted, tosses in her bonds,
        And strains against the cloud.

No scents may pause within the garden-fold;
        The rifled flowers are cold as ocean-shells;
Bees, humming in the storm, carry their cold
        Wild honey to cold cells.

                        [Alice Meynell, 1847–1922]

[b]   *Oread*

whirl up, sea –
whirl your pointed pines,
splash your great pines
on our rocks,
hurl your green over us,
cover us with your pools of fir.

                    [H.D., 1886–1961]

[c]   *Sonnet 65*

Since brass, nor stone, nor earth, nor boundless sea,
But sad mortality o'ersways their power,
How with this rage shall beauty hold a plea
Whose action is no stronger than a flower?
O, how shall summer's honey breath hold out
Against the wreckful siege of battering days,
When rocks impregnable are not so stout,
Nor gates of steel so strong, but Time decays?
O fearful meditation! where, alack,
Shall Time's best jewel from Time's chest lie hid?
Or what strong hand can hold his swift foot back?
Or who his spoil of beauty can forbid?

O, none, unless this miracle have might,
That in black ink my love may still shine bright.
        [Shakespeare]

Notes

1   R. W. EMERSON, 'The Poet', *Essays*.
2   A technical account of what I here call 'rules of transference' is given by U. WEINREICH, 'Explorations in Semantic Theory', in *Current Trends in Linguistics*, Vol. III, ed. T. A. SEBEOK, The Hague, 1966, 455–71.
3   See I. A. RICHARDS, *Philosophy of Rhetoric*, New York and London, 1936, 96.
4   *Ibid.*, 117. For this threefold division of metaphor into tenor, vehicle, and ground, I have drawn inspiration from a similar threefold scheme proposed by U. ORNAN, in a valuable article 'Shitat Nituach shel Dimuyim Sifrutiyot: Iyunim Bevayot Hasignon', *Leshonenu* (Jerusalem), 26 (1961–2), 40–7. Unfortunately, no English translation of this article is available.
5   Examples from B. GROOM, *The Diction of Poetry from Spenser to Bridges*, Toronto, 1955, 215.
6   G. ESNAULT, *Imagination Populaire, Metaphores Occidentales*, Paris, 1925, 31. Translation by S. ULLMANN, *Language and Style*, Oxford, 1964, 177.
7   W. NOWOTTNY, *The Language Poets Use*, London, 1962, 54–6, points out the vague or undeterminable character of tenor and vehicle.
8   See NOWOTTNY, *op. cit.*, 50–1, on the variety of formulae for expressing a simile.
9   Cf. NOWOTTNY, *op. cit.*, 51.
10 See ULLMANN, *op. cit.*, 83–7.
11 The last two examples are from ULLMANN, *op. cit.*, 87.
12 C. BROOKE-ROSE, *A Grammar of Metaphor*, London, 1958, 38.
13 *Ibid.*, 29.

Ten

Honest Deceptions

Our object now is to study the three tropes HYPERBOLE (the figure of over-statement), LITOTES (the figure of understatement), and IRONY. They are all connected in that in a sense they misrepresent the truth: hyperbole distorts by saying too much, understatement by saying too little, and irony often takes the form of saying or implying the opposite of what one feels to be the case.

Since the question of truth and falsehood has been raised, it is worth-while pausing here to think about the place of these notions in literature. Plato's accusation that poets merely present an illusion of real events has been an important theme in the history of literary criticism; but we no longer expect a poet to 'tell the truth' in the same sense as the historian, hoping instead that he will lead us to a more profound kind of truth which eludes bald factual statement. One of the chief devices for attaining this deeper truth is the device of fiction, whereby a writer invents an imaginary world of people and events to be manipulated at his will. We must there-fore keep separate in our minds the division between fact and fiction on the one hand, and on the other, the distinction between truth and falsehood as its applies, for example, to newspaper reports or judicial evidence. Still further, we must bear in mind that if we say hyperbole distorts the truth, we mean it belies the state of affairs we actually understand to exist either in the real world, or in the imaginary, fictional world created by the poet. So, for example, when Tamburlaine says:

I hold the fates bound fast in iron chains
And with my hand turn fortune's wheel about . . .

[*I Tamburlaine*, I.ii]

we judge this to be hyperbole by reference not to the historical Tambur-laine, but to the dramatic situation in which Marlowe's Tamburlaine utters it – viz. at the beginning of his career, when he is a brigand in charge of a mere five hundred men. We recognize it as, so to speak, 'in excess of the situation', whether that situation is factual or fictional.

H. W. Fowler defines hyperbole as the use of exaggerated terms 'for the sake not of deception, but of emphasis'.[1] The proviso that the audience or reader should be aware of the true state of affairs applies to all three figures – otherwise their effect is lost. Hence the title of this chapter is 'Honest Deceptions'. 'A little incident in which five or six people received scratches' would not be litotes (rhetorical understatement) if it were used to deceive the world as to the seriousness of a battle. But it would be if it were used by a modest soldier who wanted to underestimate his prowess, or by someone intending to deflate the boast of one of the participants, assuming the true proportions of the battle were known to his audience. Translating this into terms of effect, rather than intention, we may say that rhetorical misrepresentation must be accompanied by some evidence that it is not to be taken at its face value. As with metaphor, we usually arrive at the underlying interpretation by rejecting the literal one as unacceptable or incredible in the circumstances.

10.1 HYPERBOLE AND LITOTES

To illustrate these general points, let us now take a closer look at the two contrasting devices of hyperbole and litotes.

10.1.1 *Hyperbole*

Exaggeration in colloquial talk is often incredible because at variance with known fact. 'He's got acres and acres of garden' is an overstatement if we happen to know that the plot indicated is no more than one acre in extent. We are then able to judge that the speaker means no more than 'He has a very large garden'. In other cases, an exaggerated statement is not just incredible in the given situation but in any situation – because outside the bounds of possibility. 'She's as old as the hills' is an assertion which cannot be swallowed whole under any circumstances. The nineteenth-century humorist Sydney Smith is supposed to have said to a neighbour: 'Heat, ma'am! It was so dreadful here that I found there was nothing left for it but to take off my flesh and sit in my bones.'[2] The lady addressed would have been under no necessity to find out whether the remark was true or not, as its content was too fantastic to be believed. Such absurdities occur, with more serious intent, in literature: Miranda, in *The Tempest* [I.ii], urges her father to continue his narrative of their misfortunes with 'Your tale, sir, would cure deafness'.

Hyperbole, like the other two figures, is frequently concerned with personal values and sentiments: that is, with making subjective claims which, however exaggerated, we could not verify unless we were somehow able to get inside the cranium of the person about whom the claims are made. The addressee has to rely entirely on the general standards of society and on his knowledge of the speaker in judging the truth of such claims. When Cob, in *Every Man in His Humour* [IV.ii] says 'I do honour the very flea of his dog', he maintains that his esteem for the man is so great that it extends also to the man's dog, and not only to the dog, but even to the flea battening on the dog's blood. No one could take it upon himself to refute such an extravagant claim, which can be neither proved nor disproved. But if we change the issue from a question of truth into a question of belief, then clearly the most credulous of mortals would treat it as absurd.

Some might say the same about Hamlet's outburst, when after leaping into the open grave of Ophelia, he counters the shrill rhetoric of her brother Laertes with:

I loved Ophelia: forty thousand brothers
Could not, with all their quantity of love,
Make up my sum.
                              [*Hamlet*, V.ii]

However, Hamlet might reply that this is no exaggeration. He wants to assert that his love is limitless in quantity and unique in quality: that it can by no means be weighed against anyone else's, not even a brother's. The conversational hyperbole of 'I wouldn't go through that door for a million pounds' is of similar effect. The intention of the speaker is to tell us that however big the inducement, he would stay away: so he thinks of some enormously large figure to represent the maximum. We would scarcely expect him to agree on an exact figure (say £1,500,000) for which he would change his mind. Subjective statements of this kind may seem like exaggerations from the point of view of an onlooker, but from the speaker's viewpoint may be utterly serious.

10.1.2 *Litotes or Rhetorical Understatement*

The figure of understatement, litotes, is by no means so prominent in literature as hyperbole: perhaps because it has none of the potential absurdity of the other tropes. Whereas hyperbole is a figure which stretches, perhaps almost to breaking point, the communicative resources of the language, it is difficult to see how a failure to say *enough* about a subject can overstep the bounds of reason or acceptability. The effect of litotes therefore depends a great deal on what we know of the situation. In contrast to the hyperbole of Hamlet's harangue from the grave of Ophelia, I now quote a rather more characteristic litotes in which he describes his father:

> He was a man, take him for all in all,
> I shall not look upon his like again.
>
> [*Hamlet*, I.ii]

From what we learn by Hamlet's behaviour throughout the play, it is clear that these words do not do justice to his feelings. It is not that the statement is untrue: rather, it is true in the manner of a platitude – it reveals nothing of the emotion that Hamlet expresses elsewhere.

The term 'litotes' is sometimes reserved for a particular kind of understatement in which the speaker uses a negative expression where a positive one would have been more forceful and direct: 'It's not bad'; 'He's no Hercules'; 'She's no oil painting'; 'She's not exactly a pauper'; etc. These resemble the example from *Hamlet* in that they are not so much untrue as non-committal. They are statements which ascribe to somebody or something a particular position on an evaluative scale – in the last case, that represented by the antonymy 'rich'/'poor'.

To indicate the positive meaning 'rich', we take the term *pauper* and negate it: 'not a pauper'. But as *pauper* refers to the extreme position at the poverty end of the scale, its negation refers to the whole of the rest of the scale. The part designated by the word *rich* is only part of this remainder:

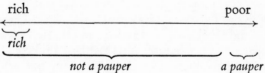

Hence, although the speaker intends us to understand 'She is rich', he leaves open, in what he says, the question of whether she is rich or not.

10.1.3 *The Uses of Hyperbole and Litotes*

In so far as they mainly apply to evaluative meaning, hyperbole and litotes serve to colour the expression of personal feelings and opinions, which may be either of a positive or a negative kind (enthusiasm, disgust, etc.). Litotes expresses an overt lack of commitment, and so implies a desire to suppress or conceal one's true attitude; but paradoxically this may, like hyperbole, be a mode of intensification, suggesting that the speaker's feelings are too deep for plain expression. Because of its two-layer significance – superficial indifference and underlying commitment – litotes is often treated as a category of irony. The ironical import is seen, for example, in the stoical flippancy of Mercutio's reference to his fatal wound in *Romeo and Juliet* [III.i]:

> 'Tis not so deep as a well, nor so wide as a church-door, but 'tis enough, 'twill serve.

Hyperbole is typically used in eulogy, and litotes in disparagement. In everyday speech, they represent antithetical postures, and tend to go with contrasting philosophical attitudes: optimism and idealism in the case of hyperbole, pessimism and cynicism in the case of litotes. An association of sex may even be suggested: hyperbole seems predominantly a characteristic of female speech and litotes of male speech, so that 'It wasn't too bad' as an expression of approval would almost certainly come from a man, and 'It was absolutely fabulous' from a woman. When we interpret such remarks as exaggerated or understated, we recognize not so much the discrepancy with truth (which may be subjective and inaccessible to observation) as the posture itself, which is revealed through expectation of character, tone of voice, and so on.

In poetry, hyperbole is often a means of celebrating human ideals – for instance, ideals of love, of religion, or (as in the example from *Tamburlaine* in §10.1.1 above) of worldly power. Perhaps it is in the expression of religious ideals that the contrast between the standards of heart and soul on the one hand and the standards of reason and common sense on the other are most apparent. When St Peter asks [Matthew 18] how often he should forgive his brother's offences, Jesus replies 'I say not unto thee, Until seven times: but Until seventy times seven', by spiritual standards, an understatement for 'always'. Similarly, when George Herbert ends a famous hymn

> Even eternity is too short
>   To extol Thee,

the sentiment is far-fetched by any standards applicable to man; but applied to God, and from a purely doctrinal point of view, it is no more than the truth.

Litotes, although not a common feature of later English verse, is a stock device of the poetry of the Anglo-Saxon period. Typical examples are 'not at all did he promise her adornments', said of the father of St. Juliana when threatening her with violent death [*Juliana*, 118]; and 'they did not care for war', said of cowards fleeing from the field of battle [*The Battle of Maldon*, 192]. This characteristic of style reflects the ethic of warfare and tribal loyalty celebrated in Germanic heroic poetry: the ideal warrior expressed himself by deeds rather than words: his use of language was reserved and defensive, communicating his attitudes by implication rather than by open declaration. In the Christian era, this ethic was adapted easily enough to the Christian heroism of saints and martyrs.

10.2 IRONY

A great deal has been written about irony, and the different connotations it assumes in such phrases as 'Socratic irony', 'the irony of fate', 'dramatic irony'.[3] These matters are irrelevant here except as a background to its purely linguistic study, which is my main concern.

10.2.1 *The Mask of Irony*

The two-level response which we noted in litotes is characteristic of linguistic irony as a whole. H. W. Fowler in *Modern English Usage* describes irony as a mode of expression which postulates a double audience, one of which is 'in the know' and aware of the speaker's intention, whilst the other is naive enough to take the utterance at its face value.[4] This seems to be a fitting account of what we understand by 'dramatic irony', i.e. a situation in which a double meaning is meant to be appreciated by the audience, but not by someone on the stage. But linguistic irony does not so much presuppose a double audience as a double response from the same audience.

The basis of irony as applied to language is the human disposition to adopt a pose, or to put on a mask. The notion of a disguise is particularly pertinent, as it brings out [a] the element of concealment in irony, and [b] the fact that what is concealed is meant to be found out. If you dress up as a rabbit at a fancy-dress ball, you do not intend to be mistaken for a rabbit. In the same way, the mask of irony is not normally meant to deceive anyone – if it does, then it has had the wrong effect. When someone takes an ironical remark at face value, we are justified in saying that he has 'failed to appreciate the irony' of it.

It is also of the essence of irony that it should criticize or disparage under the guise of praise or neutrality. Hence its importance as a tool of satire. The 'mask' of approval may be called the OVERT or DIRECT meaning, and the disapproval behind the mask the COVERT or OBLIQUE meaning.

For simplicity's sake, we may start with an example of the type of every-day irony to which we apply the term SARCASM. Sarcasm consists in saying the opposite of what is intended: saying something nice with the intention that your hearer should understand something nasty. If I had a black eye, and a friend met me in the street with the remark 'Don't you look gor-geous!', I should have to be extremely undiscerning not to realize that the reference was to my temporary disfigurement, not to my physical beauty. The reason for rejecting the overt meaning is its incompatibility with the context: in a different context, that of 'boy meets girl', the overt interpre-tation would be acceptable, if not mandatory.

We now see how irony fits into the general pattern of tropes. A super-ficial absurdity points to an underlying interpretation; and as with hyper-bole, the initial interpretation may be rejected for one of two reasons – [a] because it is unacceptable within the situation, or [b] because it would be unacceptable in any situation. The first type of incongruity is illustrated in the sarcastic utterance just cited; the second, that which is absurd or out-rageous with respect to any context, is illustrated in the following:

His designs were strictly honourable, as the saying is;
that is, to rob a lady of her fortune by way of marriage.
[Fielding, *Tom Jones*, XI, 4]

Fielding here offers a definition of *honourable* which blatantly conflicts with any definition that would be countenanced by a dictionary-maker. Since we cannot take what he says seriously, we infer that it is an exaggeration, to the point of ridicule, of a point of view which he wishes to disparage. There is an ironic contrast between the word *honourable*, and the dis-honourable conduct it is held to stand for.

The most valued type of literary irony is that which, like Fielding's, im-plies moral or ethical criticism. The kind of nonsense which the writer affects to perpetrate is incredible not because it is factually absurd, as in 'human elephant', but because it outrages accepted values:

Thrift, thrift, Horatio! The funeral baked meats
Did coldly furnish forth the marriage tables.
[*Hamlet*, I.ii]

In this speech Hamlet gives an ostensible motive for his mother's hasty re-marriage after his father's death. What he suggests is that she wanted to save the cost of a marriage banquet by using the left-overs of the funeral repast. But this is so preposterous that no one could take it seriously for a minute. Hamlet's unconcerned wordly wisdom, his apparent acceptance of the monstrously thick-skinned behaviour he attributes to his mother, is a mask which conceals his true sense of horror.

The writer most noted for this type of irony is Swift, who in the treatise from which the following passage is taken, contends with apparent gravity that the answer to the social problems in Ireland lies in cannibalism:

> I have been assured by a very knowing American of my acquaintance in London, that a young healthy child well nursed is at a year old a most delicious, nourishing, and wholesome food, whether stewed, roasted, baked, or boiled, and I make no doubt that it will equally serve in a fricassee, or a ragout.   [*A Modest Proposal*]

A serious argument in this vein would, needless to say, be unthinkable in eighteenth-century England, as in any civilized society. It is this which, de-spite Swift's dead-pan reasonableness of manner, forces us to assume an ironical interpretation.

In all these examples, it may be observed, the ironist adopts a tone which is at variance with his true point of view, and which subtly sharpens the edge of the irony. Swift methodically lists the various ways of preparing a young child for the table as if careful to anticipate a gourmet's objection that it does not offer the same culinary delights as (say) veal or venison. That is to say, he adopts the air of a rational man ready to foresee and politely refute criticism, whilst appearing oblivious to the moral objec-tions crying out for attention. In a rather similar way, Hamlet's indiffer-ence and Fielding's bland acceptance of what he takes to be customary usage are poses which exaggerate the enormity of what they say.

10.2.2 *Irony and Metaphor*

A close connection between irony and metaphor is seen in examples like this:

> Hark ye, Clinker, you are the most notorious offender. You stand *con-victed of sickness, hunger, wretchedness, and want.*[5]
> [Smollett, *Humphrey Clinker*, Letter to Sir Watkin Phillips, 24 May]

The phrase *convicted of* is so restricted in English that what follows it must designate some kind of crime or misdemeanour: 'convicted of arson', 'convicted of theft', 'convicted of riotous assembly' are acceptable English expressions, but not 'convicted of sickness', 'convicted of happiness', etc. This is, then, the kind of violation of selection restrictions which most commonly produces metaphor. From the clash of *convicted of* and *sickness*, etc., there arises the equation CRIME= MISFORTUNE, analogous to the equation of tenor and vehicle in metaphor, except that here it is the contrast between the two that is brought to our attention, rather than their likeness.

A second example comes from *King Lear*, and is spoken by Lear when he meets Edgar in the guise of a Tom o' Bedlam, and imagines him to have been brought to madness and destitution by his daughters, as in Lear's own case:

Is it the fashion that discarded fathers
Should have thus little mercy on their flesh?[6]

[III.iv]

The violation of selection restrictions here is the clash between *discarded*, which requires an inanimate object, and *fathers*, which is animate. Again, it is possible to analyse the line into overt and covert meaning on the pattern of analysis into tenor and vehicle proposed in §9.2.1:

OVERT: *Is it the fashion that* [rejected] *fathers*
COVERT: „,„ „   „   „ *discarded* [boots, etc.]

In this way, fathers become identified with outworn chattels (articles of dress, old boots, etc.), a morally outrageous implication that we cannot accept, any more than we can accept Swift's treatment of children as if they were livestock for fattening. Yet in the fictional situation, this is presumably an unconscious irony, as the demented Lear actually perceives, in the moral anarchy surrounding him, an aged father and an old boot to be equivalent. The bitterness of the irony is increased by the wording of Lear's question in such a way that discarding one's father is represented as an entirely normal thing to do.

That metaphor and irony can arise from the same linguistic source—violation of co-occurrence conditions – shows that they are both modes of interpretation; that is, they are not so much part of the text, as part of the reader's response to the text.

10.2.3 *Innuendo*

An innuendo is 'an allusive remark concerning a person or thing, especially of a depreciatory kind'.[7] This definition appears to single out a special kind of ironic statement which is remarkable for what it omits rather than for what it mentions. A woman who declared in court 'My husband has been sober several times in the past five years' might gain a divorce with little difficulty, although her declaration would technically not be an accusation at all. The secret lies in her apparent assumption that drunkenness is the natural and normal state of affairs, and that sobriety is unusual enough for its occurrence to be noted and reckoned. The contrast between overt and covert *meanings*, can here be traced to a contrast between overt and covert *presuppositions*: the speaker's eccentric presupposition that drunkenness is the rule and sobriety the exception goes against the normal presupposition that sobriety is the rule and drunkenness the exception. We interpret: 'My husband is a habitual drunkard.'

Much humour has its basis in innuendo. Here, for example, is Sydney Smith's comment on Macaulay's powers as a conversationalist: 'He has occasional flashes of silence that makes his conversation perfectly delightful.'[8] The deliberately wrong-headed assumption is that consummate excellence in a good talker consists in not talking – which Macaulay, we learn, achieved only on occasions. Hence silence in Macaulay is like sobriety in the inebriate husband, something rare enough to be remarkable.

Now let us take an example from verse: a couplet in which Pope describes the end of municipal celebrations in London:

Now night descending, the proud scene was o'er,
But lived in Settle's numbers one day more.
[*The Dunciad*, I]

'Settle's numbers' are the verses of one of Pope's lesser contemporaries. Pope tells us that Settle, far from immortalizing the event in his poetry, merely made it live in people's memory for one more day; i.e. Settle's verses were so bad as not to survive publication day. By the conjunction *but*, however, Pope suggests that this was a positive achievement on Settle's part. The ironic contrast is therefore between the common assumption 'The achievement of the poet is to immortalize the events he describes', and the assumption to which Pope seems to subscribe, 'It is an achievement for a poet to cause the events he describes to be relived for just one extra day'.

It is interesting that in all these examples, inserting the word *only* will remove the ironic mask, and make one directly aware of the writer's real attitude: 'My husband has *only* been sober several times . . .', 'He has *only* occasional flashes of silence . . .', 'lived in Settle's numbers *only* one day more'. This is because *only* has the force of 'contrary to expectation, no more than', and makes it explicit that what is described is regarded as in some way extraordinary by normal standards of judgment.

10.2.4 *Irony of Tone*

There is a kind of irony which is a matter of register (especially of tone), rather than of content. As before, let us begin by taking an illustration from the simple ironies of colloquial speech. One type of sarcasm, as noted in §10.2 above, consists in dispraise under the guise of praise ('Don't you look gorgeous'); another type, equally telling, consists in delivering an affront in a manner of unimpeachable, if not exaggerated, politeness. The crudest example is the sneering use of titles like 'Sir', 'Madam', 'your Highness', for people to whom they are clearly inappropriate. A more sophisticated example is:

> CECILY: When I see a spade I call it a spade.
> GWENDOLEN: I am glad to say I have never seen a spade. It is obvious that
> our social spheres have been widely different.
>   [Wilde, *The Importance of Being Earnest*, II]

Mock-politeness is also a common feature of the parliamentary and courtroom rhetoric:

> The Right Honourable gentleman is indebted to his memory for his
> jests, and to his imagination for his facts.
>   [R. B. Sheridan, Speech in reply to Mr Dundas]

A blunter way of putting it, 'Your jokes are stale and your facts wrong', would have been less effective, because it is part of the strategy of this type of verbal warfare to show one's superiority to one's opponent in meticulous adherence to the rules of polite behaviour, whether in parliament, in the courts, or in scholarly debate. The ceremonious address to 'the Right Honourable gentleman' in the third person preserves an air of decorum without which the insult would lose its zest.

Sarcasm of tone need not be used in direct address: it can be aimed at a third party, as in 'What does his lordship want?', said of a despotic boss. It can also be aimed at a whole class of people, or a whole society; and as such, it is the essence of the MOCK HEROIC manner in eighteenth-century poetry. Pope's two great mock heroic compositions, *The Rape of the Lock* and *The Dunciad*, satirize respectively the vanity and triviality of the court *demi-monde*, and the mental bankruptcy of the contemporary world of letters. His method of attack is to pay an apparent compliment to his sub-

ject by celebrating it in the manner of epic poetry; at the same time describing it in such an uncomplimentary manner as to make one aware of
the inappropriateness of the style to the matter. Mock heroic is by no
means entirely a stylistic question: it is a question of using all the paraphernalia of the epic, including narrative digressions, invocations of the
Muses, references to deities and supernatural beings, etc. Nevertheless,
heightened language plays an essential part in its total effect, as we see in the
following passage, which describes the altar of worthless books raised by
Cibber, the mock-hero of *The Dunciad*, in honour of the goddess Dulness:

> Of these, twelve volumes, twelve of amplest size,
> Redeemed from tapers and defrauded pies,
> Inspired he seizes; these an altar raise;
> An hetacomb of pure unsullied lays
> That altar crowns; a folio common-place
> Founds the whole pile, of all his works the base;
> Quartos, octavos, shape the less'ning pyre;
> A twisted birthday ode completes the spire.
>   Then he: 'Great tamer of all human art!
> First in my care, and ever at my heart;
> Dulness! whose good old cause I yet defend,
> With whom my muse began, and whom shall end,
>
> . . .
>
> O thou! of bus'ness the directing soul!
> To this our head like bias to the bowl,
> Which, as more pond'rous, made its aim more true,
> Obliquely waddling to the mark in view:
> O! ever gracious to perplexed mankind,
> Still spread a healing mist before the mind'.
>   *The Dunciad*, I]

The mock-heroic vein manifests itself, linguistically, in the type of incongruity called 'register mixing' in an earlier chapter (§3.2.7). There is a conflict between the predominantly high-flown style, and the occasional in-
trusion of vulgar, 'unpoetical' diction. The general elevated tone is shown
in both syntax and vocabulary. The passage opens with the run-on lines
and heavy caesuras of the Miltonic verse paragraph (see §7.5.2), and contains a typically Miltonic verbless introduction of indirect speech, 'Then
he'. The extended vocative, which begins with 'Great tamer' and con-
tinues almost to the end of the quotation, is, like the liberal use of exclamations, imitated from the hyperbolic style of the epic encomium. In

vocabulary, the clause 'An hetacomb of pure unsullied lays/That altar crowns' typifies Augustan diction in its stately, high-sounding vein, whilst *obliquely* and *pond'rous* add Latin dignity. Foregrounded elements, such as the use of rhyming couplets and lines balanced by antithesis, also contribute to the heightened style. But words like *pies*, *twisted*, and *waddling*, which no Augustan poet would use with serious intent, break through the barrier of decorum, and warn us not to take the heroic vein seriously.

The ironies of everyday speech are frequently meant in a spirit of playfulness rather than malice; and likewise the mock-heroic vein in literature is often little more than a convention providing sophisticated amusement for poet and reader. Gray's *Ode on the Death of a Favourite Cat* is far from the venomous wit of *The Dunciad*:

> Presumptuous maid! with looks intent
> Again she stretch'd, again she bent,
> Nor knew the gulf between –
> Malignant Fate sat by and smiled –
> The slippery verge her feet beguiled;
> She tumbled headlong in!

There is the same incongruity of loftiness mixed with vulgarity of tone: the exclamation 'Presumptuous maid', the parallelism of the second line, the Miltonic *nor* in the third line, and personification of Fate in the fourth line – all these contribute to epic heightening, whilst 'tumbled headlong' tumbles us headlong into bathos. Yet there is no feeling that the cat is being criticized by the use of heroic conventions: indeed, the poet seems to express by this means a half-serious (some might say sentimental) regard for the cat, and concern over her death.

In Gray's time, the mock-heroic manner had become a dominant convention; and because the incongruity no longer surprised, its satirical power was weakened. The process was not unlike that whereby a living metaphor turns, by familiarity, into a dead one. The juxtaposition of high style and low matter succeeded not just in comically inflating the matter, but ultimately in deflating the style. Not that using the convention as Gray does amounts to a disparagement of it: a writer can make good use of a convention, and still show that he is aware of its limitations *as* a convention.

Examples for discussion

Study hyperbole, litotes, and irony in relation to absurdity and figurative language
in the following passages.

a] [This is part of a speech in which Tamburlaine replies to his bride's plea that he
should spare her father and country.]

<blockquote>

Ah, fair Zenocrate! – divine Zenocrate!
Fair is too foul an epithet for thee, –
That in thy passion for thy country's love,
And fear to see thy kingly father's harm,
With hair dishevell'd wip'st thy watery cheeks;
And, like to Flora in her morning's pride,
Shaking her silver tresses in the air,
Rain'st on the earth resolved pearl in showers,
And sprinklest sapphires on thy shining face,
Where Beauty, mother to the Muses, sits,
And comments volumes with her ivory pen,
Taking instructions from thy flowing eyes;
Eyes, when that Ebena steps to heaven,
In silence of thy solemn evening's walk,
Making the mantle of the richest night,
The moon, the planets, and the meteors, light;
There angels in their crystal armours fight
A doubtful battle with my tempted thoughts
For Egypt's freedom and the Soldan's life,
His life that so consumes Zenocrate;
Whose sorrows lay more siege unto my soul
Than all my army to Damascus' walls;
And neither Persia's sovereign nor the Turk
Troubled my senses with conceit of foil
So much by much as doth Zenocrate.

[Marlowe, *I Tamburlaine*, V.i]

</blockquote>

[*b*]

<blockquote>

A monk ther was, a fair for the maistrie,[1]   165
An outridere,[2] that lovede venerie,[3]
A manly man, to been an abbot able.
Ful many a deyntee hors hadde he in stable,
And whan he rood, men myghte his brydel heere
Gynglen in a whistlynge wynd als cleere   170
And eek as loude as dooth the chapel belle.
Ther as this lord was kepere of the celle,
The reule of seint Maure or of seint Beneit,[4]

</blockquote>

By cause that it was old and somdel streit[5]
This ilke Monk leet olde thynges pace,   175
And heeld after the newe world the space.[6]
He yaf nat of that text a pulled hen,
That seith that hunters ben nat hooly men,
Ne that a monk, whan he is recchelees,[7]
Is likned til a fissh that is waterlees, –   180
This is to seyn, a monk out of his cloystre.
But thilke text heeld he nat worth an oystre;
And I seyde his opinion was good.
What sholde he studie and make hymselven wood,[8]
Upon a book in cloystre alwey to poure,   185
Or swynken with his handes, and laboure,
As Austyn[9] bit?[10] How shal the world be served?
Lat Austyn have his swynk to hym reserved!
Therefore he was a prikasour[11] aright:
Grehoundes he hadde as swift as fowel in flight;   190
Of prikyng[12] and of huntyng for the hare
Was al his lust, for no cost wolde he spare.
I seigh[13] his sleves purfiled[14] at the hond
With grys,[15] and that the fyneste of a lond;
And, for to festne his hood under his chyn,   195
He hadde of gold ywroght a ful curious pyn;
A love-knotte in the gretter ende ther was.
His heed was balled, that shoon as any glas,
And eek his face, as he hadde been enoynt.
He was a lord ful fat and in good poynt[16];   200
His eyen stepe,[17] and rollynge in his heed,
That stemed as a forneys of a leed[18];
His bootes souple, his hors in greet estaat.
Now certeinly he was a fair prelaat;
He was nat pale as a forpyned[19] goost.   205
A fat swan loved he best of any roost.
His palfrey was as broun as is a berye.

[Chaucer, *Canterbury Tales*, General Prologue]

(1) *for the maistrie:* extremely (2) a monk whose duty it was to look after estates
(3) hunting (4) Benedict (5) strict (6) *heeld . . . the space:* held his course (7) careless, neglectful (8) mad (9) Augustine (10) bids (11) hunter on horseback
(12) tracking (13) saw (14) trimmed at the edges (15) grey fur (16) condition
(17) large (18) cauldron (19) tormented

[c]

All human things are subject to decay,
And, when Fate summons, monarchs must obey:

This Flecknoe[1] found, who, like Augustus, young
Was call'd to empire and had govern'd long:
In prose and verse was own'd, without dispute   5
Through all the realms of Nonsense, absolute.
This aged prince now flourishing in peace,
And blest with issue of a large increase,
Worn out with business, did at length debate
To settle the succession of the state;   10
And pond'ring which of all his sons was fit
To reign, and wage immortal war with wit,
Cried, ''Tis resolv'd; for nature pleads that he
Should only rule, who most resembles me:
Sh——[2] alone my perfect image bears,   15
Mature in dulness from his tender years;
Sh—— alone of all my sons is he
Who stands confirm'd in full stupidity.
The rest to some faint meaning make pretence,
But Sh—— never deviates into sense.   20
Some beams of wit on other souls may fall,
Strike through and make a lucid interval;
But Sh——'s genuine night admits no ray,
His rising fogs prevail upon the day:
Besides, his goodly fabric fills the eye   25
And seems design'd for thoughtless majesty:
Thoughtless as monarch oaks that shade the plain,
And, spread in solemn state, supinely reign.
Heywood and Shirley[3] were but types of thee,
Thou last great prophet of tautology: 30
Even I, a dunce of more renown than they,
Was sent before but to prepare thy way:
And coarsely clad in Norwich drugget came
To teach the nations in they greater name.
My warbling lute, the lute I whilom strung,   35
When to King John of Portugal I sung,
Was but the prelude to that glorious day,
When thou on silver Thames did'st cut thy way,
With well tim'd oars before the royal barge,
Swelled with the pride of thy celestial charge;   40
And, big with hymn, commander of an host,
The like was ne'er in Epsom blanket toss'd.
Methinks I see the new Arion[4] sail,
The lute still trembling underneath thy nail.
At thy well sharpen'd thumb from shore to shore   45

The treble squeaks for fear, the basses roar:
Echoes from Pissing Alley Sh—— call,
And Sh—— they resound from A—— Hall,'[5]
. . .

Here stopp'd the good old sire; and wept for joy,   50
In silent raptures of the hopeful boy.
All arguments, but most his plays, persuade,
That for anointed dulness he was made.
                              [Dryden, *MacFlecknoe*]

(1) Richard Flecknoe, Irish dramatist and poetaster, an elder contemporary of Dryden.
(2) Thomas Shadwell, dramatist, and political rival of Dryden.   (3) Thomas Heywood
(c. 1574–1641) and James Shirley (1596–1666), dramatists.   (4) A Greek musician.
5) Aston Hall. The location of this, as of Pissing Alley, is in doubt.

Notes

1   H. W. FOWLER, *A Dictionary of Modern English Usage*, Oxford, 1926, 608.
2   LADY (SABA) HOLLAND, *Memoir of the Reverend Sydney Smith*, London, 1855, Vol.
    I, 267.
3   Three works of general interest on irony are J. A. THOMSON, *Irony: an Historical
    Introduction*, London, 1926; G. G. SEDGEWICK, *Of Irony, especially in Drama*, Tor-
    onto, 1948; and N. KNOX, *The Word Irony and its Context, 1500–1755*, Durham,
    North Carolina, 1961. Nothing has been written, to my knowledge, on the
    specifically linguistic aspect of irony.
4   FOWLER, *op. cit.*, 295.
5   This example is discussed in G. N. LEECH, 'Linguistics and the Figures of Rhetoric',
    in *Essays in Style and Language*, ed. R. G. FOWLER, London, 1966, 154.
6   This example is discussed from a similar point of view in W. NOWOTTNY, *The
    Language Poets Use*, London, 1962, 48.
7   *New English Dictionary*, entry for *innuendo*, II, 3.
8   LADY HOLLAND, *op. cit.*, Vol. I, 363.

Eleven

Implications of Context

In the survey of various types of linguistic deviation in Chapter 3, I failed to deal with one special kind of violation, that which arises when a piece of language is somehow at odds with the immediate situation in which it occurs.[1] One example of this came to our notice last chapter: the contextual incongruity of ironical remarks such as 'What a lovely evening' (said during a thunderstorm). Now we shall consider this general kind of deviation more carefully.

How is it possible for language to violate constraints of situation? If someone habitually said 'good-bye' on greeting people and 'hullo' when taking leave of them, his behaviour would be thought very strange; its oddity would be on a par with that of a grammatical or semantic error. This is merely an obvious example of what is common to all utterances: each use of language has what we may call IMPLICATIONS OF CONTEXT; that is, it conveys information about the kind of situation in which it would occur. Faced with the following sentences *in vacuo*,

Down, Fido.
This one's on me.
Candidates are asked to write on one side of the paper only.

most speakers of English will be able to specify fairly precisely the circumstances of their occurrence. The kind of knowledge we bring to bear in drawing these inferences is very diverse. In part, it is our sensitivity to register and dialect differences; in part it is our general knowledge of the semantics of English in relation to the society in which we live. But certain forms of language are especially important for the 'reconstruction' of situations: they are words like *I*, *you*, *this*, *that*, *now*, *then*, *here*, and *there*, which have a DEICTIC function – that is, they have the function of *pointing* to aspects of the utterance's particular environment. *I* and *you* refer directly to speaker (or author) and addressee. The other words clearly break down into two contrasting groups: *this*, *now*, and *here* mainly denote proximity (in time, place, etc.) to the speaker, and *that*, *then*, and *there* denote lack of proximity. Questions and commands also have a deictic element of meaning, since by implication they make reference to an addressee. A situational incongruity arises whenever an utterance occurs in a situation at variance with its own implications of context.

11.1 LICENCES OF SITUATION

Two traditional figures of speech, RHETORICAL QUESTION and APOSTROPHE, consist in using features of language in situations which are normally inappropriate for them. In poetry and rhetorical prose, these devices can impart a heightened dramatic quality to the language, because they transfer into an unaccustomed context the contextual implications of questions, commands, and statements which directly involve a participant other than the writer.

11.1.1 *Rhetorical Question*

A RHETORICAL QUESTION is, in a loose sense, a question which is abnormal, in that it expects no answer: 'Who cares?', 'Aren't they wonderful dresses?', 'Do you call that music?', etc. More strictly defined, it is a positive question which is understood as if equivalent to a negative statement: 'Who cares?' is an emphatic way of saying 'Nobody cares'; 'Shall I compare thee to a summer's day?' announces the poet's intention of doing no such thing. It is true that a rhetorical question produces no violent sense of incongruity. None the less, its dramatic effect arises from a feeling that the question demands an answer and is not provided with one. A negation carries more weight, it seems, if the reader is challenged to question the positive assertion, only to be overwhelmed by the realization that none but a negative answer is possible.

From this, it is easy to understand an extension to the use of the rhetorical question as a means of expressing intense conviction of a certain view:

If God be for us, who can be against us?
[Romans 8]

Moreover, it is easy to appreciate its value as a stock device of heightening, both in oratory and in poetry:

Can storied urn or animated bust
Back to its mansion call the fleeting breath?

Can Honour's voice provoke the silent dust,
Or Flattery soothe the dull cold ear of death?

This celebrated quatrain from Gray's *Elegy* illustrates the conventional use of rhetorical questions in an elevated poetic style.

11.1.2 *Apostrophe*

Historically APOSTROPHE signifies an orator's interruption of his address to his audience, in order to address some third party, who may either be present or not. Hence its use for the kind of dramatic licence whereby words are addressed to someone who is unable to hear them or reply to them:

> The bell invites me.
> Hear it not, Duncan, for it is a knell
> That summons thee to heaven, or to hell.
> [*Macbeth*, II.i]

The direct use of an imperative seems to express the intensity of Macbeth's involvement with the man he is about to murder.

The contextual absurdity of addressing someone who is unable to hear or answer is more pronounced when the addressee is dead or not even human, as in the following cases:

Address to a dead person:

> Milton! thou shouldst be living at this hour
> [Wordsworth, *London, 1802*]

Address to an animal, bird, etc.:

> O cuckoo, shall I call thee bird,
> Or but a wandering voice?
> [Wordsworth, *To the Cuckoo*]

Address to an inanimate force of nature:

> Blow, blow thou winter wind
> [Shakespeare, Song from *As You Like It*, II.vii]

Address to an abstraction:

> Hence, loathèd Melancholy
> [Milton, *L'Allegro*]

As the addressee of any verbal communication is normally assumed to be human, this last type of apostrophe attributes humanity to an abstraction, and so is conceptually equivalent to personification (see §9.2.3).

In direct address we can express our attitude to a person or thing with great subtlety, and this is perhaps the chief advantage of apostrophe for the poet. Like rhetorical question, however, it is a conventional feature of elevated, 'poetical' language.

The chief formal indicators of apostrophe are vocatives ('O cuckoo', 'loathèd Melancholy', etc.), imperatives, and second person pronouns.

11.1.3 *Routine Licences of Situation*

On the stage, certain forms of contextual incongruity may be taken as theatrical licences, accepted by convention as part of the make-believe without which dramatic art would be impossible. They include SOLILOQUY, the convention of speaking one's thoughts aloud, so that they may be 'overheard' by the audience, and ASIDES, whereby a character is understood to convey his thoughts to the audience without being overheard by other characters on stage. In poetry, too, contextual incongruities have the status of routine licences. The standard use of rhetorical question and apostrophe as adornments of a heightened style have been mentioned and illustrated already. Both figures have been so much a resort of poets in the past that they have clear overtones of 'poeticalness' (see §1.2.3), and are obvious targets for the parodist. Yet anyone who studies their use by Shakespeare should be convinced that far from being gratuitous ornaments, they can contribute much to the vigour of poetic language:

> Can this cockpit hold
> The vasty fields of France? or may we cram
> Within this wooden O the very casques
> That did affright the air at Agincourt?
> [*Henry V*, Chorus]

This would seem as tame expressed in the form of a statement as Lear's indignation would seem, if he merely talked about the elements, instead of addressing them directly:

> Rumble thy bellyful! Spit, fire! spout, rain!
> Nor rain, wind, thunder, fire, are my daughters:
> I tax not you, you elements, with unkindness;
> I never gave you kingdom, call'd you children,

You owe me no subscription: then let fall
Your horrible pleasure.
> [*King Lear*, III.ii]

A further, similar, licence in dramatic verse is the 'self-apostrophe' exemplified by Julius Caesar's dying words 'Et tu, Brute? Then fall, Caesar!'
[*Julius Caesar*, III.i]; also, the RATIOCINATIVE QUESTION, a question addressed by a speaker to himself:

Is this a dagger which I see before me,
The handle toward my hand? Come, let me clutch thee.
> [*Macbeth*, II.i]

These are less important devices, but, as the examples show, their use in
dramatic monologue can make vivid and immediate the speaker's sensa-
tions, feelings, or thoughts.

11.2 THE GIVEN SITUATION

Poetry is virtually free from the contextual constraints which determine
other uses of language, and so the poet is able – in fact, compelled – to
make imaginative use of implications of context to *create* situations within
his poems. As Mrs Nowottny says, 'the poet is both free of context and
bound to create it'.[2] To understand this added source of creativity in poetic
language, we must first consider in very general terms how to characterize
the immediate situation in which any verbal communication operates. We
shall term this the GIVEN SITUATION, in opposition to the INFERRED (or
internal) SITUATION, the world which the poet constructs within the poem.

Any particular situation in which language is used may be roughly
described by answering the following questions:[3]

1. *Who are the participants?* That is, who is the author or speaker of the
   message? To whom is it addressed? Who are relevant 'third parties' to
   the communication – for example, passive onlookers to an argument or
   debate. These three categories we may call respectively FIRST PERSON,
   SECOND PERSON, and THIRD PERSON participants.
2. *What objects are relevant to the communication?* What objects, for example,
   are mentioned in the course of the message? are present during the trans-
   mission of the message? are involved in the purpose or effect of the
   communication? Anything satisfying at least two of these three criteria
   may, for convenience, be called 'relevant'.

3. *What is the medium of communication?* Is the message written or spoken? Is it transmitted by artificial media such as telephone, radio, or television? etc.
4. *What is the function of the communication?* To inform? to educate? to persuade? to entertain? to establish social contacts? to get some practical task done?

There is no absolute merit in these four categories, but they form a convenient framework to apply to any text or utterance. To illustrate their use, here are two specimen situations from 'ordinary life', one private and one public:

SITUATION A: THE 'BACK-SEAT DRIVER'
   (1) *Participants:* a. First person – wife
                   b. Second person – husband
                   c. Third persons – anyone else in the car
   (2) *Relevant object:* a car
   (3) *Medium:* speech
   (4) *Function:* to control b's driving of (2)

SITUATION B: COMMERCIAL TELEVISION ADVERTISING
   (1) *Participants:* a. First person – advertiser
                   b. Second persons – consumers
                   c. Third persons – (perhaps) rival advertisers
   (2) *Relevant object:* a product.
   (3) *Medium:* television; speech and writing.
   (4) *Function:* To promote sales of (2) to b.

It is quite possible to use these four headings to specify classes of situations corresponding to registers, or situational varieties, of the language (see §1.1.2). However, we shall be more interested here in particular situations involving individuals: not simply 'a wife' and 'a husband' for Situation A above, but Mr and Mrs Green; not just 'a product', for Situation B but Brand X; not just 'a poet' for poetry, but Milton, Browning, or whoever it may be.

Before we leave this general plane of discussion, notice how difficult it is to specify the four situational factors for poetic discourse:

SITUATION C: POETRY
   (1) *Participants:* a. First person – a poet.
                   b. Second person – members of the reading public
                   c. Third person – ?
   (2) *Relevant objects:* ?

(3) *Medium:* mostly printed publication, but with implications of spoken performance.

(4) *Function:* ?

Under heading (1), we are able to identify, albeit vaguely, the principal participants as poet (1st person) and reader (2nd person). We are also able to say, under heading (3), that poetry tends to reach its public through the medium of print: but this is no more than a generalization based on the practice of the past few hundred years, since the medium is liable to change from age to age (witness the oral poetry of illiterate tradition, and the current movement of 'sound poetry'). It is not easy to find anything to say under the other headings. No relevant objects or third person participants can be particularized, chiefly because the subject matter of poetry is not limited in any obvious way. Nor can one point to any social or practical function of poetry, as one may, for example, for legal documents, advertisements, or educational textbooks. A poet, of course, might be able to give a personal reason for writing a particular poem, whether that of turning an honest penny or that of 'justifying the ways of God to men'; but in trying to indicate a general purpose which helps to define poetry as a genre, we find ourselves thrust back on the empty statement that 'the purpose of writing a poem is to write a poem'. Poetry shares with other kinds of pure art an 'immanence of purpose'; or to quote Halliday, McIntosh, and Strevens, 'creative writing . . . is meaningful as activity in itself, and not merely as part of a larger situation'.[4]

11.3 THE 'WORLD WITHIN THE POEM'

Because poetry is virtually unfettered by the circumstances of the given situation – the world *outside* the poem – what is of interest in a poem is rather the situation, or sequence of situations, constructed *within* the poem, through implications of context. For example, the *I* and *you* of a poem are frequently to be identified not with author and reader, the participants of the external situation, but rather with a pair of participants, real or imaginary, which the poet has decided to call 'I' and 'you' for the purpose of the poem. Sometimes a vocative identifies the assumed addressee: 'Do you remember an inn, Miranda?' [Belloc, *Tarantella*] makes it clear that for the purpose of the poem, a person called Miranda is being addressed, and not any Joan, Jim, or Harry who might form part of the poet's general public. Another Miranda comes into Shelley's *With a Guitar, to Jane*, which begins, as if it were a casual note between friends, with the names of both author and recipient:

Ariel to Miranda: – Take
This slave of Music, for the sake
Of him who is the slave of thee . . .

In these cases, it is particularly clear that a poem can have a situational existence on two levels. By virtue of being a poem, it is a communication from the poet to the world in general; but it may, as a poem, set up its own situation of address. Shelley's poem in fact has at least three situational levels, for apart from the given situation there are two inferred situations – a factual and a fictional one. The opening words 'Ariel to Miranda' make it an imaginary communication between two fictional characters from *The Tempest*; but these names are also symbolic pseudonyms for Shelley himself and Jane Williams, to whom the poem, on a personal level, is addressed. This level is clear from the title, and becomes explicit in the poem when 'Miranda' changes to 'Jane' in the last line.

This example gives a glimpse of the kind of difficulty which arises in discussing the contextual implications of a poem. In some poems, the imaginary situation is all that matters, whereas in others, a personal situation (for instance, a poet's conveying a compliment to a friend, or an insult to an enemy) assumes importance. The private situation may so dominate the poem, that one might go so far as to wonder whether there is any public given situation to be reckoned with; whether the poem should not be regarded as a personal communication between the poet and one or more of his acquaintances. However, always we come back to the definition of literature by its role; a poem *qua* work of art is addressed to nobody in particular and is not intended to serve any particular purpose. A poem which also serves as a private missive is not a contradiction in terms: it is simply a piece of language with two separate roles.

An analogy with dramatic literature may help to elucidate the relation between the given and inferred situations in a poem. A dramatist writes a play for the world at large, and each performance of that play is 'addressed to', i.e. is performed for the benefit of, a certain audience. This much is the given situation, the world outside the play. Within the play, however, the participants are imaginary dramatis personae, and the speech situation is continually changing according to which of these imaginary participants are involved, and in what way. From beginning to end, the play may be enacted without any reference to author or audience – that is, there may be no acknowledgement, within the play, that author and audience exist. Yet it would obviously be wrong, on this basis, to deny the existence and relevance of the participants of the given situation.

Another point of resemblance between poetry and drama is the way in which the given and constructed situations are allowed to interact. Although to preserve dramatic illusion, the world within a play should ideally be 'vacuum-sealed' from the world outside, various theatrical licences permit the illusion to be broken. For instance, in comedies a stage character is sometimes allowed to come out of his stage setting and address himself directly to the audience. In poetry, such licences are not unknown, but the interaction between the given and inferred situations is more likely to be one of ambivalence – for example, when one is unable to tell, from the poem, whether the poet is addressing us in his own person, or through some fictional persona.

11.3.1 *The Introduction of Inferred Situations*

The first few lines of a poem are naturally the most important for establishing an inferred situation. In what follows, therefore, we shall concentrate on the beginnings of poems. Donne's *Songs and Sonnets* will provide suitable illustrations, being excellent material for the study of contextual implications in building up the 'world within the poem', and particularly of the role in this process of deictic words, as mentioned at the beginning of this chapter. The items listed there are now listed again, with the addition of some deictic words which are common in the literature of the past centuries, but are no longer widely current. Even so, the list is not complete.

DEICTIC WORDS AND EXPRESSIONS

[a] First and second person pronouns: *I/me/my/mine, we/us/our/ours, thou/ thee/thy/thine, ye/you/your/yours.*

[b] Demonstratives: *this, that, yon(der).*

[c] Adverbs of place: *here, there, yonder, hither, thither, hence, thence,* etc.

[d] Adverbials of time: *now, then, tomorrow, yesterday, last night, next Tuesday,* etc.

[e] Adverbs of manner: *thus, so.*

Deictic words are italicized in the following examples, so that their implications of context can be more quickly appreciated:

> *I* wonder, by *my* troth, what *thou* and *I*
> Did, till *we* lov'd, were *we* not wean'd till *then*?
> [*The Good-morrow*]

Mark but *this* flea, and mark in *this*,
How little that which *thou* deny'st *me* is
    [*The Flea*]

Blasted with sighs, and surrounded with tears,
   Hither I come to seek the spring
    [*Twickenham Garden*]

Now *thou* hast lov'd *me* one whole day,
Tomorrow when *thou* leav'st, what wilt *thou* say?
    [*Woman's Constancy*]

    Busy old fool, unruly Sun,
    Why dost *thou thus*,
Through windows, and through curtains call on *us*?
    [*The Sun Rising*]

(In some cases, a deictic word plays no part in specifying the situation, because it refers to the verbal rather than the assumed extra-verbal context: for example, the *then* in *The Good-morrow* refers back to 'till we lov'd.')

The question to ask about each example is: 'What do we learn about the situation within the poem from these lines, and how do we learn it?' Even without the clues which would be provided by reading each poem to its end, we are able to postulate a fairly definite situation for each poem. Much of the burden of communication is borne by the deictic words, but there are other formal indicators as well. We have already noted in another connection that vocatives ('Busy old fool, unruly Sun') have implications of context; also imperatives ('Mark but this flea') and questions ('Why dost thou thus . . . call on us?').

Donne's lyrical poems are noted for the rhetorical force of their openings, which is due not only to his use of violently emotional language ('stark mad', 'busy old fool', 'for God's sake', etc.) but to his use of implied context. He likes to thrust the reader straight into the middle of a scene of physical or mental action; for example, a lovers' farewell:

So, so, break off this last lamenting kiss
    [*The Expiration*]

or a heated argument about the propriety of a love affair:

For God's sake hold your tongue, and let me love
    [*The Canonisation*]

or an expostulation to one's mistress on getting up in the morning:

'Tis true, 'tis day; what though it be?
O wilt thou therefore rise from me?
               [*Break of Day*]

All these examples start *in medias res*, and have not just implications of context, but 'implications of incident'. The last two examples illustrate how the start of a poem may require us to imagine a preceding verbal context. In *Break of Day*, for instance, it is quite clear that the mistress has made a practical and reasonable remark to this effect: 'It's daytime, so we'd better get up'.

Some items presuppose a preceding verbal context in a strictly formal sense. To illustrate them, we go beyond Donne. In a lyric by Sir Thomas Wyatt which begins 'And wilt thou leave me thus?', the opening conjunction signals on a purely grammatical level that the poem is the continuation of a discourse already (in the imagination) begun. *Yes* or *No* at the beginning of a poem likewise indicate an utterance (or perhaps a gesture) to which the poem is conceived as a reply:

Yes. I remember Adlestrop
               [Edward Thomas, *Adlestrop*]

No, no, go not to Lethe, neither twist
   Wolfs-bane, tight-rooted, for its poisonous wine
               [Keats, *Ode on Melancholy*]

Notice that there is a possibility here, as with questions, commands, and other forms of language which imply the give and take of conversation, that the speaker is communing with himself, instead of with another person. The full-stop after *Yes* in *Adlestrop* perhaps suggests that the poet is confirming a reflection of his own, rather than answering a question posed by someone else.

11.3.2 *Words of Definite Meaning*

The deictic words discussed in the last section have DEFINITE MEANING; when we use them, we assume that a listener or reader is able to agree with us, by observing the context, on the identity of what is referred to. 'This cat' specifies a given animal (say a tom named Magnus now sitting on the floor and observed by you and me); 'A cat' leaves the animal's identity undetermined. But there are a few other words which have definite meaning, without having the 'pointing' function of the deictics: they include the definite article *the*, and the third person pronouns *he*, *she*, *it*, and *they*.[5] These also have interesting implications of context.

'This cat' and 'the cat' are both definite in meaning, in contrast to 'a cat'; but whereas in the former we are expected to see *which* cat is meant from the context, in the latter it is assumed that there is only one cat in question. It is this *assumed uniqueness* of the object or group objects referred to that characterizes the use of *the* and the third-person pronouns. The uniqueness may arise from previous mention:

> A dog was chasing a cat up a path. *The* cat leapt over a fence. *The* dog was unable to follow *her*.

or from the fact that only one entity of the kind exists:

> *the* Milky Way
> *the* President of *the* United States
> *the* richest man in *the* world

or from subjective assumption:

> *the* cat = the cat which belongs to *our* house
> *the* postman = the man who delivers letters to *my* house
> *the* Prime Minister = the Prime Minister of *our* country.

In these last examples, we see how language mirrors the egocentric character of human experience: we treat something as unique, if, from our personal point of view, it is the only one that matters. (I exclude from consideration here the generic use of *the*, which applies uniqueness to a whole class, not to one member of a class: '*The* grizzly bear is large and ferocious.')

From this discussion of assumed uniqueness, we are now able to understand why, in the use of the personal pronoun in these well-known first lines, the poet seems to take it for granted that we have already been introduced to the female being who is the subject of each poem:

> *She* walks in beauty, like the night   [Byron]

> *She* was a phantom of delight   [Wordsworth]

> *She* dwelt among the untrodden ways   [Wordsworth]

A more extended illustration of assumed identification is provided by Yeats's *Leda and the Swan*, which is quoted in full at the end of this chapter.[6] The subject of the poem is the rape of Leda by Zeus in the guise of a swan: a fateful union which resulted in the birth of Helen of Troy, and thence in the Trojan War. It is significant, however, that nowhere in the poem (apart from the title) are Zeus and Leda mentioned except by third-person pronouns: '*He* holds her helpless', '*her* loosening thighs', 'Did *she* put on *his* knowledge', etc. In other words, it is assumed that we already, no doubt by inference from the title, know which 'he' and 'she' are intended. Moreover, apart from the two events 'A sudden blow' and 'A shudder', everything in the poem is referred to in definite terms: '*the* great wings', '*the* staggering girl', '*the* dark webs', '*the* broken wall', are some of the many instances (for such a short poem) of the definite article, and all are used without prior mention of a referent. Yeats supposes we already know the story; he omits narrative preliminaries, and concentrates on reliving, through the visionary eyes of the poet, its central experience. By plunging the reader *in medias res*, he achieves a directness of 'attack' comparable to that of Donne's poems quoted earlier in §11.3.1.

Leda and the Swan illustrates, incidentally, the importance a title sometimes has in specifying the situation within a poem. We might go so far as to say that in this case, the title provides an indispensable clue to the interpretation of the poem.

The past tense, in English, is a further indicator of definiteness of meaning – this time, with reference to time. Note the contrast between the past tense in 'I *visited* Paris' and the perfect tense in 'I *have visited* Paris': the second vaguely indicates some visit in the indefinite past, whereas the first implies that I have a definite occasion in mind. Hence when a definite past time is mentioned, the past tense has to be used instead of the perfect: 'I *visited* Paris in 1966', not 'I *have visited* Paris in 1966'. This feature of meaning accounts for a certain narrative directness – a suggestion of *in medias res* – in the opening lines of such poems as Wordsworth's *The Daffodils* ('I wandered lonely as a cloud') and Shelley's *Ozymandias* ('I met a traveller from an antique land'), where the past tense is used without any indication of when the event described took place.

11.3.3 *Fact and Fiction*

John Crowe Ransom says that 'over every poem which looks like a poem there is a sign which reads: "This road does not go through to action; fictitious"'.[7] This is one of those insightful half-truths which become less valuable when one comes down to a practical examination of what is claimed. It is true, as we have seen, that when one reads a poem, one pays heed not to the given situation, but to the situation constructed within the poem. However, it would be more accurate to say, not that all poems are fictitious, but that they leave the choice between fact and fiction open. We may choose, for instance, whether the 'I' of a poem is the poet himself, or some hypothetical mouthpiece, the poet's persona for the purpose of that poem. In Wordsworth's 'I wandered lonely as a cloud', the poet is re-counting, we presume, his own real experience. (This is biographically confirmed by a passage in Dorothy Wordsworth's journal.) On the other hand, in other poems we are clearly steered towards a fictional interpreta-tion. It would be impossible to make the mistake of thinking that Brown-ing, in dramatic monologues such as *Fra Lippo Lippi*, is speaking on his own behalf; not only are the historical circumstances projected within the poem inappropriate, but the sentiments expressed are not all of the sort one would expect from the lips of a nineteenth-century poet. Yet another case is that of Marvell's *To His Coy Mistress*:

But at my back I always hear
Time's wingèd chariot hurrying near . . .

Is this Marvell's own feeling, or is it what he projects into the mind of an imaginary impatient lover? We do not know, and moreover, in this case, it seems not to matter.

Here we have been identifying 'fictional situation' with 'inferred situa-tion'; but of course, even within the inferred situation there may be a blend of fact and fiction. Some aspects of Fra Filippo Lippi as Browning portrays him are historically true, whereas others are imaginary.

Although discussion of inferred situation has up to this point focused on lyric poetry, it is as well to notice that there are at least three different ways of introducing a fictional language situation. The following sentence, as it might occur in a novel, is an example of the NARRATIVE method:

'What a simpleton you are!' said Miles pityingly.

The equivalent according to the DRAMATIC method would be:

MILES (pityingly): What a simpleton you are!

In dramatic performance, cues and stage directions are replaced by visible happenings on the stage. In contrast to both these methods, the LYRIC, which we have been chiefly considering up to now, omits explicit mention of the speaker and other participants, leaving them to be inferred by contextual evidence. Thus the lyric equivalent of these examples is simply:

What a simpleton you are!

All three methods are used in poetry, but do not always coincide with the genres of narrative, dramatic, and lyrical poetry as generally understood.

Thus Yeats in *Leda and the Swan* uses a third person narrative method, although this poem would normally be placed in the lyric category.

It will be observed that we have now extended the concept of 'the world within the poem' to include constructed situations and events which are only 'language situations' in the sense that they are reported in language, by third person narrative. The advantage of the narrative method is that the fictional 'world' can be described directly, in the third person, rather than through the mouths of those taking part in it. This is the most explicit method, and yet, as we have seen, implications of context are not excluded from it: the use of words of definite meaning may imply a prior assumption by the author and reader in identifying the subject of discourse. It is of incidental interest that modern novelists often prefer the definite opening *in medias res*, already illustrated in *Leda and the Swan*, to a more explicit form of introduction. The first sentence of *Lord of the Flies* by William Golding, for example, runs:

> *The* boy with fair hair lowered himself down *the* last few feet of rock and began to pick his way towards *the* lagoon.

Implicit in the three italicized uses of *the* is the assumption that you are already on the spot, acquainted with the details of the scene and *dramatis personae*. This contrasts with a more traditional style of beginning a narrative, as preserved in the time-honoured formula of the fairy story:

> Once upon a time there was a king who had three beautiful daughters.

Every part of the fictional situation is here introduced by indefinite expressions: 'Once . . . a king . . . three beautiful daughters'; nothing is taken for granted at the beginning of the story.

11.3.4 *Impossible Situations*

The inferred situations created by a poet are free from constraints of reality: they do not have to obey the rules of reason, or the laws of nature. The most commonplace example of an absurdity of situation is an apostrophe (see §11.1.2), understood as an address to someone or something that by nature or circumstances is unable to hear or reply. Sometimes a lyrical poem is entirely cast in the form of an apostrophe: Donne's *The Sun Rising*, which begins 'Busy old fool, unruly Sun', is a defiant address by a lover to the sun, which comes to drive him from his bed and from his mistress in the morning. Another, similar, licence is the placing of a poem in the mouth of something or someone unable, by nature, to use language:

> I chatter, chatter, as I flow
>   To join the brimming river,
> For men may come and men may go,
>   But I go on for ever.

Tennyson's *The Brook* is in the form of a monologue spoken by the brook itself. This anomaly differs from apostrophe only in that it is the first person, not the second person, who is unqualified to act as a participant in a language situation. Such literal absurdities may be seen as an extension of the irrational aspect of poetry as dealt with in Chapter 8.

Just as Donne is fond of situations which are dramatically involving, so Thomas Hardy, in his *Satires of Circumstance*, specializes in situations which, if not contrary to reason and nature, are at least highly implausible or coincidental. He makes typically ironical use of a necessarily unreal situation in '*Ah, Are you Digging on my Grave?*', a short poem in the form of a dialogue between a dead woman and some unknown being disturbing her rest in the graveyard. She assumes in turn that the intruder is her loved one, her next of kin, and her enemy; but learns that now she is dead, they are none of them interested in her any longer. When at last her interlocutor declares himself to be her dog, her first refuge is in the conventional sentiment that pets are more devoted friends than men. But the most bitter irony comes in the final stanza, in which the dog replies:

> 'Mistress, I dug upon your grave
>   To bury a bone, in case
> I should be hungry near this spot
> When passing on my daily trot.
> I am sorry, but I quite forgot
>   It was your resting-place.'

Another ingenious use of situational absurdity is the 'paradox of address' in the title of Dylan Thomas's poem *To Others than You*, a diatribe in which the poet complains about the hypocrisy and insensitivity of his public. The title seems to say: 'This poem is addressed to all hypocrites except the particular hypocrite now reading it, whom for politeness's sake I exclude.' If one takes this to its logical conclusion, the poem is simultaneously addressed to everyone and to no one. The suggested ironical reading of the title is borne out by the oxymoron of the poem's first line, which runs: 'Friend by enemy I call you out.'

11.4 SITUATION AND ACTION

Through implications of context, a lyric composition may contain elements of a dramatic action; that is, it may imply not just a single, static situation, but a sequence of situations or events. Donne's three-stanza *jeu d'esprit* entitled *The Flea* is a simple illustration:

> Mark but this flea, and mark in this
> How little that which thou deny'st me is;
> It suck'd me first, and now sucks thee,
> And in this flea, our two bloods mingled be.

These opening lines postulate a situation in which the poet-lover, observing a flea to have bitten both himself and his mistress, uses it as pretext to urge her surrender to his desires. The second stanza, which opens as follows:

> Oh stay, three lives in one flea spare

marks a new situation: now the mistress has threatened to kill the flea. In the final stanza, which begins:

> Cruel and sudden, hast thou since
> Purpled thy nail, in blood of innocence?

yet another situation has arisen: the flea has been caught and killed. So the three stanzas represent three stages of an action – one might say, three acts of a drama – and at each stage, the poet seizes on circumstances to plead the flea's cause, and his own.

The importance of deictic items in signalling a changing situation is seen in this section of Yeats's *Easter 1916*, in which the poet ponders on the characters of his various acquaintances martyred in the Dublin Easter Rising:

> That woman's days were spent
> In ignorant good-will,
> Her nights in argument
> Until her voice grew shrill;
> What voice more sweet than hers
> When, young and beautiful,
> She rode to harriers?
> This man had kept a school
> And rode our wingèd horse;
> He might have won fame in the end,
> So sensitive his nature seemed,

So daring and sweet his thought.
This other man I had dreamed
A drunken vainglorious lout . . .

Each use of *this* or *that* ('That woman . . . This man . . . This other man')
indicates the movement of the poet's attention from one person to another,
as if he were inspecting their bodies one by one. Yet we should notice that,
as is often the case, the context projected by the poem is vague and ambi-
valent: Yeats need not be physically surveying his dead friends – he might
be perusing their names listed in the newspaper, looking at their photo-
graphs, or simply recalling them in turn as figures in a mental portrait
gallery. It is left to the reader to supply a more precise context, rather as it
is often left to the reader to fill in the gaps between the verbal hints of a
metaphor.

A different kind of dramatic implication arises when the language of a
poem suggests periodic changes of speech situation; changes, for example,
of speaker and hearer, as if in a play. Hardy's *'Ah, Are you Digging on my
Grave?'* is a straightforward instance of poetry written in the form of a
dialogue, with transitions from one speaker to another between the verses;
but the method is still lyric rather than dramatic, because the identity of
the speakers is not directly mentioned, but inferred from what they say.
Traditional ballads, too, frequently have this kind of implicit dramatic
structure, with unsignalled switches from direct to indirect speech, or
from one speaker to another. More subtle and complex implications of
dramatic performance are found in some of the poems of T. S. Eliot,
where, by subtle changes of register or dialect, as well as by more obvious
indicators of context, there emerges a varied montage of 'voices', some
like those of an impersonal chorus, others like those of stage characters:

April is the cruellest month, breeding
Lilacs out of the dead land, mixing
Memory and desire, stirring
Dull roots with spring rain.
Winter kept us warm, covering
Earth in forgetful snow, feeding
A little life with dried tubers.
Summer surprised us, coming over the Starnbergersee   8
With a shower of rain; we stopped in the colonnade,
And went on in the sunlight, into the Hofgarten,
And drank coffee, and talked for an hour.
Bin gar keine Russin, stamm' aus Litauen, echt deutsch.   12

And when we were children, staying at the archduke's,   13
My cousin's, he took me out on a sled,
And I was frightened. He said, Marie,
Marie, hold on tight. And down we went.
In the mountains, there you feel free.
I read, much of the night, and go south in the winter.
What are the roots that clutch, what branches grow   19
Out of this stony rubbish? Son of man,
You cannot say, or guess, for you know only
A heap of broken images, where the sun beats . . .

In this initial passage from *The Waste Land*, I have numbered those lines
(8, 12, 13, 19) which mark a transition between one 'voice' and another. I
leave it to the reader, however, to determine exactly how, from the evidence of the language, we recognize these changes, when they come. It is
no wonder that Lawrence Durrell, in *The Key to Modern Poetry*,[8] finds it
possible to set this part of *The Waste Land* as a radio play: the transitions
indicated above are in fact those of his version. To some extent, breaking up
the lines in this way makes the picture appear more clear-cut than it is: the
change-over marked at line 8, for instance, is gradual rather than sudden.
In the radio version, moreover, Durrell adds information about sex of
speaker, background noises, etc., which cannot be definitely gathered from
the poem as it stands. Every intelligent reader imaginatively 'furnishes' in
this way the 'world within the poem'; the inferred situation, being inexplicit, tempts us to read in details which are not overtly stated.

11.5 CONCLUSION

Having examined at some length the situational aspect of language, we are
now able to see, resuming the theme of Chapter 4, how essential implications of context are for the total interpretation of a poem. The constructed
context is in a sense the corner-stone of the interpretative process – we cannot say that we know what a poem is 'about' unless we have identified
certain landmarks of the world it portrays. Here once again, emphasis
must be given to the subjective element of interpretation: there is room
for the individual to read into a poem more than is explicitly declared.
Nevertheless, knowledge of contextual implications is an important and
necessary part of the equipment we bring to understanding a poem, as I
hope the reader will find out for himself in considering the examples that
follow.

Examples for discussion

Identify implications of context and licences of situation in the following. Consider the interpretation of each poem in terms of the inferred situation together with general linguistic foregrounding.

[a]

> And did those feet in ancient time
> Walk upon England's mountains green?
> And was the holy Lamb of God
> On England's pleasant pastures seen?
>
> And did the Countenance Divine
> Shine forth upon our clouded hills?
> And was Jerusalem builded here
> Among those dark satanic mills?
>
> Bring me my bow of burning gold!
> Bring me my arrows of desire!
> Bring me my spear! O clouds unfold!
> Bring me my chariot of fire!
>
> I will not cease from mental fight,
> Nor shall my sword sleep in my hand,
> Till we have built Jerusalem
> In England's green and pleasant land.
> [William Blake, from *Milton*]

[b]   *Leda and the Swan*
                        (See §11.3.2)

> A sudden blow: the great wings beating still
> Above the staggering girl, her thighs caressed
> By the dark webs, her nape caught in his bill,
> He holds her helpless breast upon his breast.
>
> How can those terrified vague fingers push
> The feathered glory from her loosening thighs?
> And how can body, laid in that white rush,
> But feel the strange heart beating where it lies?
>
> A shudder in the loins engenders there
> The broken wall, the burning roof and tower
> And Agamemnon dead.
>
>   Being so caught up,
> So mastered by the brute blood of the air,

Did she put on his knowledge with his power
Before the indifferent beak could let her drop?

[W. B. Yeats]

[c]   *Prayer before Birth*
I am not yet born; O hear me.
Let not the bloodsucking bat or the rat or the stoat or the
    club-footed ghoul come near me.

I am not yet born, console me.
I fear that the human race may with tall walls wall me,
    with strong drugs dope me, with wise lies lure me,
        on black racks rack me, in blood-baths roll me.

I am not yet born; provide me
With water to dandle me, grass to grow for me, trees to talk
    to me, sky to sing to me, birds and a white light
        in the back of my mind to guide me.

I am not yet born, forgive me
For the sins that in me the world shall commit, my words
    when they speak me, my thoughts when they think me,
        my treason engendered by traitors beyond me,
            my life when they murder by means of my
                hands, my death when they live me.

I am not yet born; rehearse me
In the parts I must play and the cues I must take when
    old men lecture me, bureaucrats hector me, mountains
        frown at me, lovers laugh at me, the white
            waves call me to folly and the desert calls
                me to doom and the beggar refuses
                    my gift and my children curse me.

I am not yet born; O hear me,
Let not the man who is beast or who thinks he is God
    come near me.

I am not yet born; O fill me
With strength against those who would freeze my
    humanity, would dragoon me into a lethal automaton,
        would make me a cog in a machine, a thing with
            one face, a thing, and against all those
                who would dissipate my entirety, would
                    blow me like thistledown hither and
                        thither or hither and thither

> like water held in the
> hands would spill me

Let them not make me a stone and let them not spill me.
Otherwise kill me.
[Louis MacNeice]

Notes

1 On 'immediate situation', see J. O. ELLIS, 'On Contextual Meaning', in *In Memory of J. R. Firth*, ed. C. E. BAZELL *et al.*, London, 1966, 82; also J. R. FIRTH, 'The Technique of Semantics', *Papers in Linguistics 1934–1951*, London, 1957, 30–1.
2 W. NOWOTTNY, *The Language Poets Use*, London, 1962, 43.
3 In this passage I repeat, with modifications, a situational framework presented in G. N. LEECH, *English in Advertising*, London, 1966, 32–3. This in turn was roughly modelled on an account in FIRTH, 'Personality and Language in Society', *op. cit.*, 182.
4 M. A. K. HALLIDAY, A. MCINTOSH, and P. STREVENS, *The Linguistic Sciences and Language Teaching*, London, 1964, 97–8.
5 Cf. a related discussion in LEECH, *op. cit.*, 156–8, where, however, 'deictic' is given a slightly wider interpretation.
6 M. A. K. Halliday analyses the language of the poem in detail, and comments on the unusual use of items of definite meaning, in 'Descriptive Linguistics in Literary Studies', in A. MCINTOSH and M. A. K. HALLIDAY, *Patterns of Language*, London, 1966, 56–69.
7 J. C. RANSOM, 'Poetry: a Note on Ontology', *The World's Body*, New York, 1938, 131.
8 L. DURRELL, *Key to Modern Poetry*, London and New York, 1952, 148–51.

Twelve

Ambiguity and Indeterminacy

The trouble with the word AMBIGUITY is that it is itself an instance of troublesome ambiguity. In linguistics, it has generally been used in a narrow sense which we may represent as 'more than one cognitive meaning for the same piece of language;[1] whereas in literary studies it has often been used in an extremely broad sense popularized by Empson in his witty and influential book *Seven Types of Ambiguity*: 'any verbal nuance, however slight, which gives room for alternative reactions to the same piece of language'.[2] These two senses roughly correspond to the narrow and wide senses of 'meaning' distinguished in §3.1.3. There I found it convenient to confine 'meaning' to the narrow sense of 'cognitive meaning', and to use 'significance' for the wider sense of 'all that is communicated by a piece of language'. Similarly, I shall here prefer to use 'ambiguity' in the linguists' sense, and to keep it distinct from 'multiple significance' (which is Empson's 'ambiguity').

Both ambiguity and the wider concept of multiple significance are manifestations of the MANY VALUED character of poetic language. If an ambiguity comes to our attention in some ordinary functional use of language, we generally consider it a distraction from the message and a defect of style. But if it occurs in a literary text, we tend to give the writer the benefit of the doubt, and assume that a peaceful coexistence of alternative meanings is intended. In much the same way, if two levels of symbolism can be simultaneously read into a poem, we are often inclined to accept both, as contributing to the richness of its significance.

12.1 KINDS OF AMBIGUITY

For a classification of ambiguities, we return to the framework of linguistic levels expounded in §3.1.1. There it was observed that because of many-one relationships between the levels of semantics, form, and realization, the

utterance 'His designs upset her' could be assigned four different meanings, as pictured in the following diagram:

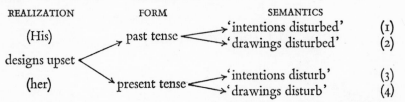

REALIZATION	FORM	SEMANTICS	
(His)	past tense	'intentions disturbed'	(1)
		'drawings disturbed'	(2)
designs upset			
(her)	present tense	'intentions disturb'	(3)
		'drawings disturb'	(4)

The branch in the path of interpretation between realization and form is
due to the HOMONYMY of the present tense and past tense of *upset* (two
different grammatical functions having the same spoken and written
realization); the branching between form and semantics is due to the
POLYSEMY (multiple meaning) of *designs* which can mean either 'intentions'
or 'drawings' in this sentence. Thus what in physical terms is 'the same
sentence' can receive any of four meanings, according to its context.
Ambiguities, it will now be clear, can originate in homonymy, polysemy,
or (as in the case of the whole sentence above) a combination of the two.

Of course, the context (either linguistic or otherwise) does not always
permit both readings of an ambiguity to be registered. 'The designs upset
her' would pick out the meaning 'drawings' for *designs*, rather than the
meaning 'intentions'.

In the past, discussion of homonymy and polysemy has been largely
confined to individual words. But it is important to realize that there are
both lexical and grammatical ambiguities:

LEXICAL HOMONYMY: (homonymy of words as items of vocabulary)
   mole (noun) = 'a small animal'
   mole (noun) = 'a spot on the skin'
   (Either meaning is possible in 'I noticed a mole')

GRAMMATICAL HOMONYMY:
   moving gates as a Modifier+Noun construction (= 'gates which
      move')
   moving gates as a Verbal+Object construction (= 'causing gates to
      move')
   (The ambiguity is apparent in 'I like moving gates')

LEXICAL POLYSEMY:
   prefer = 1. 'promote'
           = 2. 'like better'
   ('Gentlemen prefer blondes' could be ambiguous in this respect)

GRAMMATICAL POLYSEMY:

Present tense = 1. a momentary happening now

= 2. a habitually repeated event

('The centre-forward Smith kicks hard' is ambiguous in that it might refer to a single event at the time of speaking – reported, say, by a radio commentator – or to a habitual tendency.)

These are evidently distinct categories, although it is sometimes difficult to decide whether to allot marginal specimens to one category or another. The choice between lexical homonymy and lexical polysemy is especially difficult. Why should we decide, for example, that there are two separate nouns *mole* rather than two separate meanings of the same word? Traditionally, appeal has been made to etymology – that is, whether the two senses can be traced historically to the same source. However, it will be sufficient for us to rely on a rough criterion of semantic similarity. Because there is no obvious connection of meaning between *mole* and *mole*, they can be regarded as separate words.

Whether an ambiguity is perceived or not depends on the person and the context. The sentence 'I like moving gates', occurring in a normal conversation, would probably not appear ambiguous, as the context would make clear which interpretation was intended. In poetry, on the other hand, ambiguities are frequently brought to the reader's attention, and the simultaneous awareness of more than one interpretation is used for artistic effect. One reason why we recognize and tolerate more ambiguity in poetry is that we are in any case attuned to the acceptance of deviant usages and interpretations. Consider the line 'I made my song a coat', which begins Yeats's poem *A Coat*. Here is a homonymy of two grammatical constructions:

Subject + Verbal + Indirect Object + Direct Object
Subject + Verbal + Direct Object + Object Complement
I made my song a coat

The first reading is equivalent in meaning to 'I made a coat for my song', whereas the second is equivalent to 'I made my song into a coat'. Both these interpretations have an element of absurdity, and perhaps it is for that reason that both have to be reckoned with in interpreting the poem. On the other hand, if the sentence had been 'I made my son a coat', the first interpretation would have been perfectly commonplace and acceptable, and so the second, deviant interpretation would not have entered into consideration.

In discussing HOMONYMS, or words which have the same realization, it is

sometimes valuable to distinguish HOMOPHONES, or words which are pronounced alike but written differently (*boar, bore; die, dye; sea, see;* etc.), and
HOMOGRAPHS, a rather smaller class of words which are written alike but
pronounced differently (*lead, lead; bow, bow; conduct* as noun, *conduct* as
verb; etc.). These are homonyms only with respect to a particular medium
– speech or writing. Because of spelling irregularities, English contains a
large number of homophones, and accordingly many lexical ambiguities
in English are ambiguities of speech only. The pun of Belloc's epigram *On
his Books* (quoted earlier in §4.3) can, unlike Victorian children, be heard
but not seen:

> When I am dead, I hope it may be said:
> 'His sins were scarlet, but his books were *read*'.

In grammar, the situation is just the opposite: the writing system fails to
make many distinctions which are made in speech. In particular, intonation and stress are richer, as means of expressing grammatical contrasts,
than punctuation, the corresponding aspect of the writing system. This
couplet from Auden's *Out on the Lawn* is grammatically ambiguous in
writing, but not in speech:

> Lucky, this point in time and space
> Is chosen as my working place.

Assigning it one grammatical interpretation, we read it 'It is lucky that
this point . . . is chosen as my working place'; but with another structure,
it reads: 'Being lucky (i.e. because it is lucky), this point . . . is chosen as my
working place.' If we read the lines aloud, we are almost compelled, by
our choice of intonation pattern, to decide in favour of one or the other of
these readings.

In the written medium, lineation is a further fruitful source of ambiguity,
as we saw from an example by E. E. Cummings in §3.2.4. As a further
illustration, here is a verbal *trompe l'oeil* at the end of *The Right of Way* by
William Carlos Williams:

> Why bother where I went?
> for I went spinning on the
>
> four wheels of my car
> along the wet road until
>
> I saw a girl with one leg
> over the rail of a balcony

At the penultimate line, we are brought up short by the hallucination of a one-legged girl, only to realize that the grammatical construction introduced by *with* carries on into the next line.

12.2 PUNS AND WORD-PLAY

A PUN is a foregrounded lexical ambiguity, which may have its origin either in homonymy or polysemy. Generally speaking, the more blatant and contrived variety of pun is homonymic:

> Where Bentley late tempestuous wont to sport
> In troubled waters, but now sleeps in *port*.
> [Pope, *Dunciad*, IV]

Bentley, the turbulent Cambridge critic, is described in a seafaring metaphor as having reached 'port' or a place of refuge and retirement, whilst a quite unrelated type of *port* incongruously conjures up the image of an aging scholar mellowing under the influence of wine. Empson, whilst not disparaging this type of word-play, calls it 'a simply funny pun', and colourfully describes it as one which 'jumps out of its setting, yapping, and bites the Master on the ankles'.[3]

The more subtle and subdued effect of the polysemantic pun is illustrated by this passage, also discussed by Empson,[4] in which an eighteenth-century race for preferment is depicted:

> Most manfully besiege the patron's gate,
> And, oft repulsed, as oft attack the great,
> With painful art, and application warm,
> And take at last some little *place* by storm.
> [Edward Young, *Love of Fame*, Satire III]

The meaning of 'place'='position, job' is superimposed upon a sense which bears out the military metaphor, that of 'place'='location'. Because of the resemblance between the senses, their collision is less violent than that of the previous example.

What makes the homonymic pun more obtrusive and (generally) less serious than the polysemantic pun is the feeling that the poet has availed himself of an accident of language. To speakers of English, it is a matter of sheer chance that the two words *port* and *port* are pronounced and spelt the same way; but because the senses of *place* are related to one another, it does not seem unreasonable that they should be expressed by the same form.

12.2.1 *Technical Variations*

As there are various ways in which people can be made aware of an ambiguity, it is worthwhile spending some time examining the technical aspects of punning and related forms of word-play.

Punning repetition. In the puns we have so far examined, two or more senses are actually suggested by a single occurrence of the ambiguous sequence of sounds. But a double meaning can also be brought to one's attention by a repetition of the same sequence, first in one sense and then in another. So Romeo, lamenting that Cupid brings heaviness instead of gaiety, puns on *sore* and *soar*, *bound* (adj.) and *bound* (verb):

> I am too *sore* enpierced with his shaft
> To *soar* with his light feathers, and so *bound*,
> I cannot *bound* a pitch above dull woe.[5]
> [*Romeo and Juliet*, I.iv]

The device is particularly popular with Elizabethan dramatists, and is taken to extremes in a piece of dialogue from *Richard II*:

> FITZWATER: Surrey thou *liest*.
> SURREY: Dishonourable boy!
> That *lie* shall *lie* so heavy on my sword,
> That it shall render vengeance and revenge,
> Till thou the *lie*-giver and that *lie* do *lie*
> In earth as quiet as thy father's skull.
> [IV.i]

Despite the plethora of repetitions, only one ambiguity is in fact at issue here – the homonymy of the two words *lie* (as in 'lie down') and *lie* (as in 'tell lies').

Play on antonyms. One way to make a multiple meaning spring to notice is to use two words which are normally antonyms in non-antonymous senses. In the balcony scene of *Romeo and Juliet*, Juliet apologizes, in these words, for having unwittingly declared her love without being wooed for it:

> therefore pardon me,
> And not impute this yielding to *light* love,
> Which the *dark* night hath so discovered.
> [II.ii]

Light is used here in the Shakespearean sense of 'frivolous', and yet at the same time we are made aware of it as an antonym to *dark*.

The 'asyntactic' pun. In an 'asyntactic' pun, one of the meanings does not actually fit into the syntactic context. Mercutio, wounded by Tybalt, jests about his impending death:

> Ask for me tomorrow and you shall find me a *grave* man.
> [*Romeo and Juliet*, III.i]

The sinister meaning of *grave* hinted at here is that of *grave* as a noun, although in the given construction 'a grave man', it can only be an adjective.

The etymological pun. Poets, as we saw in §3.2.8, are given to using words in etymologically reconstructed senses, and this tendency sometimes shows itself in puns which bring together an etymological meaning and a current meaning of the same word. In Auden's phrase 'the distortions of ingrown virginity' [*Sir, No Man's Enemy*],[6] *distortion* can, because of its proximity to *ingrown*, be construed literally and etymologically as 'twisting out of shape', as well as in its obvious abstract sense.

Syllepsis. The rhetorical figure of SYLLEPSIS ('taking together') can be seen as a type of pun. It is a compound structure in which two superficially alike constructions are collapsed together, so that one item is understood in disparate senses:

> Here thou, great Anna! whom three realms obey,
> Dost sometimes counsel take – and sometimes tea.
> [Pope, *The Rape of the Lock*, III]

The similar constructions in this case are 'take counsel' and 'take tea'. The two uses of *take* are both idiomatic, and are plainly distinct in meaning, the one being abstract, the other concrete. The effect of the syllepsis is to suggest, ironically, that the two activities are comparable, and of equal importance.

Play on similarity of pronunciation. A 'jingle' depending on approximate rather than absolute homonymity is technically not a pun, although its effect is similar.

> A young man *married* is a man that's *marred*
> [*All's Well that Ends Well*, II.iii]

This kind of repetition differs only in the degree of similarity from that earlier called 'chiming' (§6.4.1). As with 'mice and men' and similar examples, the likeness of sound leads one to look out for a connection in sense as well. (The similarity is greater in some dialects of modern English (e.g. Scots) than in others.)

On the face of it, it seems impossible to superimpose such quasi-homonyms on the same occurrence, as one can superimpose full homonyms like *port* and *port*. Nevertheless, the 'portmanteau' technique developed with such virtuosity by Joyce is in fact a method of simultaneously suggesting expressions which sound slightly different. Joyce's blends are not words of English language at all, but grotesque and often amusing formations created by the distortion and mingling of English or foreign words. The following is a list of examples collected from the pages of *Finnegan's Wake* by Margaret Schlauch, who also provides the explanatory gloss:[7]

> *dontelleries= dentelleries* (French for lace-adorned objects; also discreet, intimate garments which 'don't tell'.)
> *erigenating= originating*; also *Erigena-ting* (from Duns Scotus Erigena, the 'Erin-born philosopher')
> *venissoon after= very soon after; venison after; Venus' son after*
> *eroscope= horoscope; Eros-scope; hero-scope*
> *Fiendish Park= Phoenix Park; Park of Fiends*
> *museyroom= museum, musing room*
> *Champs de Mors= Champs de Mars; Field of Death (Mors)*
> *herodotary= hereditary; hero-doter; Herodotus?*
> *pigmaid= made like a pig; pigmied*

12.2.2 *In Defence of the Pun*

Although maligned by popular opinion, which affects to regard the 'punster' as a pernicious bore, puns – especially those involving polysemy – have been treated seriously by poets of most periods of English literature. As foregrounded features of language they need, however, some artistic justification.

The type of pun which expresses two meanings through the same occurrence is, we might say, its own justification, for it gives two meanings for the price of one, and so adds to the poem's density and richness of significance. Empson suggests, for example, that in the following lines two unconnected interpretations of *pitch* are metaphorically applicable: that found in 'pitching a tent', and that of 'making black, covering with pitch':[8]

but soon he found
The welkin *pitched* with sullen clouds around,
An eastern wind, and dew upon the ground.
[Dryden, *Death of Amyntas*]

The two meanings can be simultaneously read into the passage without any marked incongruity, although there is no interanimating link between them.

In general, however, to justify a pun or play on words, we look for a significant connection, either of similarity or of contrast, between the meanings. In a polysemantic pun, such a connection is almost bound to offer itself, for the relationship between different senses of the same item is usually such that a derivation from one to the other can be traced by metaphor, or some other rule of transference. The two senses of *place* discussed in §12.2 are related in that the meaning of 'position, job' is an abstract extension of the locative meaning. Empson talks of a pun of this kind being 'justified by derivation'.[9]

With the homonymic pun, in contrast, less emphasis is on the semantic connection than on the ingenuity of the writer in taking advantage of an arbitrary identity of sound. In Romeo's speech quoted in §12.2.1, the cleverness of the punning repetition of *soar* and *sore*, *bound* and *bound*, seems almost an end in itself. Nevertheless, this type of pun can sometimes serve a higher purpose:[10]

and three corrupted men . . .
Have, for the gilt of France, – O guilt indeed! –
Confirm'd conspiracy with fearful France.
[*Henry V*, II, Chorus]

A double link can be discerned between the *guilt* of the traitors and the *gilt* or money they receive from the French king. There is firstly a superficial contrast between something dark and unpleasant, and something apparently bright and attractive; and secondly, there is a deeper association between lucre and evil. Both these connections are conventional, yet add point to the pun: the juxtaposition of *guilt* loads the phrase 'the gilt of France' with dark connotations.

If the contrast between the two meanings of a pun is more striking than their similarity, its purpose is probably ironical. Pope's pun on *port* (§12.2), whilst appearing to describe Bentley's retirement in the dignified metaphor of a ship reaching harbour, slily insinuates a wine-bibbing dotage. The punning on the word *fool* in *King Lear* [II.iv and elsewhere] conveys, among other things, the ironical message that the king himself is the real fool, whereas he who is called 'fool', the court jester, is the mouthpiece of wisdom.

If, on the other hand, it is the similarity between the senses that is striking, the pun is similar in force to a metaphor:

> NORTHUMBERLAND: My Lord, in the base court he [Bolingbroke] doth attend
> To speak with you; may it please you to come down.
> KING RICHARD: Down, down I come; like glistering Phaeton down,
> Wanting the manage of unruly jades.
> In the *base* court? *Base* court, where kings grow base,
> To come at traitor's calls and do them grace.
> [*Richard II*, III.iii]

Descending the walls of Flint Castle to parley with Bolingbroke, Richard seizes on the symbolic appropriateness of 'lowering' himself to treat with a treasonous subject; he reanimates the dead metaphorical connection between *base* meaning 'low down' and *base* meaning morally and socially contemptible. Many of Joyce's punning blends also depend on the perception of some analogy – for example, *museyroom*, discussed from this point of view in §4.2.2.

There may be a slight element of primitive 'word-magic' in the appreciation of a serious pun of this kind. A great deal of superstition about words, and especially over proper names, can be reduced to the conviction that because two words are alike, what they stand for must also be alike. Even in Christian literature, a trace of this feeling seems to be present in puns such as Pope Gregory's famous play on the similarity of *Angli* and *angeli*. Rather fancifully, one might imagine the saint's justification of his pun in these words: 'In a world ordered by divine providence, no aspect of language can be considered accidental. Could it not be God's especial will that this tribe of Angles, like the angels in name, should also be like them in nature? And is it not therefore especially fitting that we should convert them?'. On such grounds we might argue that the pun, far from being a superficial trick of speech, sounds primeval depths in the human mind.

12.3 OPEN INTERPRETATION

From ambiguity, we widen discussion to take in the more general topic of multiple significance: the 'many valued' view of poetic language as applied not just to cognitive meanings, but to all that a poem communicates. I have headed this section 'open interpretation', because it is important to realize that the significance of a poem is open to addition, revision, and curtailment by the knowledge, imagination, and understanding of different interpreters.

Some aspects of interpretation are obviously more personal and subjective than others. We may look at it like this. A poem offers a vast number of interpretative possibilities; some are simply theoretical possibilities which would rarely, if ever, occur to an actual reader; others are more plausible. The subjective element enters when the reader selects from this array of possibilities that interpretation, or those interpretations, which suit him best. The role of linguistics is to help us to study what possibilities exist; the role of the literary commentator, it may be suggested, is to evaluate the various possibilities, and to arrive at an informed and authoritative interpretation by rejecting some and accepting others.

To complicate the picture, some aspects of poetic significance are indefinite, in that there is no finite number of possibilities to choose from. The ground of a metaphor, for example, cannot be specified exactly: although people might agree roughly on the basis of a comparison between tenor and vehicle, there would still remain an area of vagueness. To the concept of multiple significance, therefore, we add that of INDETERMINATE SIGNIFICANCE. The whole significance of a poem could never be extracted from it by exegesis: such an undertaking would be beyond the reach of the literary commentator, and still further beyond the reach of the linguistic expert.

12.3.1 *Sources of Multiple and Indeterminate Significance*

For clarity's sake, I shall here attempt to summarize the various sources of multiple and indefinite significance in poetry which have arisen in the course of this book. No more than a rough and tentative list is offered, since the intention is merely to suggest the vastness of the problem of accounting for all that a poem is capable of communicating.

SOURCES OF MULTIPLE SIGNIFICANCE

[a] *Ordinary linguistic ambiguity*, as just discussed in §§12.1 and 12.2.

[b] *Deviations*. There are different ways of 'making sense' of the same linguistic deviation. For example, various rules of transference may be applied to the same semantic absurdity (Chapters 8 and 9).

[c] *Schemes*. The question may arise, for example, of whether to treat the relationship between two words stressed by parallelism as one of contrast or one of similarity (Chapters 4 and 5).

[d] *Implications of Context.* The 'world within the poem' may be built up simultaneously on different levels. Empson says of *The Faerie Queene* 'You can read all kinds of political and religious interpretations, indeed any interpretation that comes naturally to you, into a story offered as interesting in itself, and as giving an abstracted vision of all the conflicts of humanity'.[11] In *With a Guitar, to Jane* (see §11.3), the situation of address exists on two levels, that of Ariel to Miranda, and that of Shelley to Jane.

SOURCES OF INDETERMINATE SIGNIFICANCE

[a] *Register and dialect* (see §§1.1.1 and 1.1.2). A poem's implications of dialect and register are not clear-cut, because dialect and register distinctions themselves are not clear-cut; for example, there is no simple dichotomy between 'formal' and 'colloquial' English, but innumerable degrees of formality.

[b] *Other connotations.* The range of connotations which language has by virtue of what it refers to (see §3.1.4) is also vague and indeterminate. Who can name, for example, the exact psychological repercussions of *terrible* and *beauty* juxtaposed in Yeats's line 'A terrible beauty is born' [*Easter 1916*]? Context often gives prominence to certain attitudes and suppresses others: thus in Auden's phrase 'ingrown virginity', the unpleasant rather than pleasant associations of virginity are singled out for attention. Yet personal attitudes will always vary. This is the area of subjective interpretation *par excellence*: a person's reaction to a word, emotive and otherwise, depends to a great extent on that person's individual experience of the thing or quality referred to.

[c] *The ground and tenor of a metaphor.* Both have an indeterminate element, as described in §§9.2.1 and 9.2.2.

[d] *Implications of context.* Part of the interpretation of a poem consists in furnishing the 'world within the poem' with details which are merely inferred from implications of context: deciding, for example, what exactly is supposed to be happening in Yeats's *Easter 1916* (see §11.4). The inference can take place on a factual, as well as on an imaginary level. A person who believes that the riddle of Shakespeare's *Sonnets* has been solved will project into the poem actual historical personalities for the 'fair youth' and the 'dark lady'. The process of 'reading in' details can go on *ad infinitum*.

The interpretation of a poem is 'open' in at least two further respects. As foregrounding is by no means an all-or-none matter, personal judgment often enters in with the question of whether to consider a feature of a poem as foregrounded or not. And in the last resort, there is always a further interpretative choice – whether to find a positive interpretation for a given feature, or to reject it as vacuous or aberrant.

12.3.2 *The Analogy of Visual Arts*

These questions of interpretation may seem so bound up with language, that it may be a surprise to find that there are close parallels in the appreciation of visual arts, where one would perhaps expect less scope for ambiguity and the interference of individual judgment. The comparison will, I hope, illuminate not only the general question of artistic significance, but in particular the nature of poetic interpretation.

In *Art and Illusion*,[12] an outstanding study of the psychology of art appreciation, E. H. Gombrich explores in great detail and with great penetration the theme that understanding a picture is far from merely 'taking in' what is there on the canvas: it is projecting *into* the picture an interpretation that one accepts as the most plausible, and ignoring many other interpretations which are theoretically possible. The simplest example comes from the realm of perspective[13]:

fig. [*j*]

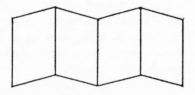

The diagram of four rhomboids, taken as a perspective drawing, is plainly ambiguous: it can be seen as a strip of folded rectanguar panels either seen from above, with the middle fold towards the front, or seen from beneath, with the middle fold towards the back. Apart from these, there is a third less obvious, but no less indisputable interpretation – that of a set of actual rhomboids joined on a flat surface. What is less easy to accept, without a study of the laws of perspective, is that this could be a three-dimensional representation of any number of irregular, and hence less probable shapes. We find it extremely difficult even to imagine these innumerable possibilities, because our minds are so used to selecting only the simplest and most reasonable reading. Not even the three regular interpretations are in practice simultaneous possibilities: context makes up our minds for us, so that we are simply not aware of having made a choice.

A comparable linguistic illustration is the 'human elephant' example, already discussed in the introduction to Chapter 9. The two words *human* and *elephant* are logically incompatible in this phrase, and so cannot both be taken in the basic zoological sense. But the question of which to take figuratively is decided by context. 'All the zoo-keepers like Jumbo – he's such a human elephant' – this picks out a literal interpretation of *elephant*; but the opposite interpretation is selected by 'Mind where you put your feet, you great human elephant!'. This second sentence also selects the meaning 'clumsy brute' rather than the other conventional metaphorical meaning of *elephant*, 'person with a long memory'. But there is the further 'submerged' ambiguity of theoretically possible interpretations which we can only bring ourselves to imagine by a special mental effort. Think, for example, of the numerous possible tenors and grounds which could establish a metaphorical connection between humans and elephants. A 'human elephant' might mean a person with large, flapping ears; or it might, perhaps, refer to a person carrying a large burden on his back as an elephant carries a howdah, or to a person who, when he blows his nose, sounds like an elephant trumpeting. Once we start thinking seriously about it, the possibilities become endless.

To show that this sort of ambivalence arises also in poetry, we may observe that Tennyson's line 'Authority forgets a dying king' [*The Passing of Arthur*] contains a literal incompatibility between *authority* and *forgets*, which may be resolved either by taking *authority* as literal and *forgets* as transferred, or *vice versa*. In the first case, we have a straightforward personification of 'authority', which forsakes, or leaves, a dying king whose will is no longer obeyed by his subjects. In the second case, *authority* may be taken as a synecdoche for 'people in authority', who literally 'forget' the king. There is an exactly corresponding ambiguity in Shakespeare's 'Crabbed age and youth cannot live together' [*The Passionate Pilgrim*, xii].

Gombrich points out how much of 'reading a picture' depends on imagining, or projecting into it, what is in fact not there.[14] A few dots and jagged strokes of paint may suggest a distant crowd of people, or a rough scribble a landscape of trees and rocks. This is similar to the way in which we project into a poem the situation suggested by a few linguistic clues. In interpreting a poem, too, we rely on the literary counterpart of what Gombrich calls 'the consistency test'[15]; that is, we discard all interpretative conjectures which do not fit in with the rest of the 'world within the poem', just as in making sense of a spatter of paint on canvas, or a couple of lines on paper, we reject those meanings which are incompatible with the 'world within the picture'. For instance, we should have to rule out some of the main interpretations of fig. [j] above if we understood the rest of the picture in which it appeared to represent an aerial panorama. But of course, in poetry as in painting, one clue can cause a revision of the whole of the rest of the interpretation – again, in the interests of consistency. Each guess in the interpretation of a poem provides a context for all the other guesses, and may either confirm or disconfirm them. Hence interpreting a work of art is not unlike interpreting the world we live in through science: the total interpretation is a theory built on individual hypotheses, and one contrary clue may cause a revision of the whole theory.

Modern painters have forced the observer into an awareness of his visual inferences by confronting him with spatial puzzles: spatial 'worlds' full of irregularities or contradictions, spatial 'worlds' denuded of conventional clues to interpretation. The special feature of cubism is, in Gombrich's words, its 'introduction of contrary clues which will resist all attempts to apply the test of consistency'.[16] The viewer, whose tendency to take the easiest path of interpretation is thus frustrated, finds himself exercising his visual imagination, and seeking some deeper level on which apparent nonsense may be turned into sense. The literary counterpart of the cubist is the 'difficult' poet who puts sentences together in such a way as to block the reader's search for an obvious interpretation, leading him to probe until he satisfies 'the consistency test' at a deeper level of interpretation. Hart Crane's 'Frosted eyes lift altars' [*At Melville's Tomb*] is a case in point. Crane had to explain to his baffled editor that this superficially nonsensical line 'refers simply to a conviction that a man, not knowing perhaps a definite god yet being endowed with a reverence for deity – such a man naturally postulates a deity somehow, and the altar of that deity by the very *action* of the eyes *lifted* in searching'.[17] Such verbal enigmas perplex our sense-making faculty until someone – ideally, as in this case, the poet himself – reveals an unforeseen interpretation.

Yet it would not do – here we must repeat the argument of §4.2.1 – to think of the poem as something locked inside the poet's mind, something of which the words on the page are simply the manifestation. The painting exists apart from what the painter intended to put into it, and the poem apart from the intentions of the poet. We have correctly been concentrating on the interpretative rather than the creative process. 'Any picture', says Gombrich, 'by its very nature, remains an appeal to the visual imagination; it must be supplemented in order to be understood.'[18] This, with minimum alteration, can be applied to verbal art. A poem exists apart from both its creator and its interpreters; but when we ask what a poem 'means' or 'communicates', we must have some interpreter in mind – and we must think of what that interpreter puts into the poem, as well as what he takes from it.

12.3.3 *Seeking the Optimal Interpretation*

We may envisage an 'optimal interpretation' of a poem either in quantitative or in qualitative terms: as the interpretation which is richest, in the sense of having the maximum amount of significance, or the interpretation which is best, on some scale of aesthetic evaluation. Of these two concepts, the second, as we shall see later in this section, implies a limitation of the first.

In this book a great deal of emphasis – perhaps too much – has been placed on the compensatory or remedial role of the reader's intelligence in making sense of what would otherwise have to be rejected as senseless or, at the least, pointless. In the discussion of symbolism (§9.2.6) we saw that this view of interpretation was not broad enough, and that the special sense-making mechanisms of poetry are not restricted to cases where the face-value interpretation is inadequate. There is a good case for supplementing the principle that 'human intelligence abhors a vacuum of sense' by the more positive principle that 'the human mind in poetry seeks *as much sense as it reasonably can*'. That is to say, in poetry all conceivable channels of communication are potentially open.

The American linguist Edward Sapir compares language to an electric dynamo able to power a lift, but normally used simply to operate a doorbell.[19] Referring to this, another noted American scholar, Uriel Weinreich, contrasts the 'desemanticized' or low-voltage use of language in conventional sayings, casual conversation, etc., with the 'hypersemanticized' or high-voltage use of language in literature.[20] Poetic language is, as Mrs Nowottny describes it in another comparison, 'language at full stretch',[21] and it is stretched to capacity not just under the threat of a failure in the communicative process, but because of a general expectation, part of the 'mental set' a reader brings to poetry, that every single feature of language is a matter of design rather than of chance or carelessness.

We may suggest, in conclusion, that the intelligent and sensitive reader of poetry looks for an optimal interpretation both quantitatively and qualitatively: he accepts as many significances as plausibly contribute to his interpretation without irrelevance or inconsistency. But clearly what is 'relevant to' or 'consistent with' a given interpretation is often a matter of aesthetic judgment: whether a given significance has a positive or negative effect on the appreciation of the poem. In the last resort, therefore, the two roles of interpretation and evaluation cannot be separated.

Examples for discussion

The following short poems are suggested as subjects for discussion ranging over every chapter of the book. Consider [a] kinds of linguistic foregrounding, [b] the interpretation of foregrounding, and [c] individual interpretations in relation to the total interpretation of each poem. Be ready to identify ambiguities and indeterminacies. Do not be afraid of paraphrase as a means of getting at *part* of the significance of a poem.

[a]   *Song*
   Still to be neat, still to be dressed
   As you were going to a feast;
   Still to be powdered, still perfumed:
   Lady, it is to be presumed,
   Though art's hid causes are not found,
   All is not sweet, all is not sound.

   Give me a look, give me a face,
   That makes simplicity a grace;
   Robes loosely flowing, hair as free;
   Such sweet neglect more taketh me
   Than all th'adulteries of art.
   They strike my eyes, but not my heart.
          [Ben Jonson, from *Epicœne, or The Silent Woman*]

[b]   *A Song*
   Lord, when the sense of thy sweet grace
   Sends up my soul to seek thy face,
   Thy blessed eyes breed such desire,
   I die in love's delicious fire.
     O love, I am thy sacrifice.
   Be still triumphant, blessed eyes.
   Still shine on me, fair suns! that I
   Still may behold, though still I die.

Though still I die, I live again;
Still longing so to be still slain,
So gainful is such loss of breath,
I die even in desire of death.
    Still live in me this loving strife
Of living death and dying life,
For while thou sweetly slayest me,
Dead to myself, I live in thee.
                 [Richard Crashaw]

[c]   *The Sick Rose*
O Rose, thou art sick!
The invisible worm,
That flies in the night,
In the howling storm,

Has found out thy bed
Of crimson joy;
And his dark secret love
Does thy life destroy.
         [Blake, from *Songs of Experience*]

[d]   *Sumum Bonum*
All the breath and the bloom of the year in the bag of one bee:
    All the wonder and wealth of the mine in the heart of one gem:
In the core of one pearl all the shade and the shine of the sea:
    Breath and bloom, shade and shine, – wonder, wealth, and – how far above
        them –
              Truth, that's brighter than gem,
              Trust, that's purer than pearl, –
Brightest truth, purest trust in the universe – all were for me
              In the kiss of one girl.
              [Robert Browning]

[e]   *An Irish Airman Foresees his Death*
I know that I shall meet my fate
Somewhere among the clouds above;
Those that I fight I do not hate,
Those that I guard I do not love;
My country is Kiltartan Cross,
My countrymen Kiltartan's poor,
No likely end could bring them loss
Or leave them happier than before.
Nor law, nor duty bade me fight,
Nor public men, nor cheering crowds,

A lonely impulse of delight
Drove to this tumult in the clouds;
I balanced all, brought all to mind,
The years to come seemed waste of breath,
A waste of breath the years behind
In balance with this life, this death.
[W. B. Yeats]

[*f*]   *Poem without a Main Verb*
Watching oneself
being clever, being clever:
keeping the keen equipoise between *always* and *never*;

delicately divining
(the gambler's sick art)
which of the strands must hold, and which may part;

playing off, playing off
with pointless cunning
the risk of remaining against the risk of running;

balancing balancing
(alert and knowing)
the carelessly hidden with the carefully left showing;

endlessly, endlessly
finely elaborating
the filigree threads in the web and bars in the grating:

at last minutely
and thoroughly lost
in the delta where profit fans into cost;

with superb navigation
afloat on that darkening, deepening sea,
helplessly, helplessly.
[John Wain]

Notes

1   In linguistics, ambiguity has often been treated in non-semantic terms: for ex-
    ample, as a purely grammatical phenomenon by N. CHOMSKY, *Aspects of the Theory
    of Syntax*, Cambridge, Mass., 1965, 21–2. Nevertheless, it can be argued that the

ultimate test of ambiguity as Chomsky understands it is whether more than one
cognitive meaning is involved.

2   W. EMPSON, *Seven Types of Ambiguity* (3rd edn), London, 1953, 1.
3   *Ibid.*, 108.
4   *Ibid.*, 108.
5   Quoted in S. ULLMANN, *Semantics: an Introduction to the Science of Meaning*, Oxford,
    1962, 191.
6   Quoted in M. SCHLAUCH, *The Gift of Language*, New York, 1955, 233.
7   *Ibid.*, 237.
8   EMPSON, *op. cit.*, 106.
9   *Ibid.*, 104.
10 Quoted in ULLMANN, *op. cit.*, 191.
11 EMPSON, *op. cit.*, 123–4.
12 E. H. GOMBRICH, *Art and Illusion*, London, 1960.
13 *Ibid.*, 222.
14 *Ibid.*, 170–203.
15 *Ibid.*, 193–4.
16 *Ibid.*, 239.
17 Letter to the Editor of *Poetry: a Magazine of Verse*; repr. in J. SCULLY, ed., *Modern
    Poets on Modern Poetry*, Fontana Library, 1966, 167–72.
18 GOMBRICH, *op. cit.*, 204.
19 E. SAPIR, *Language*, New York, 1921, 13.
20 U. WEINREICH, 'On the Semantic Structure of Language', in *Universals of
    Language*, ed. J. H. GREENBERG, Cambridge, Mass., 1963, 117–18.
21 W. NOWOTTNY, *The Language Poets Use*, London, 1962, 123.

Conclusion

A retrospective summary of this book in one or two paragraphs may help the reader who has persevered this far to see how its parts fit into a general pattern. We began, in Chapters 1 and 2, with the question 'what is special about the language of poetry?', and in particular, 'what does it mean to use language creatively?'. From there, in Chapters 3 and 4, we turned to the subject of poetic licence, and to the even broader concept of linguistic foregrounding, or 'artistic obtrusion', and saw the interpretation of poetry mainly as making sense of foregrounded aspects of language. The remaining chapters dealt with various kinds of foregrounding: Chapters 5 and 6 with repetitions of words and sounds; Chapter 7 with the conventional foregrounding of patterns in verse; Chapters 8, 9, and 10 with special modes of meaning, and the part which literal absurdity plays in their operation; Chapter 11 with the foregrounding of situation; and Chapter 12 with the foregrounding of ambiguity in puns and other uses of multiple meaning.

Certain themes have assumed prominence as this study has progressed. The notion of foregrounding has been supplemented by that of poetic language as a 'hypersemanticized' medium, in which the individual reader projects special significance wherever his critical judgment lets him do so. We have come to see the question of 'meaning' or significance in poetry from the reader's point of view as a question of interpretation, and to see interpretation as what the reader puts into a poem, as well as what he takes from it.

Finally, let us think about the part linguistic analysis plays in the total study of literary texts. It is artificial to draw a clean line between linguistic and critical exegesis: stylistics is, indeed, the area in which they overlap. Nevertheless, if such a line had to be drawn, I should draw it as follows: the linguist is the man who identifies what features in a poem need interpretation (i.e. what features are foregrounded), and to some extent (e.g. by specifying rules of transference) what opportunities for interpretation are available; the literary critic is the man who weighs up the different possible interpretations. I hasten, however, to make an amendment to this division of labour: it is better to regard linguist and critic not as different people, but as different roles which may be assumed by the same person. Every critic who appeals to linguistic evidence is acting as his own linguist; and any linguist who turns his attention to a poetic text can scarcely avoid bringing his critical judgment to bear on it. I have strayed over the line many times in this book, taking on the role of an amateur (and not particularly competent) critic. Notwithstanding, I feel that apologies are unnecessary, for the doubling of roles is inevitable. The acceptance of its inevitability might lessen the resentment of some critics against the ignorance and insensitivity of some linguists, and ease the agonized posture of some linguists who lean over backwards to avoid appearing to consult their subjective reactions to a poem.

Viewing the total significance of a poem in terms of the reader's interpretation, as we have done, disposes of the following fallacy, to which linguists on occasion have seemed to subscribe: 'Because poetry consists of language, the linguist, if he had enough leisure, could eventually give a complete explanation of a poem.' To see how wrong this is, we merely have to reflect on how many kinds of knowledge, apart from knowledge of the language, enter into the interpretation of English poetry. Comprehension of practically any poem can be influenced by biographical information, or by experience of other poems by the same writer. For example, a reader well informed on Wordsworth's life and work would be able to guess that the 'I' of an unfamiliar Wordsworth poem would be 'I, William Wordsworth the poet', rather than the fictional 'I' one would be inclined to expect in a poem by Browning. The work of some poets, such as Dryden, cannot be understood fully without a detailed social and political history of the times. A knowledge of intellectual and moral systems must be assumed in many cases – say, a knowledge of Neoplatonism in Renaissance literature. Often, interpretation also depends on familiarity with literary traditions, conventional symbolism, mythology, and so forth. We need go no further in this enumeration of relevant fields of knowledge. Scarcely any item of information on any subject can be ruled out as irrelevant to the understanding of poetry.

There is quite a widespread view – or shall I say superstition? – that to scrutinize a poem by the cold light of reason and common sense is to deprive it of the mystery, the miraculousness, which should be felt by anyone responding to a work of art. Whilst I know that nobody who has read this book subscribes to this view (anyone who held it would have given up after the Introduction), it is surely best for both linguist and critic to be silent on such matters, in deference to the words of the artist himself. I therefore gain comfort from this remark by Jean Cocteau:

> Poetry finds first and seeks afterwards. It is the quarry of exegesis which is unquestionably a Muse because it is apt to decipher our codes, to illuminate our inner darkness, and to tell us about what we were unaware of having said.[1]

In fact, this is perhaps too generous an assessment on the part of the creative writer. However much the analyst may be able to illuminate, whether by linguistic or critical exegesis, there will always remain the inexplicable residue, the marvel of creative achievement. To restore the balance, then, it is fitting that we should close with the view of another artist in words, Dylan Thomas, who above any other writer of modern times, has exhibited a magical power over the English language:

> You can tear a poem apart to see what makes it technically tick, and say to yourself, when the works are laid out before you, the vowels, the consonants, the rhymes and rhythms, 'Yes, this is *it*. This is why the poem moves me so. It is because of the craftsmanship.' But you're back again where you began. You're back with the mystery of having been moved by words. The best craftsmanship always leaves holes and gaps in the works of the poem, so that something that is *not* in the poem can creep, crawl, flash, or thunder in.[2]

Notes

1   Said at Oxford; reported by S. ULLMANN, *Language and Style*, Oxford, 1964, 99.
2   From 'Notes on the Art of Poetry' written in the summer of 1951, at Laugharne, in reply to questions posed by a student; reprinted in J. SCULLY, ed., *Modern Poets on Modern Poetry*, Fontana Library, 1966, 202.

Suggestions for Further Reading

A. Style and Literary Interpretation

['Ling.' indicates that a work is written mainly from the viewpoint of linguistic analysis; 'Lit.', that it is written mainly from the viewpoint of literary interpretation.]

ARTHOS, J. *The Language of Natural Description in Eighteenth Century Poetry.* Ann Arbor, 1949. [Lit.]

BAILEY, R. M. and BURTON, D. M. *English Stylistics: a Bibliography.* Cambridge Mass., 1968.

BARFIELD, O. *Poetic Diction.* (2nd edn.) London, 1952. [Lit.]

BROOKE-ROSE, C. *A Grammar of Metaphor.* London, 1958. [Lit.]

BROOKS, C. *The Well-wrought Urn.* New York, 1947. [Lit.]

CHATMAN, S. and LEVIN, S. R., eds. *Essays on the Language of Literature.* Boston, 1967.

DAVIE, D. *Purity of Diction in English Verse.* London, 1952. [Lit.]

DAVIE, D. *Articulate Energy.* London, 1955. [Lit.]

EMPSON, W. *Seven Types of Ambiguity.* (3rd edn.) London, 1953. [Lit.]

ENKVIST, N. E., SPENCER, J. and GREGORY, M. J. *Linguistics and Style.* London, 1965. [Ling.]

FOWLER, R., ed. *Essays on Style and Language.* London, 1966.

GARVIN, P. L., trans. and ed., *A Prague School Reader on Esthetics, Literary Structure and Style.* Washington D.C., 1958.

GROOM, B. *The Diction of Poetry from Spenser to Bridges.* Toronto, 1955. [Lit.]

HALLIDAY, M. A. K. 'The Linguistic Study of Literary Texts' in *Proceedings of the IXth International Congress of Linguists, ed.* H. G. LUNT. The Hague, 1964, pp. 302–7. [Ling.]

JAKOBSON, R. 'Linguistics and Poetics' in *Style in Language, ed.* T. A. SEBEOK. New York, 1960, pp. 350–77. [Ling.]

JAKOBSON, R. 'Grammatical Parallelism and its Russian Facet', *Language,* 42 (1966), 399–429. [Ling.]

KNOX, N. *The Word Irony and its Context, 1500–1755.* Durham, N. Carolina, 1961.

LEECH, G. N. '"This Bread I Break": Language and Interpretation', *Review of English Literature*, 6.2 (1965), 66–75. [Ling.]

LEVIN, S. R. *Linguistic Structures in Poetry*. The Hague, 1962. [Ling.]

LEVIN, S. R. 'Poetry and Grammaticalness' in *Proceedings of the IXth International Congress of Linguists*, ed. H. G. LUNT. The Hague, 1964, pp. 308–314. [Ling.]

LEVIN, S. R. 'Internal and External Deviation in Poetry', *Word*, 21 (1965), 225–39. [Ling.]

LODGE, D. *Language of Fiction*. London and New York, 1966. [Lit.]

NOWOTTNY, W. *The Language Poets Use*. London, 1962. [Lit.]

POLSKA AKADEMIA NAUK, *Poetics*, Warsaw and The Hague, *c.* 1961.

QUIRK, R. 'Poetic Language and Old English Metre', Paper 1 of *Essays on the English Language*. London, 1968. [Ling.]

RICHARDS, I. A. *Principles of Literary Criticism*. London, 1925. [Lit.]

RICHARDS, I. A. *Practical Criticism*. New York, 1929. [Lit.]

RICKS, C., *Milton's Grand Style*. Oxford, 1963. [Lit.]

STEINMANN, M., ed. *New Rhetorics*. New York, 1967.

TILLOTSON, G. 'Eighteenth Century Poetic Diction', *Essays and Studies*, 25 (1939), 59–80. [Lit.]

ULLMANN, S. *Language and Style*. Oxford, 1964.

WIMSATT, W. K. and BEARDSLEY, M. C. *The Verbal Icon*. Lexington, Ky., 1954; New York, 1958. [Lit.]

WRIGHT, K. 'Rhetorical Repetition in T. S. Eliot', *A Review of English Literature*, 6.2 (1965), 93–100.

B. *Prosody*

ABERCROMBIE, D. 'A Phonetician's View of Verse Structure' in *Studies in Phonetics and Linguistics*. London, 1965, pp. 16–25.

CHATMAN, S. *A Theory of Meter*. The Hague, 1965.

FOWLER, R. '"Prose Rhythm" and Metre' in *Essays on Style and Language*, ed. R. FOWLER, London, 1966, pp. 82–99.

FOWLER, R. 'Structural Metrics', *Linguistics*, 27 (1966), 49–64.

GROSS, H. *Sound and Form in Modern Poetry*. Ann Arbor, 1964.

GROSS, H., ed. *Modern Essays on Prosody*. New York, 1966.

HALLE, M. and KEYSER, S. J. 'Chaucer and the Study of Prosody', *College English*, 28.3 (1966), 187–219.

LOTZ, J. 'Metric Typology' in *Style in Language*, ed. T. A. SEBEOK. New York, 1960, pp. 135–48.

POPE, J. C. *The Rhythm of Beowulf*. New Haven, 1942.

SAINTSBURY, G. *A History of English Prosody*. 3 Vols. London, 1906–10.

SHAPIRO, K. and BEUM, R. *A Prosody Handbook*. New York, 1965.

SPROTT, S. E., *Milton's Art of Prosody*. Oxford, 1953.

WIMSATT, W. K. and BEARDSLEY, M. C. 'The Concept of Meter: an Exercise in Abstraction', *PMLA* 74 (1959), 585–98.

C. *General Linguistics and the English Language*

[Works marked 'Advanced' assume a fair knowledge of linguistics.]

ABERCROMBIE, D. 'Syllable Quantity and Enclitics in English' in *Studies in Phonetics and Linguistics*, London, 1965, pp. 26–34.

CHOMSKY, N. 'Degrees of Grammaticalness', in *The Structure of Language*, ed. J. A. FODOR and J. J. KATZ. Englewood Cliffs, N.J., 1964, pp. 384–89. [Advanced.]

CHOMSKY, N. *Aspects of the Theory of Syntax*. Cambridge, Mass., 1965. [Advanced.]

CRYSTAL, D. and DAVY, D. *Investigating English Style*. London, 1969.

ELLIS, J. O. 'On Contextual Meaning' in *In Memory of J. R. Firth*, ed. C. E. BAZELL *et al.* London, 1966, pp. 79–95.

FIRTH, J. R. *Papers in Linguistics 1934–51*. London, 1957. [Especially 'Personality and Language in Society', pp. 177–89, and 'Modes of Meaning', pp. 190–215.]

GIMSON, A. C. *An Introduction to the Pronunciation of English*. London, 1962.

GLEASON, H. A. *Linguistics and English Grammar*. New York, 1965.

HALLIDAY, M. A. K., MCINTOSH, A. and STREVENS, P. *The Linguistic Sciences and Language Teaching*. London, 1964.

JESPERSEN, O. *Growth and Structure of the English Language*. (9th edn.) Oxford, 1948. [Especially Chapter 10.]

KATZ, J. J. 'Semi-sentences' in *The Structure of Language, ed.* J. A. FODOR and J. J. KATZ. Englewood Cliffs, N.J., 1964. [Advanced.]

MCINTOSH, A. and HALLIDAY, M. A. K. *Patterns of Language*. London, 1966.

O'CONNOR, J. D. *Better English Pronunciation*. Cambridge, 1967. [Especially Chapter 6.]

QUIRK, R. *The Use of English*. (2nd edn.) London, 1968.

ROBERTS, P. *English Sentences*. New York, *c.* 1962.

ROBINS, R. H. *General Linguistics: an Introductory Survey*. London, 1964.

SCHLAUCH, M. *The Gift of Language*. New York, 1955. [Especially Chapter 9.]

ULLMANN, S. *Semantics: an Introduction to the Science of Meaning*. Oxford, 1962.

WEINREICH, U. 'On the Semantic Structure of Language' in *Universals of Language*, ed. J. H. GREENBERG. Cambridge, Mass., 1963, pp. 114–71. [Advanced.]

WEINREICH, U. 'Explorations in Semantic Theory' in *Current Trends in Linguistics*, Vol. III, ed. T. A. SEBEOK. The Hague, 1966. pp. 395–477. [Advanced.]

WRENN, C. L. *Word and Symbol*. London, 1967.

D. *Rhetoric*

[The works listed here are chiefly relevant because they document the tradition of rhetoric from classical times up to the present day.]

ATKINS, J. W. H. *Literary Criticism in Antiquity*. 2 Vols. Cambridge, 1934.

ATKINS, J. W. H. *English Literary Criticism: the Medieval Phase*. Cambridge 1943.

ATKINS, J. W. H. *English Literary Criticism: the Renaissance*. London, 1947.

BAIN, A. *English Composition and Rhetoric*. 2 Vols. London, etc., 1887.

BROOKS, C. and WARREN, R. P. *Fundamentals of Good Writing: a Handbook of Modern Rhetoric*, London, 1952.

GRIERSON, SIR H. *Rhetoric and English Composition*, London, 1944.

PUTTENHAM, G. *Arte of English Poesie, ed.* G. D. WILLCOCK and A. WALKER. Cambridge, 1936.

WILSON, T. *Wilson's Arte of Rhetorique, 1560, ed.* G. H. MAIR. Oxford, 1909.

E. *Miscellaneous Publications of More General Interest*

ELIOT, T. S. *Selected Prose*. Penguin Books, 1953.

FOWLER, H. W. *A Dictionary of Modern English Usage*. Oxford, 1926.

GOMBRICH, E. H. *Art and Illusion*. London, 1960.

HOTOPF, W. H. N. *Language, Thought, and Comprehension: a Case Study of the Writings of I. A. Richards*. London, 1965.

POUND, E. *A.B.C. of Reading*. London, 1951.

RANSOM, J. C. *The World's Body*. New York, 1938.

RICHARDS, I. A. *Philosophy of Rhetoric*. New York and London, 1936.

SCULLY, J., ed. *Modern Poets on Modern Poetry*. Fontana Library, 1966.

SHUMAKER, W. *Literature and the Irrational*. Englewood Cliffs, N.J., 1960.

SKELTON, R. *Poetry* (Teach Yourself Books). London, 1963.

WELLEK, R. and WARREN, A. *The Theory of Literature*. London, 1949.

General Index

A **bold face** number is used to distinguish a reference where the meaning of a term
is mentioned or discussed.

Index of Sources of Examples for Discussion

Leech, Geoffrey N
    A linguistic guide to English poetry [by] Geoffrey N.
Leech. Harlow, Longmans, 1969.

    xvi, 240 p. illus. 23 cm. (English language series)   30/–
                                                B 69–13722

    Bibliography : p. [229]–232.

235310

    1. English poetry—History and criticism. 2. Poetics. 3. English
language—Style. I. Title.